LITERATURE AND THE POLITICS OF FAMILY IN SEVENTEENTH-CENTURY ENGLAND

A common literary language linked royal absolutism to radical religion and republicanism in seventeenth-century England. Authors from both sides of the civil wars, including Milton, Hobbes, Margaret Cavendish, and the Quakers, adapted the analogy between family and state to support radically different visions of political community. They used family metaphors to debate the limits of political authority, rethink gender roles, and imagine community in a period of social and political upheaval. While critical attention has focused on how the common analogy linking father and king, family and state, bolstered royal and paternal claims to authority and obedience, its meaning was in fact intensely contested. In this wide-ranging study, Su Fang Ng analyzes the language and metaphors used to describe the relationship between politics and the family in both literary and political writings and offers a new perspective on how seventeenth-century literature reflected as well as influenced political thought.

SU FANG NG is Assistant Professor of English at the University of Oklahoma.

LITERATURE AND THE POLITICS OF FAMILY IN SEVENTEENTH-CENTURY ENGLAND

SU FANG NG

CAMBRIDGE
UNIVERSITY PRESS

CAMBRIDGE UNIVERSITY PRESS
Cambridge, New York, Melbourne, Madrid, Cape Town, Singapore,
São Paulo, Delhi, Dubai, Tokyo

Cambridge University Press
The Edinburgh Building, Cambridge CB2 8RU, UK

Published in the United States of America by Cambridge University Press, New York

www.cambridge.org
Information on this title: www.cambridge.org/9780521123723

© Su Fang Ng 2007

First published 2007
This digitally printed version 2009

A catalogue record for this publication is available from the British Library

ISBN 978-0-521-87031-3 Hardback
ISBN 978-0-521-12372-3 Paperback

Contents

Acknowledgments

First, and foremost, I am grateful to Michael Schoenfeldt, who supervised this work when it was a dissertation. Mike believed in the project's ambitions and provided encouragement and guidance with patience and generosity. My other teachers also gave invaluable suggestions and support. I thank John Knott for his unfailing good humor, Linda Gregerson for her ability to reinvigorate one's enthusiasm for the work, and Julia Adams for her astute comments from a historical sociologist's perspective.

This work would not have been completed without the generous support of a number of institutions. The University of Michigan gave me funding at several crucial points in my graduate career, most notably an Andrew W. Mellon candidacy fellowship and a Rackham Predoctoral Fellowship – the latter gave me a year's funding to finish the dissertation. When I was beginning my research, a travel grant from the English Department and the Robin I. Thevenet Summer Research Grant from the Women's Studies Program at Michigan made it possible for me to read in the archives of the Library of the Society of Friends in London. That same summer, I also benefited from a workshop held in Finland organized by the Network of Interdisciplinary Women's Studies in Europe; the cost of attendance was defrayed by a fellowship from the Institute for Research on Women and Gender and the Center for European Studies at the University of Michigan. As a faculty member at the University of Oklahoma, I am grateful for research support from my department, from the College of Arts and Sciences, and from the office of the Vice-President for Research. My department gave me a semester's release time from teaching, while the College and University provided for four summers of research and writing in the form of Junior Faculty Summer Fellowships and Junior Faculty Research Program Grants. This research was supported in part by a grant from the Oklahoma Humanities Council and the National Endowment for the Humanities. (Findings, opinions and conclusions do not necessarily represent the views of the OHC or the NEH.) The grant helped to cover the cost of traveling to

Washington, DC, where I was able to consult the extensive archives of the Folger Shakespeare Library. I also want to thank the Newberry Library for awarding me a Short-Term Fellowship for Individual Research that made it possible for me to spend a month working in their wonderful collection in Chicago. No work of this kind can be done without libraries. I would like to thank the staff of the Harlan Hatcher Graduate Library at the University of Michigan, the Library of the Society of Friends in London, the library at the University of Mainz, the Bates College library, Bizzell Library at the University of Oklahoma, the Folger Shakespeare Library, and the Newberry Library.

I have benefited from the suggestions and help of a number of people at various stages. The anonymous readers for the press read the manuscript with great care and challenged me to think more deeply about my subject. My book is the better for their detailed and astute comments and suggestions. My editor, Ray Ryan, was also helpful in shepherding the manuscript through. Several of my colleagues at Oklahoma offered crucial aid in bringing this book to completion: Daniel Cottom, Ronald Schleifer, and Daniel Ransom. They not only advised on the manuscript but also assisted with other professional concerns. Given the many demands on his time, Dan Cottom, in particular, has been very gracious in his willingness to mentor a junior colleague. Others from whose conversations I have learnt include Martha Skeeters, Daniela Garofalo, Peter Barker, and Melissa Stockdale. At Michigan, the following people have either commented on parts of the work or have otherwise helped facilitate it: Karla Taylor, Valerie Traub, Sarah Frantz, Elise Frasier and Mary Huey. I also learnt much from seminars with Bill Ingram, Simon Gikandi, John Kucich, and Yopie Prins. Elsewhere, I am grateful for the friendship of Lovalerie King and Wendy Wagner, even though their specialties are remote from mine. I presented early drafts of the book at the Renaissance Law and Literature conference at Wolfson College, Oxford in 1998, the International Margaret Cavendish Conference in 2001, the British Milton Seminar in 2000, and at the Seventh and Eighth International Milton Symposiums in 2001 and 2005. For their comments, questions, and encouragement, I thank these conference audiences, whom I shall collectively name the tribe of Miltonists. I would also like to thank Richard Rowland for suggesting that I look at Nathaniel Lee's *Lucius Junius Brutus*. The final manuscript was prepared while I was at the Radcliffe Institute for Advanced Study, where I had the research assistance of Casiana Ionita. I am grateful for permission to reuse some of the material I first published as "Marriage and Discipline: The Place of Women in Early Quaker Controversies," *The Seventeenth Century* 18.1

(2003): 113–40. I would also like to remember here the kindnesses of Julie Abraham, Trudier Harris, Bill Gruber, and in particular, the late Georgia Christopher, who a long time ago gave me encouragement when I needed it. It remains to thank Kenneth Hodges for his wit and intelligence. He has lived with this project since its inception, and has been unfailingly supportive and incredibly generous; this book is as much his as it is mine. Finally, I dedicate this book to my parents, Ng Kim Nam and Chan Lai Kuen.

Introduction: strange bedfellows – patriarchalism and revolutionary thought

In 1615 James I ordered the publication of *God and the King*, which supported the obligation to take the oath of allegiance: the work announces itself to be "Imprinted by his Maiesties speciall priuiledge and command."[1] Attributed to Richard Mocket, at the time warden of All Souls, Oxford, the pamphlet defends divine right absolutism by making the patriarchal analogy linking father and king. Cast in the form of a dialogue, *God and the King* wastes little time in preliminaries. After a brief greeting, Philalethes, just come from a catechism, launches into a justification of monarchical authority by way of the fifth commandment. A good cathechumen, he recites the lesson that the names of father and mother include all other authorities, especially royal authority. The injunction to honor father and mother also mandates obedience to kings. Extrapolating from Isaiah 49:23, which "stile[s] Kings and Princes the nursing Fathers of the Church," Philalethes concludes, "there is a stronger and higher bond of duetie betweene children and the Father of their Countrie, then the Fathers of priuate families."[2] The tract insists on obedience to kings based on the "natural" and divinely sanctioned subjection of children to parents. Enjoying considerable royal patronage, *God and the King* appeared in both English and Latin, and in James's lifetime was reprinted in London in 1616 and in Edinburgh in 1617. James commanded all schools and universities as well as all ministers to teach the work, and directed all householders to purchase a copy. This command was subsequently enjoined by both the Scottish privy council and general assembly in 1616. The analogy also worked in reverse. While the king claimed paternal authority, fathers claimed to be kings of their domains in domestic handbooks. John Dod and Robert Cleaver's *Godlie Forme of Householde Government*, first published in 1598, and reprinted

---

[1] [Richard Mocket], *God and the King: or, A Dialogue shewing that our Soueraigne Lord King IAMES, being immediate vnder God within his DOMINIONS, Doth rightfully claime whatsoeuer is required by the Oath of Allegeance* (London, 1615), title page.

[2] *Ibid.*, 2–3.

numerous times, compares fathers to monarchs: "A Householde is as it were a little commonwealth," and the father-husband is "not onely a ruler but as it were a little King, and Lord of all."[3] Dod and Cleaver were not the only ones to enthrone the father as sovereign in the household. William Gouge's *Of Domesticall Duties* (1622), another popular puritan handbook, traces the origin of state and church back to it. Gouge makes similar claims that "a familie is a little Church and a little common-wealth, at least a lively representation thereof"; moreover, the family is a "schoole wherein the first principles and grounds of gouernment and subiection are learned: whereby men are fitted to greater matters in Church or common-wealth."[4] No matter their focus, these prescriptive works argue from the analogy to claim obedience to authority.

These pamphlets were but a few examples of texts turning to the widely used metaphor of family or household to conceptualize social organization. Susan D. Amussen goes so far as to claim that "the distinction between 'family' and 'society' was absent from early modern thought."[5] Among his many examples, Christopher Hill includes Walter Ralegh's comparison of the King to "the master of the household," Oxford and Cambridge "undergraduates [who] were urged to look upon their tutor as though he were head of their family," and the radical Digger leader, Gerrard Winstanley, speaking of a "bigger family, called a parish."[6] Besides bolstering the social order, the family-state analogy importantly supported the political order. Lancelot Andrewes preached in a sermon before James that patriarchal and royal rule were the same: "*Jus Regium* cometh out of *jus Patrium*, the Kings right from the Fathers, and both hold by one Commandement."[7] Robert Bolton argued that "before Nimrod, fathers and heads of families were Kings," and because in those days "men lived five or six hundred yeares . . . [it was] an easie matter for a man to see fifty, yea a hundred thousand persons of his posterity, over whom he exercised paternall power, and by consequence, soveraigne power."[8] Johann Sommerville says, "Many writers – including [John] Donne, [Roger] Maynwaring,

[3] John Dod and Robert Cleaver, *A Godlie Forme of Householde Government* (London, 1612), sig. A7, L8v.

[4] William Gouge, *Of Domesticall Duties: Eight Treatises* (London, 1622), sig. CIV, 18.

[5] Susan D. Amussen, "Gender, Family and the Social Order, 1560–1725," in Anthony J. Fletcher and John Stevenson, eds., *Order and Disorder in Early Modern England* (Cambridge: Cambridge University Press, 1985), 196.

[6] Christopher Hill, "The Spiritualization of the Household," in *Society and Puritanism in Pre-Revolutionary England* (London: Secker & Warburg, 1964), 459, 461, 464.

[7] Lancelot Andrewes, *A Sermon Preached before His Maiestie, on Sunday the Fifth of August Last, at Holdenbie, by the Bishop of Elie, His Maiesties Almoner* (London, 1610), 13.

[8] Robert Bolton, *Two sermons preached at Northampton* (London, 1635), 15.

[Robert] Willan, [John] Rawlinson and [Richard] Field – endorsed the view that Adam's power had been kingly."[9] Even in the Elizabethan period, similar ideas were articulated by Hadrian Saravia, born in Flanders but naturalized as an Englishman in 1568, who argued that the "first governments were paternal" (*prima imperia fuisse paterna*) and that the "father's power is kingly" (*patriam potestatem regiam*).[10] Later Saravia became a translator of King James's Authorized Version of the Bible, and his work was republished in 1611 at the height of the controversy over the nature of political authority between James and Catholics like Cardinal Bellarmine. But the representative English text of political patriarchalism is Robert Filmer's *Patriarcha: The Naturall Power of Kinges Defended against the Unnatural Liberty of the People.* Written some time between 1635 and 1642 in the years leading up to the civil wars, it circulated in manuscript until it was first published in 1680, nearly thirty years after the author's death, to support the Tory position in the Exclusion Crisis. Influenced by Jean Bodin, Filmer codified the patriarchalist position for the English, asserting that fatherly sovereignty was absolute. He made the link between paternity and sovereignty literal by deriving monarchical power from the fact of fatherhood. Tracing sovereignty back to Adam, he claimed it descended to kings through an unbroken succession of natural fathers and so was to "succeed to the exercise of supreme jurisdiction."[11]

In both social and political patriarchalism the family-state analogy has been read as fundamentally conservative and authoritarian, if not absolutist. The underlying assumption is that the family was rigidly hierarchical, as depicted by Lawrence Stone's influential *The Family, Sex, and Marriage in England 1500–1800*.[12] Recent decades, however, have witnessed challenges to the account of the family as an authoritarian institution. Questioning Stone's narrative of the change in the family from authoritarianism to "affective individualism," Ralph Houlbrooke and others argue that relations in the family before the eighteenth century were more affectionate than Stone allowed, and that these relations changed little between the fifteenth and the eighteenth centuries.[13] This led to challenges to the traditional account

[9] J. P. Sommerville, *Royalists and Patriots: Politics and Ideology in England 1603–1640*, 2nd edn (London and New York: Longman, 1999), 32.
[10] Hadrian Saravia, *De imperandi authoritate*, in *Diversi tractatus theologici* (London, 1611), 167.
[11] Sir Robert Filmer, *Patriarcha and Other Writings*, ed. Johann P. Sommerville (Cambridge: Cambridge University Press, 1991), 10.
[12] Lawrence Stone, *The Family, Sex, and Marriage in England 1500–1800* (New York: Harper & Row, 1977).
[13] Ralph Houlbrooke, *The English Family, 1450–1700* (London and New York: Longman, 1984); E. P. Thompson, "Happy Families," *Radical History Review* 20 (1979), 42–50; Lois G. Schwoerer,

of domestic patriarchalism. Reassessing claims of patriarchal oppression, Margaret Ezell suggests women had more authority than has been acknowledged, given the high number of widowed women and orphaned children – at least one child in three lost his or her father before reaching adulthood.[14] In a fatherless society, wives managed estates and arranged marriages. Even arch-patriarchalist Robert Filmer, who praises the virtues of a good wife in an unpublished work, upon his death left the management of his estate to his wife rather than to his many brothers or to his grown sons.[15]

Beyond the domestic sphere, literary critics and historians interpret family tropes to emphasize closeness rather than distance between ruler and subject. Taking new historicist literary critics to task for assuming that Stuart representation of the nurturing father is "an ideological concealment of oppressive power relations," Debora Shuger argues the image of the father is part of the emergence of the loving family in the sixteenth century as a defense mechanism "in response both to the increasingly mobile and competitive conditions of Renaissance society and to the rather arbitrary power of the state."[16] In his history of early modern youths, Paul Griffiths similarly suggests courts and guilds employed familial rhetoric when arbitrating between masters and servants "to support an 'imagined' ordered household: . . . to cultivate a mood of inclusion to lighten the sense of differentiation and distance upon which their authority depended."[17] The affective family, however, still maintains the top-down structure of the authoritarian family. While Jonathan Goldberg's *James I and the Politics of Literature*, singled out for opprobrium by Shuger, describes the monarch as the center who becomes subverted but whose subversion is ultimately contained, Shuger's own reading of James, overly optimistic about the absence

"Seventeenth-Century Englishwomen: Engraved in Stone?" *Albion* 16 (1984), 389–403; and Eileen Spring, "The Family, Strict Settlement, and the Historians," in G. R. Rubin and David Sugarman, eds., *Law, Economy and Society, 1750–1914: Essays in the History of English Law* (Abingdon, Oxon.: Professional Books, 1984), 168–91. For the affective family, see Steven Ozment, *When Fathers Ruled: Family Life in Reformation Europe* (Cambridge, Mass.: Harvard University Press, 1983); and Linda A. Pollock, *Forgotten Children: Parent-Child Relations from 1500 to 1900* (Cambridge: Cambridge University Press, 1983). In contrast, J. C. D. Clark, disagreeing with Stone, argues that patriarchalist and divine-right political doctrines as well as a hierarchical social order based on paternalism remained in place in England until 1832 (*English Society, 1688–1832: Ideology, Social Structure, and Political Practice during the Ancien Régime* [Cambridge: Cambridge University Press, 1985]).
[14] Margaret J. M. Ezell, *The Patriarch's Wife: Literary Evidence and the History of the Family* (Chapel Hill: University of North Carolina Press, 1987), 18.
[15] "In Praise of the Vertuous Wife" is published in Ezell, *The Patriarch's Wife*, Appendix I, 169–90.
[16] Debora Kuller Shuger, *Habits of Thought in the English Renaissance: Religion, Politics, and the Dominant Culture* (Berkeley: University of California Press, 1990), 235.
[17] Paul Griffiths, *Youth and Authority: Formative Experiences in England 1560–1640* (Oxford: Clarendon Press, 1996), 292.

of coercion, depicts a consensual society. Despite apparent differences, however, both emphasize uses of the analogy to consolidate monarchical or paternal power, whether coercive or benevolent.

While these revisions show a complex relation between family and state even within patriarchalist thought, the pervasive modern assumption that the family-state analogy is intrinsically patriarchal needs to be challenged. The most useful and thorough discussion to date is Gordon Schochet's *Patriarchalism in Political Thought*: Schochet studies the history and forms of patriarchalism in early modern England and the sudden emergence in the seventeenth century of political theory that uses familial reasoning as direct justification of political obligation, rather than simply as a bolster to social order or criterion for membership in a political community. While the study resists reducing patriarchalism into one form, it nonetheless maintains a distinction between patriarchalism and contractarianism, with the family-state analogy a strategy of patriarchalism. This view is also implicit in Johann Sommerville's study of the struggle between absolutism and constitutionalism, *Politics and Ideology in England 1603–1640*. This is partly because patriarchalist writers tended to use the familial origin of society – an important strand of this logic is the supposed fact that God gave dominion to Adam, the first father – as evidence for their argument that the king rules by paternal power. Moreover, scholars who see a sharp divide between patriarchalism and contractarianism adhere too closely to John Locke's influential (and negative) account of patriarchalism in *The Two Treatises of Government* (1698). Filmer's *Patriarcha* has come to be seen as the representative text of patriarchalism because Locke and other Whig writers chose it as the target of their attack during the Exclusion Crisis.[18] The opposition between social contract theory and patriarchalism was less absolute than Whig history would have us believe. The two discourses were in dialogue about the nature of family and state.

The use of the familial metaphor need not lead only to a patriarchal conclusion. R. W. K. Hinton points out that Sir Thomas Smith's *De Republica Anglorum* describes marriage as a partnership, emphasizing consent and cooperation in both family and political society.[19] Even political texts arguing for patriarchalism indicate ways in which the family-state analogy can be used within a political theory of voluntary association or social

[18] The major studies of Filmer are James Daly, *Sir Robert Filmer and English Political Thought* (Toronto: University of Toronto Press, 1979); and Gordon J. Schochet, *Patriarchalism in Political Thought: The Authoritarian Family and Political Speculation and Attitudes Especially in Seventeenth-Century England* (New York: Basic Books, 1975).
[19] R. W. K. Hinton, "Husbands, Fathers and Conquerors," *Political Studies* 15 (1967), 292–93.

contract.[20] Although he does not pursue the point, Schochet admits that "Althusius's conception of the political community as a voluntary association seriously undermined the main thrust of the moral patriarchal theory."[21] Indeed, analogical use of the family could support politics that were or had the potential to be oppositional to the crown. During the interregnum, in justifying a limited use of civil power in religion in *The Humble Proposals . . . for the . . . Propagation of the Gospel* (1652), the Independents asserted, "the magistrate must be a nursing father to the church," and proposed "the establishment of congregationalism as the national discipline."[22] John Rogers refused to exclude civil magistrates from adjudicating in religious matters, arguing, "it is [the civil magistrate's] duty to provide for and encourage the faithful preachers and professors of the Gospel, and to be a nursing father to the church of Christ."[23] By calling the magistrate a nursing father, the Independents and Rogers were appropriating for the magistrate the patriarchal power to rule, putting them in conflict with the king. Comparing Moses to the commonwealth, the parliamentarian Henry Marten asserted that the House of Commons "were the true mother to this fair child" and therefore the "fittest nurses."[24] Such parliamentary appropriations of the parental metaphor were mocked in a series of satiric pamphlets by the royalist Sir John Birkenhead, who wittily asked, "Whether the House of Commons be a widow, a wife, a Maid, or a Commonwealth?"[25] From a royalist point of view, in believing itself to be the entire commonwealth, the Commons herself was a widow who murdered her royal husband, and ultimately a whore, a common woman neither maid, wife, nor widow.

The pamphlet war over the regicide demonstrates how authors exploited the inherent contradictions of the family-state analogy for political debate. In defending monarchy, royalists depicted Charles as a father betrayed by disloyal children. In the popular *Eikon Basilike* (1649), which appeared immediately after the regicide, the ghostly voice of Charles reproached his

[20] While her essay does not go so far as to identify republican uses of the family-state analogy, Constance Jordan distinguishes among several different uses of Aristotle that vary in their commitment to patriarchy ("The Household and the State: Transformations in the Representation of an Analogy from Aristotle to James I," *Modern Language Quarterly* 54 [1993], 307–26).

[21] Schochet, *Patriarchalism*, 36.

[22] Arthur E. Barker, *Milton and the Puritan Dilemma, 1641–1660* (Toronto: University of Toronto Press, 1942), 221–22.

[23] John Rogers, *A Vindication of that Prudent and Honourable Knight, Sir Henry Vane, From the Lyes and Clumnies of Mr. Richard Baxter* (London, 1659), 14.

[24] Samuel Rawson Gardiner, *The History of the Commonwealth and Protectorate, 1649–1660*, 4 vols. (London and New York: Longmans, Green, 1903), 1:243.

[25] John Birkenhead, *Paul's Church-Yard, Centuria Secunda* (London, 1652), 7.

people for their failure to show him proper filial obedience. Two of the most significant defenses of the king, Claude de Saumaise's *Defensio Regia pro Carolo I* (May 1649) and Pierre du Moulin's *Regii Sanguinis Clamor ad Coelum Adversus Paricidas Anglicanos* (August 1652), made the case that killing the king was patricide. In his tract commissioned by Charles II, Saumaise, better known by his Latinized name, Salmasius, tracing the growth of the state from its origins as a family unit, went even further to assert that because the king took precedence over fathers as an *über*-father, the killing of kings was more heinous a crime than homicide or patricide. The defenders of the new English republic took the claims of royalist patriarchalism seriously enough to respond to them. As polemicist for the English commonwealth, John Milton answered the three tracts by reworking the family trope, alternately suggesting in *Eikonoklastes* that the king was insufficiently caring as a father and arguing in the *First Defence* that the people were parents to kings.

At the root of the family-state analogy was not a single ideology but a debate. With a long history dating back to the ancient world, the analogy's meaning was not stable. From the start, the exact relation between family and society had been disputed. Plato claimed that the various arts of kingship, statesmanship, and householding were equivalent.[26] But Aristotle disagreed, arguing in the first book of *Politics* for an "*essential* difference" between families and kingdoms and between fathers and rulers.[27] Cicero, however, believed the family fundamental to the state: in *De Officiis*, he writes, "For since it is by nature common to all animals that they have a drive to procreate, the first fellowship exists within marriage itself, and the next with one's children. Indeed that is the principle of a city and the seed-bed, as it were, of a political community [*seminarium rei publicae*]."[28] Seventeenth-century authors could appeal to different conceptualizations of the relation between family and state for a variety of political ends. The family-state analogy proved to be enduring and its deployment was not simply a mark of social conservatism. Rather, it was a sign of the politicization of literature. For the argument by analogy was a powerful mode of analysis. Noting the pervasiveness of analogues in the early modern period, Kevin Sharpe suggests that the historian of political ideas needs to go beyond canonical texts of political philosophy, for "in a system of correspondences

---

[26] Plato, *The Statesman*, ed. Harold N. Fowler (London, 1925), 259:3, 12.

[27] Aristotle, *The Politics of Aristotle*, trans. Ernest Barker (Oxford: Clarendon Press, 1946; reprint, 1958), 2, emphasis in original.

[28] Cicero, *On Duties*, ed. M. T. Griffin and E. M. Atkins (Cambridge: Cambridge University Press, 1991), I:54, 23.

[where] all [is] related to all," the language of treatises on subjects from gardening to the body was "politicized at every turn."[29]

In tracking the many varied permutations of the family-state analogy, this study finds the analogy a supple vehicle for political debate, used to imagine a range of political communities from an absolutist monarchy to a republic. As such, the family-state analogy was a political language as defined by the Cambridge contextualist approach to politics and not a worldview in the sense understood by older intellectual history. Political argument was conducted in a variety of idioms or "languages" such as, for instance, the language of common law. A political language was a "mode of utterance available to a number of authors for a number of purposes."[30] According to J. G. A. Pocock, to identify such languages one looks, among other things, for evidence "that diverse authors employed the same idiom and performed diverse and even contrary utterances in it" and for its recurrence in a variety of texts and contexts.[31] The ubiquity of the family-state analogy suggests it was such an idiom. Open to appropriation, it allowed a range of authors to make contradictory claims. It was found in a wide array of texts of different kinds and genres – including domestic manuals, political theory, controversial tracts, private letters, court masques, prose narratives, lyric and epic poetry. From this perspective, the family went beyond functioning as extra-discursive "common ground" for interpreting discursive events to take on discursive form in contemporary political and literary discourses.[32]

By examining the field of discourse defined by its use, this study historically contextualizes the family-state analogy to offer a better sense of the political debates. Instead of interpreting canonical texts of political theory as timeless, addressing perennial questions, Pocock, Quentin Skinner, John Dunn and others practicing the contextualist approach place texts within historical contexts in order to identify what authors might be doing in writing. They shift the scholar's focus from intention to performance, viewing "participants in political argument as historical actors, responding to one another in a diversity of linguistic and other political and historical contexts that gave the recoverable history of their argument a very rich texture."[33] Thus, in his edition of Locke's *Two Treatises of Government*, Peter

[29] Kevin Sharpe, *Remapping Early Modern England: The Culture of Seventeenth-Century Politics* (Cambridge: Cambridge University Press, 2000), 101.
[30] J. G. A. Pocock, *Virtue, Commerce, and History: Essays on Political Thought and History, Chiefly in the Eighteenth Century* (Cambridge: Cambridge University Press, 1985), 10.
[31] *Ibid.*
[32] Nancy Armstrong and Leonard Tennenhouse, *The Imaginary Puritan: Literature, Intellectual Labor, and the Origins of Personal Life* (Berkeley: University of California Press, 1992), 69.
[33] Pocock, *Virtue, Commerce, and History*, 3.

Laslett shows how the work was Locke's intervention in the Exclusion Crisis, rather than simply a theoretical work on social contract removed from considerations of everyday politics. The attention to performance derives from J. L. Austin's "speech-act" theory, which strives to discover the force of an utterance; in other words, what might someone be doing by saying something, which Austin calls the "illocutionary" force of utterances.[34] With reference to Ludwig Wittgenstein's assertion that "words are deeds," Skinner argues that beyond reading for content we need to attend to "illocutionary acts" – how authors were participating in contemporary debates.[35] The history of political thought is thus reconceived as a history of political discourse that is also a history of political action. Texts, whether primarily political or literary, do not simply describe or record history; they also create it. In a magisterial study, David Norbrook employs such methods to reconstruct painstakingly a narrative of the emergence of republican literary culture: "An approach through speech-acts points us away from closed systems of thought into dialogue, into the constant invention of arguments and counter-arguments." For Norbrook, this approach better elucidates early modern English culture where "monarchy was being reinvented in response to recurrent challenges."[36] Likewise, the sheer range of contradictory uses to which the family-state analogy and family metaphors were put demand a reexamination that does not presuppose that such metaphors constituted a unified symbolic system.

The evidence suggests a contentious public sphere. As England entered civil war in the early 1640s and censorship laws came to an end, the intensified flurry of pamphleteering created a new Habermasian literary public where battles were fought as often in print as on the field.[37] This public was probably not one but many: Nigel Smith speaks of a public space "permeated by private languages."[38] Each was a community, no matter how ill-defined, asserting itself in the marketplace of ideas. At the same time, massive dislocations of the political system and fragmentation of the Christian *communitas* into numerous separate churches made new ways of conceptualizing identity both possible and increasingly urgent. No wonder

---

[34] J. L. Austin, *How to Do Things with Words* (Cambridge, Mass.: Harvard University Press, 1962), 99.

[35] See Skinner's essays in James Tully, ed., *Meaning and Context: Quentin Skinner and his Critics* (Princeton: Princeton University Press, 1988).

[36] David Norbrook, *Writing the English Republic: Poetry, Rhetoric and Politics, 1627–1660* (Cambridge: Cambridge University Press, 1999), 11.

[37] This reading public is suggested by Sharon Achinstein, *Milton and the Revolutionary Reader* (Princeton: Princeton University Press, 1994).

[38] Nigel Smith, *Literature and Revolution in England, 1640–1660* (New Haven: Yale University Press, 1994), 25.

political theories proliferated in the period. It is in response to the chaos
of civil war that Thomas Hobbes wrote *Leviathan* (1651), the founding
work of the modern discipline of political science. Theories of society were
intimately connected with contemporary events. In the particular circumstances, with a weakened central authority, theories could and were put into
practice, whether on a national scale like the republican commonwealth of
the interregnum, or on a more modest scope like the sectarian churches.
As the English debated the limits of political authority in a period when
civil wars put pressure on old forms of government, old forms of worship,
and old ways of thinking, the family-state analogy as a common political language underwent various permutations, taking on both absolutist
and revolutionary aspects. With it, authors challenged old communities
and constituted new ones (imagined and real), finding new affiliations and
forging new collective identities.

In linking history with literature, this study is also indebted to a literary-
critical movement known as new historicism or cultural materialism.
Emphasizing historical contextualization, new historicism, like the contextualist approach in politics, was influenced by postmodernist ideas about
the constitutive role of language or discourse in social and political relations, particularly Michel Foucault's ideas of power. With beginnings in the
1980s, new historicism/cultural materialism has had a profound influence
on Anglo-American literary studies but critics point to significant flaws, in
particular the arbitrariness of its use of anecdotes in place of historical narrative. It has become unfashionable to practice new historicism, such that
historicist critics prefer to dissociate themselves from it. Thus, in his major
revision of Goldberg's new historicist reading of Jacobean literature, Curtis
Perry describes his own work as "part of an ongoing movement in Renaissance studies towards the reconsolidation of the considerable advances of
new historicism with old historical narratives of individual agency."[39] Whatever its name, historicist literary criticism as currently practiced has turned
firmly away from old literary history, which viewed history as merely the
background to the study of a distinct sphere of autonomous works of
art. While hoping to avoid the pitfalls of early forms of new historicism,
this study is unabashedly historicist in blurring the boundaries between
historical and literary material.

---

[39] Curtis Perry, *The Making of Jacobean Culture: James I and the Renegotiation of Elizabethan Literary
Practice* (Cambridge: Cambridge University Press, 1997), 6. A recent collection of essays on literature
and history coined a new term not far different from the old: Robin Headlam Wells, Glenn Burgess,
and Rowland Wymer, eds., *Neo-Historicism: Studies in Renaissance Literature, History, and Politics*
(Cambridge: Cambridge University Press, 2000).

More specifically, historicist criticism, whether in history of political thought or literary criticism, challenges an older intellectual history. In this view, the family was but one part of a system of analogies. Correspondences go beyond the family to extend to everything from astronomy to zoology in interlocking microcosms and macrocosms. Such analogical habits of thought constructed the universe as a hierarchical chain of being extending from God to the smallest grain of sand.[40] Arthur Lovejoy developed what he called a history of ideas with the aim of identifying important philosophical ideas and describing the historical movement of these "unit-ideas." In *The Great Chain of Being*, he plotted through two thousand years of Western history the influence of the neo-platonist philosopher Plotinus' notion that all creation formed a chain of being. Taking this idea that the Renaissance worldview saw the universe as hierarchical, E. M. Tillyard applied it to literature. Renaissance preoccupation with analogies, or correspondences, and the harmonies they imply, were assumed to denote a consensual society.[41] But despite reading them in history, the "unit-ideas" remain fairly static; they are identifiable because unchanging. As Michael Bristol points out, "the ideas that migrate in this way do not experience change; their meaning, or intellectual character, is not affected by specific deployment within any historical context."[42] For Tillyard, who describes the analogies and similitudes of the chain of being as a "hovering between equivalence and metaphor," the sliding from simile to analogy and to metaphor of correspondences like the family and state only confirms the existence of an all-encompassing worldview. This study, however, views such blurring of categories as evidence of the family as a common political language as well as a language capable of expressing conflict. A metaphor collapsing tenor and vehicle can be challenged by being exposed as an inexact analogy. This is precisely how the parliamentarian Henry Parker responded to the royalist family metaphor. Minimizing its evocative power by reducing it to mere analogy, he denies that the king is like the father in every detail: "The father is more worthy than the son in nature, and the son is wholly a debtor to the father, and can by no merit transcend his dutie, nor challenge any thing as due from his father . . . Yet this holds not in the relation betwixt King and Subject, for its more due in policie, and more strictly to be chalenged, that

---

[40] Arthur Lovejoy, *The Great Chain of Being: A Study of the History of an Idea* (Cambridge, Mass.: Harvard University Press, 1936); E. M. W. Tillyard, *Elizabethan World Picture* (London: Chatto & Windus, 1943).

[41] James Daly, "Cosmic Harmony and Political Thinking in Early Stuart England," *Transactions of the American Philosophical Society* 69, pt. 7 (1979).

[42] Michael D. Bristol, *Shakespeare's America, America's Shakespeare* (London and New York: Routledge, 1990), 147.

the King should make happy the People, than the People make glorious the King."[43]

While revisionist historians stress the elements of early Stuart society that emphasize order and consensus, a framework of shared meanings and linguistic conventions also lent themselves to conflict. As Richard Cust and Ann Hughes note, the structural anthropology of Claude Levi-Strauss shows that human societies tend to see the world in terms of polarities and so "seventeenth-century English people had available several intellectual frameworks within which conflict rather than consensus was normal."[44] This included the vocabulary of misrule in discourses on witchcraft or the notion of *concordia discors*, or harmony in discord, that allowed for beliefs in "a sovereign king and a sovereign common law, or absolute royal prerogatives and absolute rights to property" to coexist.[45] Cust and Hughes's example of the body analogy for polity, for example, shows that while body parts ideally function together in a hierarchical harmony, a healthy body was achieved through purgation. As an ideal, consensus "could only be achieved through vigilance, struggle and sometimes conflict."[46] Like the body, the family's hierarchy could be conceived in a number of ways that could come into conflict with each other. Because the early modern family did not conform to a single model, the family metaphor in the period did not have a single meaning. It supported absolute monarchy as well as contractual, voluntaristic, and participatory forms of government. What meanings seventeenth-century authors ascribed to family depended on their political beliefs. While some seventeenth-century authors identified the king as *pater patriae*, others identified a wide range of subjects and potential (or actual) authorities, such as Parliament or even dissenting churches.

The meaning of the family metaphor depended on context, for it was a conceptual vehicle by which writers debated political issues. Once the focus shifts from recovering meaning to reconstructing linguistic action by read-ing texts in historical contexts, the historian of political thought moves away from an exclusive focus on canonical texts and the elite stratum of society, formerly the subjects of intellectual history. Quentin Skinner suggests that

---

[43] Henry Parker, *Observations upon Some of His Majesty's Late Answers and Expresses* (London, 1642), 184–85.

[44] Richard Cust and Ann Hughes, "Introduction: After Revisionism," in Cust and Hughes, eds., *Conflict in Early Stuart England: Studies in Religion and Politics, 1603–1642* (London and New York: Longman, 1989), 17.

[45] Stuart Clark, "Inversion, Misrule and the Meaning of Witchcraft," *Past and Present* 87 (1980), 98–127; Derek Hirst, *Authority and Conflict: England, 1603–1658* (Cambridge, Mass.: Harvard University Press, 1986), 87.

[46] Cust and Hughes, "Introduction: After Revisionism," 17.

intellectual historians should study canonical texts "in broader traditions and frameworks of thought" and "to think of the history of political theory not as the study of allegedly canonical texts, but rather as a more wide-ranging investigation of the changing political languages in which societies talk to themselves."[47] This entails a widening of perspectives beyond narrow disciplinary categories. Political discourse was not confined to any one subject or even genre. Nigel Smith uncovers a proliferation of genres in the English Revolution while David Norbrook canvasses a wide range of republican texts, aiming to remove "canonical writers like Milton and Marvell from their timeless pantheon and . . . setting them in the political flux along with many much less well-known contemporaries."[48] Textual negotiations over the meaning of the family-state analogy cut across disciplines, canons, and genres, as this study shows. Because analogy was a fundamental early modern form of reasoning, the literary modes of analogy and metaphor were employed also in non-literary works. What is traditionally considered literature, or fiction, was in productive transactions with other discourses, political and historical, through the common and widespread use of the family-state analogy. Tracking the family-state analogy across genres, this study reads literary texts with non-literary ones as framing contexts for each other. Beyond the traditional texts of political philosophy, my focus on literary works and the more ephemeral texts of the period provides another perspective on the social and political uses of the familial metaphor. In particular, this study follows, from his early polemical tracts to his late epic, the career of a major author of the century, Milton, juxtaposing him with high political theorists like Hobbes and with royalist women and sectarian communities to show the metaphor's sustained power.

By widening our perspective to read literary texts alongside political or philosophical ones, we see more clearly the links between seemingly separate discourses. One with great political significance was religion. Not only were "high" and "low" culture inextricably linked, so too were the sacred and profane. Sometimes they were confused as when James I, referring to his close political advisor, George Villiers, the Duke of Buckingham, declared, "Christ had his John and I have my George."[49] Other times one served as foundation for the other: Mocket's *God and the King* concludes that kings are nursing fathers of the commonwealth from the interdependence

---

[47] Quentin Skinner, *Liberty before Liberalism* (Cambridge: Cambridge University Press, 1998), 101, 105.
[48] Smith, *Literature and Revolution in England*; Norbrook, *Writing the English Republic*, 9.
[49] Reported in a letter from the Spanish Ambassador Gondomar to the Archduke Albert, 2/12 October 161?, quoted in S. R. Gardiner, *History of England from the Accession of James I to the Outbreak of the Civil War, 1603–1642*, 10 vols. (London: Longmans, Green, 1883–84), III:98.

of religious community and civil society. Not only did political and religious discourses merge, religion was a crucial component of the causes of the civil wars, as revisionist historians in particular have shown.[50] Revisionists, however, are not the only ones who have noted the importance of religion in the English Revolution. In his *History of England*, long the traditional account, Samuel R. Gardiner argues that constitutional issues were less important than the religious issues that divided Parliament.[51] Puritanism became a revolutionary force as Charles I's support of Arminianism, which "adopted a persecuting attitude towards established Calvinism and generated xenophobic hostility," increasingly marginalized Calvinism: "the redefinition of puritanism, which implied that Calvinism was subversive, tended to become a self-fulfilling prophecy."[52] Puritanism became politicized such that the godly commonwealth stood in contradistinction to the absolutist monarchy. In placing the mid-century revolution in the context of wider European religious wars, Jonathan Scott argues, "*What* the English revolution was was belief – radical belief."[53] His focus on the revolutionary power of radical belief follows the lead of Gardiner and of Christopher Hill.[54] According to Scott, "Laudianism was counter-reformation Protestantism," but the distinction was difficult to discern and instead provoked fears of popery.[55] On the one hand, the monarchy was defensive about limits reformation religion might place on its power; on the other hand, the king's opponents' concern for the survival of parliaments became linked to Protestantism. After the Long Parliament forced Charles to abandon Arminianism, the nation did not return to the Elizabethan (and Jacobean) religious settlement that had accommodated a plurality of religious opinion. Instead, puritans pushed for further reformation with revolutionary consequences. In large part, religious belief went hand in hand with political action.

Intimately connected to politics, religious discourse intersected as well with literary discourse. Derek Hirst finds an "interweaving of matters ecclesiastical and expressive in the Restoration" so that literary style becomes indicative of religious belief: the "plain style" is preferred by the godly

[50] J. S. Morrill, "The Religious Context of the English Civil War," *Transactions of the Royal Historical Society*, 5th ser., 34 (1984), 155–78.

[51] Gardiner, *History of England*, x:11–12.

[52] L. J. Reeve, *Charles I and the Road to Personal Rule* (Cambridge: Cambridge University Press, 1989), 97.

[53] Jonathan Scott, *England's Troubles: Seventeenth-Century English Political Instability in European Context* (Cambridge: Cambridge University Press, 2000), 34. Earlier, Morrill made the case for the civil wars as the last of the European religious wars ("The Religious Context").

[54] Christopher Hill, *The World Turned Upside Down: Radical Ideas During the English Revolution* (London: Temple Smith, 1972).

[55] Scott, *England's Troubles*, 29.

while N. H. Keeble notes that university sermons in 1660 detected fanaticism in homespun metaphor and allegory typical of uneducated preachers.[56] Hirst points to an incident where even a young child was able to observe the overlapping discourses of religious controversy and theater such that "ecclesiastical controversialists and the poet laureate appeared to be in colloquy": John Humfrey was discussing whether conscience had a greater authority than a magistrate in relation to a pamphlet by Samuel Parker, future bishop of Oxford, titled *A Discourse of Ecclesiastical Polity*, when "a little Boy, about ten years of age, being carried belike to a Play [John Dryden's *Tyrannick Love*] that week, which being never at one before, had made some impressions in his mind, *Why Mother*, says he, to her standing by, [John] Lacy [the male lead] *hath confuted this Book; for he acting the Tyrant, said in the Play, That conscience was a greater King than he.*"[57] The same subject – whether the king had sovereignty over subjects' conscience, a matter with considerable political import – was discussed in both religious pamphlets and in popular plays.

Furthermore, literary and philosophical texts separated by politics were united by their choice of metaphor. This study explores the works of both royalists and radicals, finding not a strict division between the two groups but rather innovative adaptations of the metaphor. However diverse their politics, seventeenth-century authors shared literary conventions, and authors as different as John Milton, Margaret Cavendish, and the designers of court masques used the same metaphor to describe very different forms of ideal government. Reading them together exposes the literary and social assumptions that make the analogy between family and state so compelling as a shared, though contested, discourse to people across the political spectrum. Benedict Anderson has provocatively defined nations as "imagined communities," and in the seventeenth century, while people used similar ways of imagining, the images of community ended up strikingly different.[58] In reading these various "canons" in relation to each other, this study shows the points of contact between "high" political theory and

[56] Derek Hirst, "Making All Religion Ridiculous: Of Culture High and Low: The Polemics of Toleration, 1667–1673," *Renaissance Forum: An Electronic Journal of Early-Modern Literary and Historical Studies* 1.1 (1996), par. 6 (http://www.hull.ac.uk/renforum/v1no1/hirst.htm); N. H. Keeble, *The Literary Culture of Nonconformity in Later Seventeenth-Century England* (Leicester: Leicester University Press, 1987), 234–44.
[57] Hirst, "Making All Religion Ridiculous," par. 15; John Humfrey, *A case of conscience whether a nonconformist, who hath not taken the Oxford Oath, may come to live at London, or at any corporate town, or within five miles of it, and yet be a good Christian* (London, 1669), sig. B, 9.
[58] Benedict Anderson, *Imagined Communities: Reflections on the Origin and Spread of Nationalism*, rev. edn (London, 1991). For the discursive basis of early modern nationalism, see Richard Helgerson, *Forms of Nationhood: The Elizabethan Writing of England* (Chicago: University of Chicago Press, 1992).

more popular manifestations of political thought in other texts – literary and ephemeral.

Contestation over the analogy demonstrates also cultural continuities between the first half of the seventeenth century and the second half. Arbitrarily dividing the seventeenth century, literary history calls the early part of the century the Renaissance and declares everything after 1660 part of the long eighteenth century. In fact, English culture did not suddenly in 1660 become something totally different. Period divisions are merely convenient fictions. We cannot too quickly consolidate a narrative about the Revolution that ends with the Restoration in 1660. As Laura Knoppers reminds us, Milton's last major poems were published after the Restoration and they must be seen as texts of resistance, very much attuned to contemporary events, not solely as texts looking back on the past Revolution.[59] Restoration texts like *Paradise Lost* or the writings of Margaret Cavendish look back to the earlier seventeenth century as well as point forward. Literature we tend to divide into different categories – royalist *versus* republican, Renaissance *versus* Restoration, poetry *versus* political theory – was actually united by this habit of linking family and state, and thus there was a larger, more vigorous political debate than is often recognized.

Last, but not least, a discussion of patriarchalism cannot ignore gender. As the power of the king was contested, so too the power of the father. The intimate link between patriarchalism and patriarchy is most evident in the early modern domestic handbooks, which attempted to elevate the father in recreating absolutist hierarchies in the household. But the concept of patriarchy, as applied to a social system, is newer than we might imagine. The *OED* gives as its first reference to this meaning of the word a text from the early seventeenth century. Earlier, the word patriarch and other forms of the word referred to rulers of the Old Testament tribes of Israel and to their perceived inheritor, the church. Defenders of political patriarchalism turned to the Bible as their primary text, transferring such patriarchal powers that have been ascribed to Adam or Abraham or church fathers to the king and to male heads of households. If kings had paternal power, then fathers were said to be like kings. But as Margaret Ezell points out, seventeenth-century domestic patriarchalism was a literary phenomenon, "a concept of power derived from a literary source, the bible, and codified in written documents."[60] Like kingly authority, paternal authority cannot be taken for granted. In terms of the history of patriarchalism,

---

[59] Laura Lunger Knoppers, *Historicizing Milton: Spectacle, Power, and Poetry in Restoration England* (Athens: University of Georgia Press, 1994).
[60] Ezell, *The Patriarch's Wife*, 16.

the republican challenge to absolutism was at its heart also a challenge to the rule of the father, and so a challenge, even if a partial one, to patriarchy. While some scholars have argued that the universalist language of the Habermasian public sphere excluded women and that republicanism was inherently masculinist, often such critiques needed to take into account women who resisted marginalization into the private sphere.[61] Indeed, some women, as David Norbrook argues, "did indeed assume that certain spheres of discourse were universal, rather than specifically masculine, and hence vigorously claimed inclusion."[62]

It is a mistake to think of patriarchalism or patriarchy as a monolithic system. It too has a history and changes over time. Patriarchalism – both political and domestic – has two vulnerable points. What do you do about other men? What do you do about class? First, even if the father is the ultimate authority in the home, we still need to decide who is superior among a group of patriarchs. The tragedy of King Lear, as Shakespeare wrote it, was his inability to accept that his daughter's bond of duty to her father was inevitably limited by a similar bond to a husband, and each could only have half her love and half her care and duty. Secondly, the class system means that some women had authority over some men. Early modern society was a complex system of intersecting gender and class hierarchies. It was not, and has never been, a simple case of all women being oppressed by all men. There was, too, the authority of age, giving older women authority over younger men, to upset that strict binary. These vulnerabilities were easily exploited as the English Revolution expanded the scope for women's participation in church and state. My first chapters suggest the gendered nature of political thought in the masques of queens, in Milton's language of masculine liberty, in Hobbes's gendered contest in the state of nature, and in the debate over republican fatherhood. The chapters in the second half feature women more prominently by examining their political ideas, whether in their fiction or in their participation in separatist churches.

In the history of patriarchalism, the seventeenth century was a particularly important moment when patriarchy was extended into a political system and gendered differences were turned into an explicit system of government. The history of patriarchalism was central to patriarchy in its early modern articulation. Both early modern patriarchy and patriarchalism

[61] See Hilda L. Smith, *All Men and Both Sexes: Gender, Politics, and the False Universal in England, 1640–1832* (University Park: Pennsylvania State University Press, 2002).
[62] David Norbrook, "Women, the Republic of Letters, and the Public Sphere in the Mid-Seventeenth Century," *Criticism* 46.2 (2004), 224. His examples are Margaret Cavendish and Anna Maria van Schurman, who both entered into the republic of letters through their writings.

were not consistent ideologies. While revolutionary politics did not go hand in hand with progressive notions of gender, the debate over the family-state analogy also involved a debate over gender. In this debate, gender and class differences were used to turn the tables on patriarchalists. In debunking absolutist patriarchalism, early modern authors also debunked domestic patriarchy. In doing so, they expanded the possibilities for political action, reconceptualized authority, and redefined gender roles.

PART I

Revolutionary debates

CHAPTER I

Father-kings and Amazon queens

FATHER-KINGS

James I, perhaps England's most learned king, not only commissioned but also wrote treatises on divine-right kingship in which he frequently resorted to the analogy linking father and king to explain monarchical duties and authority. His *Trew Law of Free Monarchies* asserts, "The King towards his people is rightly compared to a father of children."[1] In *Basilicon Doron*, the good king is a "naturall father and kindly Master" to the people, while a tyrant is a "step-father and an vncouth hireling" (20). While aware that not all kings are good, James's comparison between a tyrant and a stepfather reveals a marked tendency to employ family analogies. Instead of a sharp distinction, tyrant and good king are on a continuum. James advises Prince Henry to stamp out dissent by turning himself into the people's only father: "Suffer none about you to meddle in any mens particulars, but like the Turkes Ianisaries, let them know no father but you, nor particular but yours" (*Basilicon Doron*, 38). Given the early modern association of Turkishness with tyranny, the reference to Turkish janissaries elides the categories of kings and tyrants. James's ingrained habit of naturalizing kings as fathers appears too when he describes the coronation: "By the Law of Nature the King becomes a naturall Father to all his Lieges at his Coronation" (*Trew Law*, 65). Kings literally become fathers when they ascend the throne. Going beyond analogy, James substitutes the king for biological fathers of families.

In James's patriarchal state, the people have no right to rebel. Even a tyrannical father (or king) commands absolute obedience: "Yea, suppose the father were furiously following his sonnes with a drawn sword, is it lawfull for them to turne and strike againe, or make any resistance but by flight?" (*Trew Law*, 77). Because flight is the only resistance permitted,

---

[1] King James VI and I, *Political Writings*, ed. Johann P. Sommerville (Cambridge: Cambridge University Press, 1994), 76. Further references to James's works are from this edition and cited parenthetically.

the subject's independent action is greatly limited. James often simply calls subjects children, conflating the two to obscure their analogical relation. This is particularly true of sections on the duty of subjects, which maintain that kings are literally, not just analogically, fathers. When speaking of fatherly love, however, James's language asserts the king's royal identity by highlighting the analogy: one passage is composed almost entirely of "As . . . so" sentence constructions, beginning with "And as the Father of his fatherly duty is bound to care . . . [for] his children; euen so is the king bound to care for all his subiects" (*Trew Law*, 65). In discussing royal authority, James retains the name of king and adds to it the name and authority of father. In detailing the duty of children, he defines subjects as children to construct them as dependent, immature, and incapable of resistance.

Such assertions in *Trew Law* and other works have been read as evidence of James's absolutist tendencies by historians and literary scholars alike. Jonathan Goldberg's *James I and the Politics of Literature*, long the influential account of Jacobean literature, depicts a court-centered universe of discourse, in which James's royal articulations constitute power networks. Assuming an authoritarian father-king, Goldberg turns the literary sphere into a version of an absolutist political sphere. Among historians, the question of absolutism in the early Jacobean period provoked a heated debate. The traditional view detects an increasingly absolutist English monarchy, following continental trends. Revisionist historians, however, challenge the long-standing historical framework erected by Samuel R. Gardiner's monumental *History of England* to argue there was no "high road to civil war."[2] According to Conrad Russell and others, seventeenth-century England was "unrevolutionary," characterized by consensus rather than ideological conflict.[3] The story of an absolutist court pitted against a proto-democratic Parliament, anti-Marxist revisionists claim, is a Whig interpretation of history.[4] At the start of the seventeenth century, revisionists argue, the English did not understand absolutism to mean unlimited monarchical power. Rather, it implied a monarch who was independent of foreign rule,

[2] Samuel R. Gardiner, *History of England from the Accession of James I to the Outbreak of the Civil War, 1603–1642*, 10 vols. (London: Longmans, Green, 1883–84); G. R. Elton, "A High Road to Civil War?" in C. H. Carter, ed., *From the Renaissance to the Counter-Reformation: Essays in Honor of Garrett Mattingly* (New York: Random House, 1965), 325–47.

[3] Conrad Russell, "Parliamentary History in Perspective, 1604–1629," *History* 61 (1976), 1–27, *Parliaments and English Politics 1621–1629* (Oxford: Clarendon Press, 1979), *The Causes of the English Civil War* (Oxford: Clarendon Press, 1990), and *Unrevolutionary England* (London: Hambleton Press, 1990).

[4] Herbert Butterfield, *The Whig Interpretation of History* (New York: Norton, 1965).

deriving authority from God, so that a monarch could be absolute and still shared sovereignty with Parliament.[5] In rereading early Stuart history, revisionists recuperated James's reputation, revealing him to be a politic king able to work effectively with Parliament. Paul Christianson argues that by the time of his speech to Parliament on 21 March 1610, James had learned to speak the discourse of the common law, couching his absolutism in constitutionalist terms while J. P. Kenyon asserts that James "was careful always to operate within the framework of the Common Law."[6] The recent more nuanced interpretations of James are needed correctives to the old picture of an inflexible and incompetent king.

However, in abandoning Gardiner's paradigm, revisionists have not been able to explain adequately how the civil war started. Critics of revisionism emphasize, even beyond the issue of religion, the "role of principle" or ideology, pointing to the prominence of Parliament as an elected body, for coordinated political strategizing suggesting the formation of an "opposition" or several, and for the political energy and initiative of the gentry in the Commons.[7] Even if he did not put absolutism into practice, James spouted absolutist rhetoric inconsistent with the constitutionalist views of common lawyers and many parliamentarians of his day, rhetoric that connects James to continental modes of thought.[8] Quarrelling with Attorney General Edward Coke over the king's prerogative in interpreting the law, James favored the Roman maxim *rex est lex loquens* while Coke, who undertook the massive task of compiling case law in his *Reports*, insisted that *judex est lex loquens*; refusing to revise his *Reports*, the lawyer was stripped of his position of chief justice.[9] Rejecting Coke's argument that common law also governs the king, James maintained the "King is aboue the law, as both the author and giuer of strength thereto" (*Trew Law*, 75). Jenny

---

[5] James Daly, "The Idea of Absolute Monarchy in Seventeenth-Century England," *Historical Journal* 21 (1978), 227–50.

[6] Paul Christianson, "Royal and Parliamentary Voices on the Ancient Constitution, c. 1604–1621," in Linda Levy Peck, ed., *The Mental World of the Jacobean Court* (Cambridge: Cambridge University Press, 1991), 71–95; J. P. Kenyon, *The Stuart Constitution: Documents and Commentary* (Cambridge: Cambridge University Press, 1969), 8.

[7] Derek Hirst, "Revisionism Revised: The Place of Principle," *Past and Present* 92 (1981), 81; Thedore K. Rabb, "Revisionism Revised: The Role of the Commons," *Past and Present* 92 (1981), 55–78.

[8] Charles Howard McIlwain, "Introduction," *The Political Works of James I* (New York: Russell & Russell, 1965); and J. P. Sommerville, "James I and the Divine Right of Kings: English Politics and Continental Theory," in Peck, ed., *Mental World*, 55–70.

[9] In his parliamentary speech of 1607, James claims, "*Rex est Iudex*, for he is *Lex loquens*" (*Political Writings*, 171). For Coke's relation to James, see Richard Helgerson, *Forms of Nationhood: The Elizabethan Writing of England* (Chicago: The University of Chicago Press, 1992), ch. 2; and Catherine Drinker Bowen, *The Lion and the Throne: The Life and Times of Sir Edward Coke* (Boston: Little, Brown, 1957).

Wormald points out that by 1577 the royal Scottish library contained a copy of Guillaume Budé's *Institut du Prince* and Jean Bodin's *République*, both of which offered absolutism in contrast to his populist tutor George Buchanan's contractualism that insisted on the right to remove tyrants from the throne.[10] She finds James's use of common law language merely a "veneer, overlaying his very different approach."[11] James's view of kingship was perceived as a change from Elizabethan practice. At the end of the seventeenth century, James Welwood argues that James was seeking absolute power: "As she [Elizabeth] was far from invading the *Liberties of her Subjects*, so she was careful to maintain and preserve her own *just Prerogative . . .* [while James] grasp'd at an *Immoderate Power*, but with an ill Grace; and if we believe the Historians of that time, with a design to make his People *little*."[12]

Perhaps the most untiring revisionist critic is Glenn Burgess, who believes the opposition between absolutism and constitutionalism a false dichotomy: instead, a broad consensus agreed that the king was accountable only to God and thus irresistible, but he was also bound by the laws.[13] Equally indefatigable is Burgess's staunchest opponent, Johann Sommerville, who protests that Burgess's distinctions rest on such narrow definitions that it is hard to find absolutists on the continent let alone in England.[14] While Burgess emphasizes how absolutist-sounding definitions of sovereignty became qualified to conform to what he calls the mainstream consensual view, Sommerville highlights the perception of contemporaries alarmed by these statements. Lately we are moving beyond this impasse. In a recent collection of essays honoring Conrad Russell, the editors so revised revisionism – claiming that Russell did not eschew long-term structural explanations nor was he unaware of ideological conflict – that little of it seems recognizable.[15] Similarly, essays in the volume portray a society riven by ideology with national politics considerably influencing local. Post-revisionists incorporate the insights of revisionism without discarding

---

[10] J. P. Sommerville, "James I and the Divine Right of Kings," 56; Jenny Wormald, "James VI and I, *Basilikon Doron* and *The Trew Law of Free Monarchies*: The Scottish Context and the English Translation," in Peck, ed., *Mental World*, 43.

[11] Jenny Wormald, "James VI and I: Two Kings or One?" *History* 68 (1983), 205.

[12] James Welwood, *Memoirs of the Most Material Transactions in England, for the Last Hundred Years, Preceding the Revolution in 1688* (London, 1700), 18–19.

[13] Glenn Burgess, *Absolute Monarchy and the Stuart Constitution* (New Haven: Yale University Press, 1996).

[14] J. P. Sommerville, "Revisionism Revisited: A Retrospect," in *Royalists and Patriots: Politics and Ideology in England 1603–1640*, 2nd edn (London and New York: Longman, 1999).

[15] Thomas Cogswell, Richard Cust, and Peter Lake, eds., *Politics, Religion and Popularity in Early Stuart Britain: Essays in Honour of Conrad Russell* (Cambridge: Cambridge University Press, 2002).

the useful features of Gardiner's paradigm. Neither the extreme polarizing of debate nor the collapsing of ideological difference is helpful. Because the family-state analogy was a language of debate, opposing discourses employing the metaphor share features with one another while having points of disagreement. As Derek Hirst says,

> A common political language, whether it is used to address the divinity of kingship or the importance of the past, is not therefore a sign that all assumptions are shared. Indeed, one of the most marked features of that language may have helped to uncover discordant elements in the vaunted harmony.[16]

It is not by denying the existence of absolutism – real or theoretical – that we complicate the picture of the Stuart monarchy but by paying attention to the debate. In literary studies, Curtis Perry's recent challenge to Goldberg, for instance, maintains the king's centrality while still recognizing the varied and ambivalent nature of James's influence, thus allowing for individual agency and "the possibility of genuine opposition to the dominant social order."[17] A crucial node of the debate, the figure of the father functioned as a vehicle for discussing the extent and limits of paternal and royal power. A closer examination of James's own varied uses of the family-state analogy reveals it not to be completely in his control but rife with internal contradictions. James was not able to sustain fully his absolutist rhetoric.

Moreover, early modern understanding of monarchy itself contained contradictions, as Glenn Burgess shows with the notion of double prerogative.[18] The king had two sorts of powers: ordinary and absolute prerogative. Within ordinary prerogative, kings must conform to common law; absolute or extraordinary prerogative supplemented common law, supporting monarchical acts in areas where common law had no force. Disputes arose from disagreements over whether particular acts fell under the king's absolute prerogative, such as the case of the imposition of custom duties debated in the parliamentary sessions of 1610 and 1614. James's critics, like James Whitelocke, did not deny his absolute prerogative but felt it did not apply to the case. Burgess suggests that the Jacobean consensus accommodated a variety of political languages and worked so long as these languages were not used inappropriately. In fact, such "consensus" was already fissured. As Derek Hirst points out, absolute prerogative came into play in states

---

[16] Hirst, "Revisionism Revised," 83.
[17] Curtis Perry, *The Making of Jacobean Culture: James I and the Renegotiation of Elizabethan Literary Practice* (Cambridge: Cambridge University Press, 1997), 6.
[18] Glenn Burgess, *The Politics of the Ancient Constitution: An Introduction to English Political Thought, 1603–1642* (University Park: The Pennsylvania State University Press, 1993), 139–78.

of emergency when to preserve the state the king could take action as he
alone saw fit. But because there was no clear way of deciding whether the
situation was an emergency, difficulties arose when Charles used such prerogative powers to raise revenue (a domestic matter governed by ordinary
prerogative) and turned extraordinary into ordinary use.[19]

As such, even revisionists detect a drift toward absolutism in the Caroline period: while James took care to operate within the law, Charles
I sought to bend it, pushing the constitutional framework to its breaking
point. In the case of the forced loan, for instance, Charles attempted to alter
the existing constitution with arbitrary imprisonment, extra-parliamentary
taxation, and martial law. To curb the king's absolutist innovations, Parliament responded with the 1628 Petition of Right. Having the force of
a statute, the Petition more clearly defined and revised royal prerogative,
with the consequence that under Charles the law became "less a vehicle
of social cohesion and more an instrument of political dissent."[20] His dis-
comfort with ambiguity made him unsuited to ruling with a constitution
that depended on blurred distinctions. Charles came to rely more on non-
parliamentary forms of government and eventually in 1629 did away with
parliaments altogether. His rhetoric was also polarizing: in the summer
leading to his personal rule, Charles complained to the French ambassador
Chateauneuf of being attacked by Parliament and denigrated parliamentary leaders as "puritans, enemies of monarchs, and . . . republicans."[21]
Although constitutional royalists – moderates committed to the rule of
law – continued to support the mixed constitution and attempted to negotiate a settlement in the 1640s, the former consensus could not be sustained.[22]

Ideologically, Charles saw himself following in his father's footsteps.[23]
The official policy of his government in the *Constitutions and Canons Ecclesiasticall* of 1640 upholds James's absolutist views. Translating theory into
practical duties and rights, the *Constitutions* gives the king "absolute power
over the lives and consciences of his subjects," not allowing any form,
even defensive, of resistance against the king.[24] Charles also resorted to

[19] Derek Hirst, *Authority and Conflict: England, 1603–1658* (Cambridge, Mass.: Harvard University
    Press, 1986), 27.
[20] L. J. Reeve, *Charles I and the Road to Personal Rule* (Cambridge: Cambridge University Press, 1989),
    21.
[21] *Ibid.*, 132.
[22] David Smith, *Constitutional Royalism and the Search for Settlement, c. 1640–1649* (Cambridge:
    Cambridge University Press, 1994).
[23] Reeve, *Charles I*, 174–75; David Mathew, *Scotland under Charles I* (London: Eyre and Spottiswoode,
    1955), 26.
[24] George F. Sensabaugh, *That Grand Whig Milton* (Stanford: Stanford University Press, 1952), 10.

the family-state analogy to support divine-right monarchy. In the sermon preached before the king in 1627, Roger Maynwaring calls for obedience in support of the forced loan: "For, as a *Father* of the Countrey, hee commands what his pleasure is."[25] Charles ordered Maynwaring's sermon, as well as the absolutist cleric Robert Sibthorpe's, to be published, in spite of Archbishop Laud's caution, with the inscription, "By His Majesties Special Command." Maynwaring's sermon rehearses commonplaces about the reciprocal bonds of relations between God and man, husband and wife, parents and children, and masters and servants to conclude that from those arose the "most *high, sacred,* and *transcendent Relation,* which naturally growes betweene *The Lords Anointed,* and their loyall *Subiects*: to, and ouer whom, their lawfull *Soueraignes* are no lesse then *Fathers, Lords, Kings,* and *Gods* on earth."[26]

Claiming that kings, superior even to angels, participate in God's omnipotence, Maynwaring's sermon connects religious and political obedience. While James spoke of kings as gods, he did not tinker with the earlier Elizabethan religious accommodation, but maintained an inclusive church. Unlike his father, Charles promoted Arminians like William Laud and attempted to force religious uniformity. His religious innovations had effects similar to his political novelties: his "passion for definition in religious matters – his search for unity through uniformity – forced others to define their own positions."[27] Resistance to Arminianism would define it as crypto-popery and associated it with arbitrary government and divine-right monarchy. Laud promoted the idea of episcopacy *jure divino*. Bishop Joseph Hall continued justifying the church's authority from divine right in his *Episcopacy by Divine Right, Asserted* (1641); in it, he made liberal use of the maternal metaphor, imagining Christians as dutiful sons of the church.[28] In turn, Charles himself would come to associate Presbyterianism with sedition: "all popular Reformation" is "little better than Rebellions."[29] Making explicit what James only implied, Charles and his supporters put James's theory into practice with disastrous consequences.

Charles's attempt to fix one interpretation to such uncertain notions as the monarch's double prerogative exposed its inherent contradictions. Just as these contradictions could be exploited by a resisting Parliament,

[25] Roger Maynwaring, *Religion and Alegiance: In Two Sermons* (London, 1627), sig. D2, 19.
[26] *Ibid.*, sig. B2–B2v, 3–4.   [27] Smith, *Constitutional Royalism*, 32.
[28] Joseph Hall, *The Works of the Right Reverend Joseph Hall D. D.*, ed. Philip Wynter, rev. and corrected, vol. IX (Oxford: Clarendon Press, 1863; reprint New York: AMS Press, 1969).
[29] *The Papers which passed at Newcastle betwixt His Sacred Majestie and Mr Al[exander] Henderson: concerning the change of Church-Government* (1649), 38. Cited in Smith, *Constitutional Royalism*, 129.

so too could the contradictions in family metaphors. The mystical union between king and country supported by the idea of the king's two bodies, for instance, ruptured under scrutiny. For inherent to the king's two bodies was a doubleness in monarchy, making possible the fiction of an immortal sovereign who was above the law.[30] But the differences between the king's natural body and his political one could also be emphasized. The man occupying the seat of monarchy could be separated from the institution. When taken to its logical end, Charles was tried for treason, transformed from father of his country to its tyrant. The hierarchies of family relations themselves could clash. Although Maynwaring's sermon describes the hierarchies, or "bonds of relations," as though they were mutually supportive and fitted together seamlessly in a unified system of correspondences, in fact one hierarchy could be used to contest another. Interestingly, in summing up the monarch's multiple roles of "*Fathers, Lords, Kings*, and *Gods*," he neglects to include one hierarchy. The bond of relation between husband and spouse, though mentioned earlier, does not reappear in the litany of monarchical roles. The absence is suggestive of how gender was a crucial fracture in the consensual system of correspondences. Later Whig authors like John Locke would exploit it, pointing out that the biblical command is to obey both father and mother, to challenge patriarchalism. For now, before the civil wars, any conflict arising from gender was kept largely at bay or at worst only appeared in mild forms of discord such as in kings' relations with queens.

JAMES AND THE CONTRADICTIONS OF FAMILY ROLES

James's apparently rigid definition of family roles is belied by his varied and sometimes contradictory uses of family metaphors. His book of advice to the prince is a significant example of this inconsistency. *Basilicon Doron*'s idealized portrait of a father teaching his (silent) son contains a suppressed contradiction. James presents kings and fathers as having speaking roles; but the silence and submissiveness required of the reader is a position that Prince Henry as future king only uneasily occupies. The ambiguity of Henry's role is most evident in the passage where James advises Henry on how to behave after James's death. While Henry may succeed to the throne, he does not necessarily assume the infallible authority of the father-king but

---

[30] Ernst H. Kantorowicz, *The King's Two Bodies: A Study in Mediaeval Political Theology* (Princeton: Princeton University Press, 1957).

must continue honoring his parents, including his mother: "And if it fall out that my Wife shall out-liue me, as euer ye thinke to purchase my blessing, honour your mother: . . . beginne not, like the young lordes and lairdes, your first warres vpon your Mother" (*Basilicon Doron*, 47). James warns him, "O inuert not the order of nature, by iudging your superiours, chiefly in your owne particular!" (*Basilicon Doron*, 47). Is this admonition meant for Henry as prince? Does it apply when he is king? James even includes Henry's former teachers and childhood governors among the superiors he must honor, though they would be his subjects: "Honour also them that are *in loco Parentum* vnto you, such as your gouernours, vp-bringers, and Præceptours" (*Basilicon Doron*, 47). Pulled in two directions, Henry must cultivate "trew humilitie" (*Basilicon Doron*, 47) while imitating his father, the absolute king. These exhortations are not necessarily contradictory; the contradiction is in distance between the roles of father and son that James creates for himself and for Henry, making it difficult to imagine Henry an absolute king.

Dying at eighteen from typhoid, Henry never did have to contend with the contradiction of playing the roles of both son and father-king. James, however, did. While not yet king of England, he corresponded with Elizabeth to press his case as her heir. As such, he needed to present himself as her spiritual son. While in most of his letters to Elizabeth James signs himself brother and cousin (occasionally also friend), James calls Elizabeth "mother" and calls himself her "son" in letters during a crisis precipitated by the murder of Lord Russell, son of the Earl of Bedford, killed during a meeting of English and Scottish wardens of the Middle March, which jeopardized the developing Anglo-Scottish alliance.[31] Upon hearing of the murder, James hastily wrote Elizabeth protesting his innocence. Addressing Elizabeth as "Madame and mother," James calls her "mother" a second time in the body of the letter.[32] Wanting to preserve good relations with England, James constructed himself as Elizabeth's inferior, as her son, to appease her anger while still emphasizing their familial closeness.

James did not always play the part of a supplicating son, though he did swallow his pride in accepting Elizabeth's explanation that she did not intend the execution of his natural mother, Mary Queen of Scots. In a sonnet written for Elizabeth, James uses, among others, metaphors of marriage and of brotherhood:

[31] G. P. V. Akrigg, ed., *Letters of King James VI & I* (Berkeley and Los Angeles: University of California Press, 1984), 64–66, letters 15 and 16.
[32] *Ibid.*, 64, letter 15.

Full oft contentions great arise, we see,
Betwixt the husband and his loving wife
That sine they may the firmlyer agree
When ended is that sudden choler strife.
Yea, brethren, loving other as their life,
Will have debates at certain times and hours.
. . .
Een so this coldness did betwixt us fall
To kindle our love as sure I hope it shall.[33]

The indiscriminate use of family metaphors here – Elizabeth as both brother and spouse – suggests the malleability of family roles when used as tropes to represent a close relationship. The connotations of brother and of spouse are very different, of course. When James calls Elizabeth brother, he acknowledges that they both possess royal status, but he also suggests that they are roughly equals. When James calls Elizabeth his spouse, the roles are ambiguously assigned. Elizabeth's gender makes her more like a wife, but the power dynamics between her and James makes the other identification a strong possibility. Wisely, James does not make the comparisons explicit, avoiding the double shoals of presumption and excessive concession. (Later, he would make the mistake of comparing Elizabeth with Vergil's Dido, and had to work hard to smoothe her ruffled feathers.)[34]

James's indiscriminate use of family metaphors is not simply the effect of political strategy. Another example, from late in his reign, is his relations with his last favorite, George Villiers, duke of Buckingham. There the varied family configurations in which he imagined himself with Buckingham come from intense emotions. His addresses to Buckingham as "My only sweet and dear child" and himself as "your dear dad" are consonant with his tendency to literalize the analogy of king as father.[35] Although, given his three surviving children, it is peculiar for James to call Buckingham his only child, Buckingham fits readily into the analogy as subject-child. But in one well-known letter that has confused scholars, James anticipates a reunion with Buckingham as "a new marriage ever to be kept hereafter." He confesses: "for, God so love me, as I desire only to live in this world for your sake, and that I had rather live banished in any part of the earth with you than live a sorrowful widow's life without you. And so God bless you,

---

[33] *Ibid.*, 72, letter 19, lines 5–10, 13–14.   [34] *Ibid.*, 128, letter 51.
[35] See letters 179, 180, 182, 188–202, 205–12, 214–15, 221–26 in *ibid.* (372–442, *passim*). Letters 189–211, written to both Buckingham and Prince Charles when they were on the romantic quest to woo the Spanish Infanta, address them as "My sweet boys."

my sweet child and wife, and grant that ye may ever be a comfort to your dear dad and husband."[36] Scholars have speculated on James's homosexual relations with his male favorites.[37] Here desire may intensify James's feelings with the effect of shifting his metaphors for Buckingham from son to wife. The shifts again suggest malleability in James's use of family metaphors. By naming Buckingham his wife, James allows Buckingham a closer, perhaps more equitable, relation, if his use of the marriage trope here is anything like in his letters to Elizabeth. There is further slippage when James refers to himself as widow. Although the word "widow" can have a common gender in the period, when he imagines himself a grieving widower, James sees himself as dependent in some ways on Buckingham, thus reversing, even if only slightly, the ordinary hierarchy. Nor can James's letters to Buckingham be entirely contained as private communications because of the public nature of its transmission. They may be more correctly viewed as semi-public, given that a number of the letters were also addressed to or from a third party. More importantly, his relationship with Buckingham was never entirely private. When Buckingham accompanied Charles on the mission to Spain, one satirist commented, "Buckingham, his spouse, is gone / And left the widowed king alone."[38] Having seeped into the public realm to acquire new connotations, the king's language is employed to satirize an ostensibly private relation with great public consequence. Later, the same accusation would be leveled against Charles, leaving the ship of state "Not governed by the master, but his mate;"[39] the term "mate" for Buckingham casts sexual aspersions at his relationship with the king. As Lena Cowen Orlin notes: "The rage for analogy explains the permeability during the English Renaissance of discourses that today seem categorically distinct."[40]

Besides the way that family metaphors sometimes fit only uneasily, there are other dissonances in the figure of the absolutist father-king, among

[36] *Ibid.*, 431, letter 218.
[37] For James's homosexuality, see Godfrey Davies, "The Character of James VI and I," *Huntington Library Quarterly* 5 (1941–42), 33–63; Maurice Lee, Jr., *Great Britain's Solomon: James VI and I in his Three Kingdoms* (Urbana and Chicago: University of Illinois Press, 1990), particularly ch. 8; David M. Bergeron, *Royal Family, Royal Lovers: King James of England and Scotland* (Columbia: University of Missouri Press, 1991), 28–31, 160–87; and Bruce R. Smith, *Homosexual Desire in Shakespeare's England: A Cultural Poetics* (Chicago: University of Chicago Press, 1991).
[38] Norman K. Farmer, "Poems from a Seventeenth-Century Manuscript with the Hand of Robert Herrick," Supplement to *Texas Quarterly* 16 (1973), 144–45.
[39] "On the Duke, 1628," in Frederick W. Fairholt, ed., *Poems Relating to George Villiers, Duke of Buckingham and his Assassination by John Felton, August 23, 1628*, Percy Society, Early English Ballads, vol. xxix (London: Percy Society, 1850), 77.
[40] Lena Cowen Orlin, *Private Matters and Public Culture in Post-Reformation England* (Ithaca: Cornell University Press, 1994), 10.

them its dual nature. James tries to combine both a "nourish father" and an absolutist king who cannot be resisted even if he is tyrannical. In *The Trew Law of Free Monarchies*, this potentially contradictory combination means that James has to describe the function of a king not once but twice. First, he describes the love and care that a father-king would give his subjects (as children) in a long passage that makes ample use of the analogy of king as father: "And as the Father of his fatherly duty is bound to care for the nourishing, education, and vertuous gouernment of his children; euen so is the king bound to care for all his subiects" (65). Here James emphasizes the good, loving father who sacrifices for his children, whose every act is done for their welfare, even putting himself in danger to protect them. Oddly enough, this passage on the fatherly love of kings is followed by a direct quotation from 1 Samuel 8: 9–20, in which Samuel warns the Israelites that if they ask for a king, the king will take away their possessions and make servants of their children. Eschewing the conventional interpretation of the verses as a prophecy of Saul's future tyranny, James interprets them as an exhortation of obedience: "to prepare their [the Israelites'] hearts before the hand to the due obedience of that King, which God was to giue vnto them; and therefore opened vp vnto them, what might be the intollerable qualities that might fall in some of their kings, thereby preparing them to patience, not to resist to Gods ordinance" (*Trew Law*, 67). James explicates each of the verses at great length in defense of the right of kings to do as they wish.[41] The subtitle of the work, *The Reciprock and Mvtvall Dvetie Betwixt A Free King, and His Naturall Subiects*, suggests a mutuality in the relationship between a king and his subjects, but by the end of *Trew Law* James has redefined reciprocity as the absolute obedience of subjects to their king. Positioned at the top of the hierarchy, he also claims the right to change the hierarchy at will, arguing that a father (and king) may ignore the laws of primogeniture:

Now a Father may dispose of his Inheritance to his children, at his pleasure: yea, euen disinherite the eldest vpon iust occasions, and preferre the youngest, according to his liking: make them beggers, or rich at his pleasure; restraine, or banish out of his presence, as hee findes them giue cause of offence, or restore them in fauour againe with the penitent sinner: So may the King deale with his Subiects. (*Trew Law*, 182)

Making only the barest of effort to justify ignoring natural order, James emphasizes the father-king's will. While the verses from Samuel are used to insist on subjects' duty to obey, the analogy of the "nourish father" finally simply describes the character of the ideal king. It is not some obligation he is compelled to meet. With boundless power, the king cannot be restricted by his duty.

James's most prominent self-fashioning was as father-king. But in his writings and speeches he employed a range of familial tropes. Imagining himself variously in the position of father, husband, and son, his unrestricted use of the metaphor could lead to contradiction. Even within an absolutist, court-centered framework, the metaphor had a range of potentially incompatible expressions. This was no more evident than in James's use of the marital metaphor, where gender difference exacerbated the dissonances. In his first speech to the English Parliament, James I recommends the union of his two kingdoms in terms of marriage:

What God hath conioyned then, let no man separate. I am the Husband, and all the whole Isle is my lawfull Wife; . . . I hope therefore no man will be so vnreasonable as to thinke that I that am a Christian King vnder the Gospel, should be a Polygamist and husband to two wiues. (136)

Pleading for the union, James puts himself in the dangerous position of being seen as a polygamist, at least politically. His choice of metaphor highlights his divided loyalties, especially unfortunate at a time when the English feared that James was favoring his Scottish courtiers. But he also uses the marriage trope to refer to England and Scotland as potential spouses. Arguing for the Instrument of Union, James compares it to the terms of jointure that must first be agreed upon before marriage:

Vnion is a mariage: would he not bee thought absurd that for furthering of a mariage betweene two friends of his, would make his first motion to haue the two parties be laid in bedde together, and performe the other turnes of mariage? Must there not precede the mutuall sight and acquaintance of the parties one with another, the conditions of the contract, the Ioincture to be talked of and agreed vpon by their friends, and such other things as in order ought to goe before the ending of such a worke? (163)

If England and Scotland are going to be spouses, who will play which role? A question about hierarchy and power, it has vast ramifications in areas as diverse as law and religion. James is forced to concede to his English Parliament: "you [the English] are to be the husband, they [the Scottish] the wife: you conquerors, they as conquered, though not by the sword, but by the sweet and sure bond of loue" (164). Though couched in the language of spousal love, the relationship remains hierarchical. Nonetheless, the lines of authority remain in question when the king who is married to both England and Scotland wants the two kingdoms to be married, raising again the specter of polygamy.

The potential contradictions of occupying different roles were, however, largely kept in abeyance. James only referred to himself as son in the period before he ascended the English throne and in private letters to Elizabeth. Nonetheless, the contradictions alert us to how other authors may come to appropriate the family metaphor to further political agendas different from, even opposed to, that of the Stuart monarchy. Because it raises the question of gender, marriage as a trope poses particular problems when employed in conjunction with the analogy of king as father. Royal marriages thus become another source of inconsistent portrayals of family relationships.[42]

AMAZON QUEENS

With the establishment of the Stuart dynasty, England once more had queen consorts, something not seen during the long decades of rule by an unmarried queen. Coming from other European monarchies, Stuart queens followed common continental practice in setting up their own court, which constituted another source of royal patronage and political power. Since they arrived with other royal alliances, they had scope to define their own style and roles. This Anna of Denmark and later Henrietta Maria accomplished through extensive use of masques and court entertainments.

Anna's popular reception in Scotland as an alternative source of patronage or as a center around which could form an oppositional court is evident from the rhetoric of her entry into Edinburgh in 1590. In the Butter Tron pageant presented to Anna, female performers hailed her as their maternal protector: "We will treat you as our mother / And you shall be our brave refuge."[43] One speech reminds Anna to "bear royal children with honour, / and also become a woman of intelligence / whose virtues will shine both inwardly and outwardly. / You will inspire your lord to good deeds / and convert the people to the fear of God."[44] While emphasizing her wifely duty to her king, the invocation of Anna as mother suggests too a power, like James's, conceived in parental terms. Mother to future royal heirs, she is also mother of her people and country. If the father-king fails

---

[42] For a study of marriage metaphors in the union debates, see Anne McLaren, "Monogamy, Polygamy and the True State: James I's Rhetoric of Empire," *History of Political Thought* 25.3 (2004), 446–80.

[43] David Stevenson with Peter Graves, trans., *Scotland's Last Royal Wedding: The Marriage of James VI and Anne of Denmark* (Edinburgh: John Donald Publishers, 1997), 111.

[44] *Ibid.*, 110.

to protect his people, they can turn to the mother-queen. Although the rhetoric of motherhood may not have subversive intent, the openness of the family analogy to appropriation can potentially destabilize the king's power. Anna's reception as maternal protector was not simply a symbolic gesture. She came to Scotland with royal authority, allied to kings in her own right as daughter of one and sister of another. Unafraid to oppose the king, Anna was a self-assertive, independent, and politically adroit queen. From all accounts, she frequently clashed with her husband, often over the guardianship of her children, particularly the Prince of Wales. Although dismissed by historians as frivolous, Anna's adeptness at political maneuvering in the factional Scottish court suggests otherwise. As Leeds Barroll points out, in her dispute with Sir John Maitland, the powerful chancellor, Anna "managed . . ., at age of eighteen, to align with her against Scotland's chancellor . . . such disparate figures as the duke of Lennox, the earl of Mar, the earl of Bothwell . . ., and Alexander Sixth Lord Home, creating a near crisis whose seriousness is confirmed by a number of contemporary assessments."[45]

In masques Anna found a means by which to shape her public self-representation. Dancing roles featuring independent, warrior women, she put family metaphors under pressure and tested their symbolic value for the king's absolutist principles. The martial aspects of Anna's masques subverted Jacobean ideals of passive femininity and challenged the king's patriarchal politics.[46] Beyond the feminist subversion of the masques discussed by recent scholars, the masques contributed to an inconsistent

---

[45] Leeds Barroll, *Anna of Denmark, Queen of England: A Cultural Biography* (Philadelphia: University of Pennsylvania Press, 2001), 18. Earlier biographies of Anna include Ethel Carleton Williams, *Anne of Denmark: Wife of James VI of Scotland, James I of England* (London: Longman, 1970); Agnes Strickland, *Lives of the Queens of England, from the Norman Conquest*, 6 vols. (London: Bell and Daldy, 1864–65), IV:62–65; and the *Dictionary of National Biography* entry by Adolphus William Ward. See also Barroll, "The Court of the First Stuart Queen," in Peck, ed., *Mental World*, 191–208; "Theatre as Text: The Case of Queen Anna and the Jacobean Court Masque," in Augusta Lynne Magnusson, C. Edward McGee, and J. Leeds Barroll, eds., *The Elizabethan Theatre XIV: Papers Given at the International Conference on Elizabethan Theatre Held at the University of Waterloo, Ontario, in July 1991* (Toronto: P. D. Meany, 1996), 175–93; and "Inventing the Stuart Masque," in David Bevington and Peter Holbrook, eds., *The Politics of the Stuart Court Masque* (Cambridge: Cambridge University Press, 1998), 121–43.

[46] Besides Barroll's work, scholarship attentive to the queen as the center of an alternative court includes Barbara Lewalski, *Writing Women in Jacobean England* (Cambridge, Mass.: Harvard University Press, 1993); and Clare McManus, *Women on the Renaissance Stage: Anna of Denmark and Female Masquing in the Stuart Court (1590–1619)* (Manchester: Manchester University Press, 2002). See also Marion Wynne-Davies, "The Queen's Masque: Renaissance Women and the Seventeenth-Century Court Masque," in S. P. Cerasano and Marion Wynne-Davis, eds., *Gloriana's Face: Women, Public and Private, in the English Renaissance* (Detroit: Wayne State University Press, 1992), 79–104; and Suzanne Gossett, "'Man-Maid, Begone!': Women in Masques," *English Literary Renaissance* (1988), 96–113.

portrayal of family dynamics, undermining James's self-appointed role as father-king.[47] The English masques visually represented the doubleness of monarchy: with Anna dancing as powerful female figures before the king, in the symbolic representation monarchical power becomes feminized, bifurcated, even dispersed. If the rhetoric of maternity in the 1590 Edinburgh entry hints at the queen as an alternative locus of power, the English masques do the same by adopting the different strategy of emphasizing her independence. In personating royal and divine female figures, Anna presents her obedience to her husband as deriving from consent rather than submission. The dynamics of the masques emphasize her choice to obey, not James's power to compel obedience. Ultimately, the masques unlink the queen from the king, such that she does not easily fit into the hierarchical structures of patriarchalism.

In the masques written by Samuel Daniel, Anna danced roles distinctly martial in character.[48] This martial representation minimizes her subordination to James as queen consort to present her as a sovereign and active force. In his dedicatory letter to Lucy, Countess of Bedford, Daniel praises Anna as "a most magnificent Queene; whose heroicall spirit, and bounty onely gave it [the masque] so faire an execution as it had"[49] as part of a comprehensive construction of Anna as warrior queen. In the first masque, *The Vision of the Twelve Goddesses* (1604), the first goddess to appear is Juno, wife of the most powerful Olympian god and the goddess of marriage, seemingly the predictable choice for a queen consort to play. Anna chose instead to play Pallas Athena "in a blew mantle, with a silver imbrodery of all weapons and engines of war, with a helmet-dressing on her head, and presents a Launce and Target" (190). Athena's association with war – sometimes she is depicted bearing a shield with the Gorgon's head – and

---

47 Reading for female agency in Anna's performances, McManus pursues a complementary argument, arguing that "James's court . . . figured its authority through the gendered construct of the patriarchal family, . . . ; in contrast, Anna's court danced an image of female community and of a continuity of queenship in performances such as *The Vision*, *Blackness* and *Queens*" (*Women on the Renaissance Stage*, 139). Recent scholarship on the masques emphasizes their polyvocality: see essays in Bevington and Holbrook, eds., *Politics of the Stuart Court Masque*, especially Martin Butler, "Courtly Negotiations," 20–40, and Hugh Craig, "Jonson, the Antimasque and the 'Rules of Flattery,'" 176–96.

48 Although I identify the masques by the poet who composed the script, I assign Anna an important role as author, or instigator, of the masques, with themes and governing ideas stemming from Anna herself. As Jonson writes, in the case of *Blackness*, "it was her majesty's will to have them blackamores at first" (Stephen Orgel and Roy Strong, eds., *Inigo Jones: The Theatre of the Stuart Court*, 2 vols. [London: Sotheby Parke Bernet; Berkeley and Los Angeles: University of California Press, 1973], 1:90).

49 Samuel Daniel, *The Complete Works in Verse and Prose of Samuel Daniel*, ed. Rev. Alexander B. Grosart, vol. III (London and Aylesbury: Hazell, Watson, & Viney, 1885), 187. Further references to *Vision* are from this edition and cited parenthetically.

her status as virgin make her the opposite of Anna as a married queen. *Vision* is replete with allusions to Elizabeth, including the role of Pallas as iconic of England's own virgin queen.[50] By deploying such an icon, Anna's masque imagery works against a consistent representation of patriarchal family politics.

In *Tethys Festival* (1610), celebrating the investiture of Henry as Prince of Wales, martial imagery is coupled with a maritime theme to highlight Anna's sovereign power. As Tethys, Anna presents to the king a trident, "the seal / And ensign of her [Tethys/Anna] love and of your [Neptune/James] right."[51] Because the trident is a substitute – given the nautical conceit of the masque – for a scepter, Anna can be seen as submitting to the king. Yet, it must pass hands from Anna to James (strictly speaking, the trident is presented by Tethys' representative, Triton). With the trident bearing a double meaning, Anna's submission comes out of choice (her "love") rather than solely compulsion (his "right"). Moreover, as a symbol of rule the trident is part of the constellation of images associated with Anna in the overall design of the masque. Above each side of Tethys' throne is "a great trident," whose presence in the course of the masque continues to assert Anna's sovereignty (194, line 183). Finally, the action puts Anna in a position mirroring the king's. Her throne, the focal point of the masque, mimics the king's centrality as prime spectator. While Anna dances in the masque, at various points she also sits on her throne as spectator. After the first dance, "Tethys withdraws and reposes her upon the mount under the Tree of victory, entertained with music and this song" (195, lines 271–72). This is repeated after the second dance, when she again becomes a spectator "entertained with another song" (195, lines 288–89). Although the masque is generally understood to have one perspective and structured for the benefit of the king as primary spectator in the audience, in this case the queen is another primary spectator. By thus positioning the queen, the masque makes clear the doubled nature of the audience, usually idealized as one, and therefore the duality of monarchy.

Monarchy's doubleness is again suggested in Ben Jonson's paired *Masque of Blackness* (1605) and *Masque of Beauty* (1608) by the alienness of the queen. Much ink has been spilled on the subject of the queen and her ladies' disguising themselves as "blackamores."[52] Sir Dudley Carleton's oft-quoted

---

[50] McManus, *Women on the Renaissance Stage*, 100–11.

[51] Strong and Orgel, eds., *Inigo Jones*, 1:194, lines 134–35. References to masques other than *Vision* are from this edition and cited parenthetically.

[52] See Bernadette Andrea, "Black Skin, The Queen's Masques: Africanist Ambivalence and Feminine Author(ity) in the Masques of *Blackness* and *Beauty*," *English Literary Renaissance* 29.2 (1999),

comment reveals the anxieties the masque stirred up at court: "Instead of vizzards, their Faces, and Arms up to the Elbows, were painted black, which was Disguise sufficient, for they were hard to be known; *but it became them nothing so well as their red and white, and you cannot image a more ugly Sight, then a troop of lean-cheek'd Moors.*"[53] The anxieties partly stem from incongruity between the masquers' identity and their role. In and of herself, the black lady need not provoke anxieties, having been used as an emblem of royal power in James IV of Scotland's tournament of the wild knight and the black lady in 1507 and 1508. Presiding over the ceremonies of entry, James IV's black lady is the "displaced, feminized version of the king – as a double and opposite," but one who is ultimately contained by the king as wild knight.[54] In contrast to James IV's black lady, whose identity is unknown, Anna as the black lady makes such containment more difficult. It resists one interpretation available to James IV, who lays claim to the powers of alien femininity by asserting identity with the black lady. Her own identity as queen means that Anna could claim royal power by taking on the black lady's identity herself. The representation of racial others brings to the fore the queen's own foreignness, which in turn construes her as an unassimilable part of monarchy, tending to divide the crown. Its staging may reflect negatively on James, himself a foreigner in England. The presence of aliens unsettles Jacobean family politics: James's position is troubled by the presence of another patriarch, Niger, the alien king whose daughters seek the English monarch. Concerned "To do a kind and careful father's part, / In satisfying every pensive heart / Of these my daughters" (91, lines 117–19), Niger is a powerful father-king who challenges James's self-representation as supreme father.

While not as overly martial, the paired masques, *Blackness* and *Beauty*, reverse the normal roles of male suitor and female beloved: actively pursuing their desire, the daughters of Niger endure foreign travel to find the king of Albion. *The Masque of Beauty* even portrays them as valiant and adventurous questing protagonists: they stop en route to rescue four other maidens imprisoned by Night. In the *Masque of Queens* (1609), Anna returns again to strong female roles. Her ladies dance as heroic queens,

246–81; Hardin Aasand, "'To Blanch an Ethiop, and Revive a Corse': Queen Anne and *The Masque of Blackness,*" *Studies in English Literature* 32 (1992), 271–85; and Kim F. Hall, *Things of Darkness: Economies of Race and Gender in Early Modern England* (Ithaca: Cornell University Press, 1995), ch. 3.

[53] Sir Dudley Carleton to Sir Ralph Winwood in C. H. Herford, Percy and Evelyn Simpson, eds., *Ben Jonson*, 11 vols. (Oxford: Clarendon Press, 1925–52), x:448.
[54] Louise Olga Fradenburg, *City, Marriage, Tournament: Arts of Rule in Late Medieval Scotland* (Madison: University of Wisconsin Press, 1991), 263.

including Penthesilea, Queen of the Amazons. Other characters are similarly endowed with a masculine spirit: even the married Hypsicratea "so loved her husband as she was assistant to him in all labours and hazards of the war, in a masculine habit" (136, lines 546–47). These martial queens, Amazonian in character, if not in habit, are visual reminders of the queen's sovereign power. The Amazon may in fact be a trope particularly favored by Anna.[55] In a 1617 portrait, Paul van Somer painted the queen in hunting costume; revealingly, the contemporary French term for a riding habit was *amazone*. Stephen Orgel connects the queen's clothing in this portrait with James's distaste for women in masculine habit: James instructed the London clergy "to inveigh vehemently and bitterly in their sermons against the insolency of our women, and their wearing of broad-brimmed hats, pointed doublets, their hair cut short or shorn, and some of stilettos or poniards."[56] Although Anna was not wearing broad-brimmed hats, pointed doublets, or short hair in the masques, nonetheless, in displaying a "heroical spirit" she played the manly part.

Anna's final masque does not continue the pattern of Amazonian personae. At first glance, *Love Freed From Ignorance and Folly* (1611) contrasts with the others, giving the queen and her ladies more passive roles. Dancing the parts of the Daughters of Morn, they are trapped by the Sphinx, symbolizing ignorance. The answer to the Sphinx's riddle is Albion: "Britain's the world the world without. / The King's the eye, as we do call / The sun the eye of this great all" (233, lines 270–72). Not only is the king the key to the women's release, the masque locates disorder in the female Sphinx. While this dynamic suggests a gendered hierarchy sustaining James's position as patriarch and king, there are some undercurrents. Although the queen as the Sphinx's prisoner is in a passive position, once released, the Daughters of Morn form a brightly lit tableau on an upper stage, as appearing from the clouds.[57] Such a tableau gives Anna a heavenly, even divine, aspect, as she is seated on a throne, possibly opposite James in the audience. While the rhetoric of the masque speaks of James as the sun,

---

[55] For the Amazon in early modern drama, see Simon Shepherd, *Amazons and Warrior Women: Varieties of Feminism in Seventeenth-Century Drama* (New York: St. Martin's Press, 1981).

[56] Norman E. McClure, *Letters of John Chamberlain*, 2 vols. (Philadelphia: The American Philosophical Society, 1939), II:286–87, quoted in Stephen Orgel, *Impersonations: The Performance of Gender in Shakespeare's England* (Cambridge: Cambridge University Press, 1996), 83. In an earlier essay, Orgel discusses family dynamics in the masque though he underplays the subversiveness of the queen's role ("Jonson and the Amazons," in Elizabeth D. Harvey and Katharine Eisaman Maus, eds., *Soliciting Interpretation: Literary Theory and Seventeenth-Century English Poetry* [Chicago: University of Chicago Press, 1990], 131, 133).

[57] See Orgel and Strong's notes on the design of "Scene 2: The Release of the Daughters of the Morn" (*Inigo Jones*, I:234–36).

it is Anna and her ladies, aided by stage lights, who are bathed in light. Thus, visually, there is a substitution of queen for king.

The appearance of the Sphinx troubles a simple patriarchal reading of the masque, despite how the wise male priests of the muses defeat the female Follies, offspring of the Sphinx. The masque's narrative of a queen freed from the clutches of the Sphinx after a riddle is correctly answered must surely recall the story of Oedipus and the Sphinx. Oedipus' reward for overcoming the Sphinx is the kingdom of Thebes and Jocasta as wife. Not recognizing his father, Oedipus earlier killed Laius in a quarrel; also unbeknownst to him, Jocasta is his mother, thus fulfilling the prophecy that he will kill his father and marry his mother. The presence of the Sphinx reminds the audience of how father–son and husband–wife relationships can become badly distorted, even horrifyingly incestuous. Indeed, in the masque the Sphinx acts as barrier separating king and queen. Although the separation is finally overcome, the patriarchal text of the masque is subtly undercut by the threat posed by the Sphinx. To a greater or lesser extent, Anna's masques challenge James's vision of family and state. On stage, Anna's royal brilliance eclipses James's sovereignty, if only for the duration of the performance. Preferring to fashion for herself the image of a powerful, heroic, and martial queen, she would rather play the Amazon.

Anna's refashioning of Elizabeth I's martial self-representation into Amazonian performances would be continued by Henrietta Maria, queen consort to Charles. From the beginning, Henrietta Maria was a more transgressive female performer. Her Shrove Tuesday 1626 masque broke two important taboos: the queen had a speaking part and some of her women "were disguised like men with beards."[58] Arguing that this masque was a "theatrical overturning of Salic law, the arrogation of masculine role just brinking upon, or brushing up against male rule," Sophie Tomlinson perceived a female-centered Caroline court disrupting traditional gender hierarchies through performance.[59] Ultimately, Henrietta Maria would pose more of a threat to patriarchal structures in her intimacy with the king when she became his closest advisor after Buckingham's death. In civil war propaganda, she was attacked as an undesirable influence on the king because of her Catholicism. The attacks were not without cause: when Henrietta Maria was betrothed to Charles, the Pope wrote to urge her to

[58] As reported by John Chamberlain in G. E. Bentley, *The Jacobean and Caroline Stage*, 7 vols. (Oxford: Clarendon Press, 1948–61), IV:549.

[59] Sophie Tomlinson, "She that Plays the King: Henrietta Maria and the Threat of the Actress in Caroline Culture," in Gordon McMullan and Jonathan Hope, eds., *The Politics of Tragicomedy: Shakespeare and After* (London and New York: Routledge, 1992), 189.

be the Esther to English Catholics, the Clothilde "who subdued to Christ her victorious husband."[60] Charles's Arminianism appeared to be crypto-Catholicism as her own masques took on aspects of the Catholic mass. It is unsurprising that religion would become a destabilizing force when Henrietta Maria's performances were influenced by two related French courtly fashions with Catholic origins.

The first, *préciosité*, is a set of manners and literary taste developed in Parisian salons, of which one of the most influential and best-known was led by Catherine de Vivonne, better known as Mme de Rambouillet. In the salons, where relations between men and women were governed by the ideal of *honnête amitié*, a code that excluded passion though not sexual attraction, women gained considerable power in setting social fashions. French discourses about women were varying, however, and their particular contours shifted rapidly in the first half of the seventeenth century.[61] Strictly speaking, the term *précieuse* was invented in the early 1650s to mock the pretensions of a group of young women in Paris but came to be applied without prejudice to all women in Parisian salons, though scholars have argued for continuity between the *précieuses* of the 50s and their counterparts in salons from the turn of the century.[62] Ian Maclean traces the development of the secular *précieuse* ideal of the heroic, independent, and active woman from the *honnête femme*, which ultimately developed from the Catholic religious ideal of woman. Erica Veevers suggests that while her rival Lady Carlisle practiced a politically engaged salon version of *préciosité*, Henrietta Maria's particular strand was the neoplatonic, religious model. Acquired from the courtly circles dominated by her mother, Marie de Medici, her *préciosité* was influenced by Devout Humanism, a Counter-Reformation movement, which invested women with neoplatonic qualities such as beauty, virtue, and love so that they can enable social harmony and promote religion.[63] Underlying the queen's cult of platonic love in her court entertainments was a devotion to the Virgin Mary with platonic ideals present in both.

At the same time, a second fashion developed: the ideal of the *femme forte*, the figure of the heroic woman of Anne of Austria's regency (1643–52). Its

---

[60] Cited in Alison Plowden, *Henrietta Maria: Charles I's Indomitable Queen* (Stroud: Sutton, 2001), 20.

[61] Carolyn Lougee, *Le Paradis des Femmes: Women, Salons and Social Stratification in Seventeenth-Century France* (Princeton: Princeton University Press, 1976); Ian Maclean, *Woman Triumphant: Feminism in French Literature, 1610–1652* (Oxford: Clarendon Press, 1977); Joan DeJean, *Tender Geographies: Women and the Origins of the Novel in France* (New York: Columbia University Press, 1991).

[62] Lougee, *Le Paradis des Femmes*, 7.

[63] Erica Veevers, *Images of Love and Religion: Queen Henrietta Maria and Court Entertainments* (Cambridge: Cambridge University Press, 1989), 2–3, 75–109, *passim*.

paradoxes arise from the perceived frailty of the female sex so that a woman who overcomes the weaknesses of her sex becomes a cause for wonder. The *femme forte*'s strength is contrasted with the rest of womanhood. Ian Maclean suggests that the *femme forte* was largely created by male writers and the *précieuse* by women writers.[64] While concurring, Joan DeJean points out ways in which women's actions lend themselves to be understood as *femme fortes*. The Amazonian figure, for instance, found a contemporary reincarnation in Barbe d'Ernecourt, Comtesse de Saint-Baslemont, a warrior poet who dressed as a man, defended her property while her husband was away at war, and seemed to have fought for her neighbors as well through the late 1630s and early 1640s.[65] Henrietta Maria's own mother, Marie de Medici, commissioned Reubens to render her life in mythic and heroic terms in a series of large paintings executed between 1622 and 1625.[66] Again, the *femme forte* was associated with Catholic beliefs, with antecedents in the Marian literature on the Virgin as *the* exceptional woman. Moreover, this literature compares Mary to a warrior to stress her heroic and military qualities.[67] In her deployment of both neoplatonic *préciosité* and *femme forte*, Henrietta Maria crafted a distinctly Catholic identity at odds with a Protestant conception of the English monarchy.

The English monarchy became tainted with Catholicism in its reliance on the masque for its self-representation. Henrietta Maria's Neoplatonism appeared too in Charles's masques to promote his ideology of divine-right kingship. The mythologizing of the king and queen's marriage as ideal love in the masques became a metaphor for the mutual love of king and people and thus the unity of the kingdom. In their magnificent edition of Inigo Jones's designs for the masques, Stephen Orgel and Roy Strong discuss the masques as uniting love and power, while in his study of Caroline court literature, Kevin Sharpe argues for a "politics of love."[68] The masques idealize the queen as beauty and emphasize the king's role as lover. In *Love's Triumph Through Callipolis*, performed on Twelfth Night 1631, the king played the heroic lover overcoming the base passion of Cupid, while in *Tempe Restored* (1632), the queen played the personification of "Divine Beauty." In *The*

[64] Maclean, *Woman Triumphant*, 117.
[65] DeJean, *Tender Geographies*, 24–33. For a contemporary biography of Barbe d'Ernecourt, see Jean-Marie de Vernon, *L'Amazone chrestienne, ou les avantures de Madame Saint-Balmon* (Paris: Gaspar Méturas, 1678).
[66] DeJean, *ibid.*, 20.   [67] Maclean, *Woman Triumphant*, 71–74.
[68] Kevin Sharpe, *Criticism and Compliment: The Politics of Literature in the England of Charles I* (Cambridge: Cambridge University Press, 1987), 265 ff.; Martin Butler, *Theatre and Crisis, 1632–42* (Cambridge: Cambridge University Press, 1984); and Graham Parry, *The Golden Age Restor'd: The Culture of the Stuart Court, 1603–42* (Manchester: Manchester University Press, 1981).

Temple of Love (1635), she acted the part of Indamora, who reestablishes the temple of Chaste Love "by the influence of her beauty" (3), and in *Salmacida Spolia* (1640), Charles was Philogene, "Lover" of his people. The masques emphasize the civilizing effects of licit, marital love. The zenith of this valorization of the matrimonial union is Thomas Carew's representation of the king and queen as twins and Hermaphrodite in *Coelum Britannicum* (1634), in which they are addressed as "Bright glorious twins of love and majesty" (46): Jupiter himself "to eternise the memory of that great example of matrimonial union which he derives from hence, hath on his bedchamber door and ceiling, fretted with stars, in capital letters engraven the inscription of CARLOMARIA" (275–79);[69] and the queen is the king's "royal half" (870). They are complementary halves that make one whole: Carlomaria rather than Charles *and* Maria. Alluding to the biblical notion that marriage makes man and wife "one flesh," the twinning of king and queen raises fears that the king is unequally yoked to a Catholic spouse.

As the decade of the 1630s drew to an end, even as the king's critics grew louder, the court made increasingly exaggerated nationalistic claims for the reforming virtue of chaste marriage on the kingdom. These claims were accompanied by Henrietta Maria's assertion of her public role through her self-representation as a heroic woman. Her version of the *femme forte*, however, is fused with and changed by her marriage to Charles. She is not a solitary martial woman but one with an idealized male partner. In William Davenant's *Salmacida Spolia*, Henrietta Maria, as an Amazon, links the cult of marriage with the ideal of the *femme forte*. The last masque performed by the royal couple, *Salmacida Spolia* was staged in January 1640 only a month after writs had been issued for Parliament to meet in April after eleven years of Charles's personal rule. The masque was performed by king and queen together, unlike other masques presented by one to the other. A remarkable instance of a joint effort, with Henrietta Maria's mother as principal spectator, *Salmacida Spolia* portrays the king as Philogenes, or "Lover of his People," dispelling civil discord and triumphant over war: discovered seated on the "Throne of Honour" (345), the king presides over "captives bound, in several postures, lying on trophies of armours, shields, and antique weapons" (348–49).[70] The queen appears last with "her martial ladies" (385–86); all were in "Amazonian habits of carnation, embroidered with silver, with plumed helms, baldrics with antique swords hanging by their sides" (393–96). The resemblance between antique weapons that the

---

[69] Momus, who speaks these lines, was played by Carew himself.

[70] Sharpe suggests Davenant is advising the king to follow a policy of peace rather than to respond to the Scottish rebellion with force (*Criticism and Compliment*, 251–56).

ladies carry and the ones lying at the king's feet visually suggests the king's conquest of the queen, especially since she is his reward for establishing peace in the kingdom (18–21). However, this explanation is found only in the printed text. Because the meaning of a masque cannot be controlled by any one person, the printed explanation may well be an attempt to contain Henrietta Maria's assertion of military and political power. In performance, the queen appears last and descends from above the king, which may make her more important. She has the more active role: she is armed while he is not. While the *femme forte* in marriage is expected to be dutiful and constant, the place of marriage in the discourse is vexed.[71] The queen is expected to have moderating effects on the king: in the masques, she embodies beauty attracting his virtue, and in their perfect love the royal couple both regulate themselves and rule the kingdom justly. Nonetheless, in her active part as a *femme forte*, she transforms that supporting role into a public one for herself. The masque presents an acceptable way for the queen to pose as a *femme forte* consonant with Stuart politics of marriage. It rewrites the legend of the Amazons to depict marital mutuality: the women dancing as Amazons come willingly to the men instead of being forced to yield. Henrietta Maria transforms the *femme forte*, the individually heroic woman, into the heroic wife.

As heroic wife, the queen was viewed as an important political advisor to the king. In a poem written soon after *Salmacida Spolia*, Davenant urges Henrietta Maria to counsel Charles to adopt a conciliatory policy:

> Madam; so much peculiar and alone
> Are Kings, so uncompanion'd in a Throne,
> That through the want of some equality
> (Familiar Guides, who lead them to comply)
> They may offend by being so sublime,
> As if to be a King might be a crime.
> All less then Kings no more with Kings prevaile,
> . . .
> To cure this high obnoxious singleness.[72]

This language gives the queen considerable power. While other counselors are his subordinates, she is equal to the king. This equality has been viewed with alarm by the anti-court faction. The puritan William Prynne's indictment of the stage in *Histriomastix* (1633) is more accurately an attack on female-dominated court drama and its connections to Catholicism; Prynne

---

[71] Maclean, *Woman Triumphant*, 110–11, and, on the question of marriage more generally, 88–118.
[72] Davenant, "To the Queen," in *The Shorter Poems, and Songs from the Plays and Masques*, ed. A. M. Gibbs (Oxford: Clarendon Press, 1972), 139–40, lines 1–7, 11.

views Henrietta Maria as a fifth columnist "in the Kings own bed and bosome for their [Catholics'] most powerful Mediatrix."[73] Nonetheless, whether her influence was positive or negative, Henrietta Maria changed the tenor of the monarchy. While Anna of Denmark merely played the Amazon, Henrietta Maria was actually engaged in a war. The civil war afforded her ample opportunity for active roles: she took on the part of a military commander and bravely made her escapes from parliamentary forces; writing to Charles, she jokingly called herself "her she-majesty, generalissima."[74] In playing and living as contemporary Amazons – even if only a heroic wife – Stuart queen consorts well and truly departed from the model of the single, absolute father-king.

INTERPRETING SUBJECTS

Queen consorts' unsettling representations of sovereignty are but one example of how reiteration of family tropes did not exactly duplicate a single model of the analogy. While the family metaphor gained power from repetition in multiple contexts, as frequent assertions buttressed the king's authority, its universality was a double-edged sword. It was appropriated for other ends even by the monarch's own subjects. This was especially true when the king's own words were widely disseminated.

A prolific writer, James consistently labored to get his works in print and distributed to his subjects. He seemed to have found in words his preferred means of representing, even exerting, royal authority.[75] In the preface to James's collected works, the editor Bishop Montagu claims that James's words themselves can act on the conscience of men "so far as . . . there have been [those] that have been converted by them."[76] Royal words are speech-acts; the king rules by them. If James's words become acts because "vttered from so eminent a place . . . [they] might with greater facilitie be conceiued," conversely his subjects are expected, in fact commanded, not to speak.[77] In *Paraphrase Upon the Book of Revelations*, James warns

---

73 *The Popish Royall Favourite, or A Full Discovery of his Majesties Extraordinary Favours to and Protections of Notorious Papists, Priests, Jesuits . . .* (London, 1643), Sig. G4, 56. Cited in Veevers, 108.

74 M. A. E. Green, *Letters of Queen Henrietta Maria, including the private correspondence with Charles the First* (London: R. Bentley, 1857), 222.

75 For James's writings as attempts to affirm his divine right, see Kevin Sharpe, "The King's Writ: Royal Authors and Royal Authority in Early Modern England," in Sharpe and Peter Lake, eds., *Culture and Politics in Early Stuart England* (Stanford: Stanford University Press, 1993), 117–38.

76 *The Workes of the Most High and Mighty Prince James* (London, 1616), preface.

77 *A Remonstrance for the Right of Kings, and the Independence of Their Crownes*, in McIlwain, ed., *Political Works of James I*, 169.

readers against private interpretations of scripture, though he himself freely deciphers the imagery of Revelation. Claiming divine inspiration, James speaks in the words of St. John, "and [God] said unto me write and leave in record what thou hast seen."[78] He presents his reading as "a mediation of God's word" while Revelation's status as a text of revolution explains his interest in providing "an authorised royal reading of its ambiguities and opacities."[79] The king's authorized reading silences his subjects. Claiming the Psalms as royal prayers because David was king, James generalizes it to the whole of scripture as "most properly of any other, belongeth the reading thereof vnto Kings" (*Basilicon Doron*, 13). Trying to forestall the potential conflict in authority between the monarch and the church, he asserts that the king's office is "mixed, betwixt the Ecclesiasticall and ciuill estate: For a King is not *mere laicus*" (*Basilicon Doron*, 52).

James's theory of the divine right of kings thus encompasses authorship. In part, the printed book leaves no space for any other voice. Conceived as silent, admiring auditors, his subjects are expected to play the part of obedient children. But his attempt to exert authority through texts leaves him open to interpretation. James Doelman argues James's majesty suffered from overexposure when his English subjects, quoting from *Basilicon Doron*, appropriated his words in attempts to advise and to govern the king: "his pageantry of the written word raised expectations, but ultimately it gave over to his subjects the power to interpret and direct their own king."[80] Appropriating also the family-state analogy, some of his subjects called the country, or the church, or Parliament their mother, to claim that their loyalties lay elsewhere. James himself was aware that his subjects could oppose him by using maternal metaphors: "And first it is casten vp by diuers, that employ their pennes vpon Apologies for rebellions and treasons, that euery man is borne to carry such a naturall zeale and duety to his commonwealth, as to his mother" (*Trew Law*, 78).

During the civil wars, the family-state analogy was used far more belligerently, as the responses to *Eikon Basilike* (1649) show. Although Charles was not an author like his father, the one text ascribed to him was far more popular than anything James had published. The King's Book, as it was popularly known, combines a narrative of the causes of the civil war and meditative prayers to present a defense of Charles's actions. *Eikon Basilike* articulates the Stuart myth of society as a tightly knit and hierarchical family with the king compared to Old Testament patriarchs and

[78] *Ibid.*, 65.   [79] Sharpe, "The King's Writ," 125.

[80] James Doelman, "'A King of Thine Own Heart': The English Reception of King James VI and I's *Basilicon Doron*," *The Seventeenth Century* 9 (1994), 7.

imagined as "father of his country".[81] The first response, the anonymous *Eikon Alethine* (1649), meaning "Truthful Image," calls Charles's paternity into question, arguing that *Eikon Basilike* was actually authored by a cleric.[82] Its frontispiece, showing a hand pulling back a curtain to expose a doctor of divinity, and its epigram make the argument plain:

> The Curtain's drawne; All may perceiue the plot,
> And Him who truely the blacke Babe begot:
> Whose sable mantle makes me bold to say
> A Phaeton Sol's charriot rulde that day.
> Presumptuous Preist to skip into the throne,
> And make his King his Bastard Issue owne.

The allusion to the Greco-Roman myth of Phaeton, who tries to drive his father Apollo's chariot but loses control of the chariot and scorches the earth, responds to the many comparisons *Eikon Basilike* makes between the sun and king as well as to charges that the king's enemies are trying to usurp his place. Even if it maintains the father–son hierarchy (the rightful driver, Apollo, versus the incompetent son), the verse redirects the accusation of usurpation at *Eikon Basilike*. As a forgery, *Eikon Basilike*, like Phaeton, pretends to be something it is not. The other analogy, the stock comparison of author and father, is even more damning. It is not just a matter of impersonation or anti-theatrical criticism.[83] *Eikon Alethine* boldly suggests that the king was cuckolded to attack the ideological basis of Stuart monarchy.

In his absolutist interpretation of the family metaphor, James revived the family-state analogy as a vital way of thinking about social order. His legacy is not much spoken of, in part because of the long shadow

---

[81] Philip A. Knachel, ed., *Eikon Basilike: The Portraiture of His Sacred Majesty in His Solitudes and Sufferings* (Ithaca: Published for The Folger Shakespeare Library by Cornell University Press, 1966), 35.

[82] *Eikon Alethine, The Pourtraicture of Truths most sacred Majesty truly suffering, though not solely. Wherein the false colours are washed off, wherewith the Painter-Steiner had bedawbed Truth, the late King and the Parliament, in his counterfeit Piece entituled EIKON BASILIKE* (London, 1649). His chaplain, John Gauden, probably put together the book from Charles's notes, substantially rewriting and editing. For his pains, Gauden received the bishoprics of Exeter and, later, Worcester from Charles II after the Restoration, and neither Edward Hyde, the Earl of Clarendon, nor George Digby, the Earl of Bristol, denied his claim in his letters to them. See Francis F. Madan, *A New Bibliography of the "Eikon Basilike" of King Charles the First* (London: Quaritch, 1950); Christopher Wordsworth, *Documentary Supplement to "Who Wrote Eikon Basilike?", including Recently Discovered Letters and Papers of Lord Chancellor Hyde, and of the Gauden Family* (London: J. Murray, 1825); and Hugh Trevor-Roper, "*Eikon Basilike*: The Problem of the King's Book," *History Today* 1 (1951), 7–12.

[83] For anti-theatrical criticism in royalist tracts, see Lois Potter, *Secret Rites and Secret Writing: Royalist Literature, 1641–1660* (Cambridge: Cambridge University Press, 1989), 179–82.

that Elizabeth cast, but when seventeenth-century authors employed the family-state analogy, they were responding in some way to James and the terms of the analogy set by him. Resisting authors and royalist followers alike turned away from the figure of the father-king to celebrate brothers, mothers, and even wifely female monarchs. As a result, they created a rich seventeenth-century tradition of varied, even contradictory, representations of the interrelations of family, state, and society, one made possible by James's own creative and compelling articulation of the political significance of family ties.

CHAPTER 2

Milton's band of brothers

CHRISTIAN FRATERNITY

Tracing the causes of the civil wars, Thomas Hobbes argues in *Behemoth* (1682) that the people were "corrupted" by a number of "seducers": his comprehensive list includes Presbyterian ministers, "Papists," sectarians grouped under the name of "Independents," "men of the better sort" well versed in the classical canon and especially works on ancient republics, the cities, particularly London, war-mongers seeing economic opportunity, and the ignorant people themselves.[1] Much has been made about Hobbes's view that the universities were hotbeds of radicalism, and consequently, the focus has been on his remarks about classically educated men reading Livy and fomenting revolt. Less has been said about Hobbes's other groups. Notably, Presbyterians headed his list, followed by two other religious factions. This is not entirely surprising since Hobbes argues in *Leviathan* (1651) that religion could be used to deceive the people. But is there more to this than Hobbes's dislike of religious fanaticism? In the second dialogue of *Behemoth*, speaker B, having been suitably instructed by speaker A, declares, "I understand now, how the Parliament destroyed the peace of the kingdom; and how easily, by the help of seditious Presbyterian ministers, and of ambitious ignorant orators, they reduced this government into anarchy."[2] Furthermore, in the last dialogue, Hobbes gives to speaker B his famous judgment of the relative merits of Salmasius's *Defensio Regia* and Milton's *First Defence*: "They are very good Latin both, and hardly to be judged which is better; and both very ill reasoning, hardly to be judged which is worse; like two declamations, *pro* and *con*, made for exercise only in a rhetoric school by one and the same man. So like is a

[1] Thomas Hobbes, *Behemoth, or the Long Parliament*, ed. Ferdinand Tönnies (Chicago: University of Chicago Press, 1990), 2–4.
[2] *Ibid.*, 109.

49

Presbyterian to an Independent."[3] Hobbes deliberately shocks his readers
by equating Salmasius, defender of monarchies, and the regicide Milton.
But the link he makes between Presbyterianism and republicanism requires
careful consideration when dealing with an author like John Milton whose
twenty-year career of pamphleteering involved issues ranging from church
government to regicide. Although it was in church politics that Milton first
contended with family metaphors, his theme in the antiprelatical tracts of
manly citizens oppressed by effeminate and corrupt governors would be
developed further in the regicide tracts. His engagement with the familial
arguments of defenders of Episcopacy like Joseph Hall laid the foundation
for his later contest with Stuart family myths. Moving from court to pulpit,
and back again, the family metaphor proved extremely flexible, particularly
in Milton's hands as he fragmented the royalists' supporting metaphor and
turned it into new and startling configurations.

Puritanism became a revolutionary force in response to an increasingly
authoritarian court. Charles I's support for Arminianism, popularly perceived as crypto-popery, greatly deepened religious divisions. Because of
its emphasis on hierarchy and order, Arminianism, "can thus be seen as a
response to the 'popular', activist and participatory elements in Puritanism;"
as Richard Cust and Ann Hughes points out, "In turn the Arminian stress
on obedience within a strictly ordained hierarchy harmonized with an
authoritarian or absolutist view of monarchy."[4] With significant political
implications, religion was an important factor in revolutionary events of
the mid-century that used to be called the Puritan Revolution. Milton's
antiprelatical tracts were part of puritan demand for further reformation of the church. Parliamentary debates in the 1640s concerned linked
issues of religion – questions of religious settlement and toleration – and
the constitution.[5] Michael Walzer argues, "it was the Calvinists who first
switched the emphasis of political thought from the prince to the saint
(or the band of saints) and then constructed a theoretical justification
for independent political action. What Calvinism said of the saint, other
men would later say of the citizen: the same sense of civic virtue, of discipline and duty, lies behind the two names."[6] While puritans can no

---

[3] *Ibid.*, 163–64.
[4] Richard Cust and Ann Hughes, "Introduction: After Revisionism," in Cust and Hughes, ed., *Conflict in Early Stuart England: Studies in Religion and Politics 1603–1642* (London and New York: Longman, 1989), 24.
[5] Ernest Sirluck, "Introduction," *Complete Prose Works of John Milton*, ed. Sirluck, vol. II, 1643–1648 (New Haven: Yale University Press, 1959), 1–136.
[6] Michael Walzer, *The Revolution of the Saints: A Study in the Origins of Radical Politics* (Cambridge, Mass.: Harvard University Press, 1965), 2.

longer be seen as innovators – Margo Todd, for instance, shows that they depended on humanism for their social ideas – nonetheless they forged what Todd calls "Christian humanism" by creatively borrowing ideas like the *vita activa*, which lent themselves to revolutionary ends.[7] The puritan emphasis on active citizenship meant that it would be easy for an author like Milton to move from espousing Presbyterian ideas to republican ones. Humanist ideas form the lynchpin connecting puritanism and republicanism.

The question of when Milton became republican is a vexed issue, depending very much on how one defines republicanism in the English context. Perhaps the earliest date that everyone can agree on is 1649 with the publication of Milton's *Tenure of Kings and Magistrates*. Some scholars detect a nascent republicanism in the antiprelatical tracts. Zera Fink suggests that even as early as 1641 in *Of Reformation* Milton borrowed from Polybius the theory that a stable constitution consists of a mix of monarchy, aristocracy, and democracy, and that "the nobility, the wise and the good, the aristocratic element, should dominate."[8] These features, argues Fink, were unchanging in Milton's thinking. Janel Mueller also stresses the mixed state as a feature of Milton's republicanism. Relying on Michael Mendle's argument that the Presbyterian Scots were leading proponents of mixed government, she finds a similar commitment to the mixed constitution in *Of Reformation*'s vocabulary.[9] Martin Dzelzainis, however, believes the theory of the mixed constitution too widely disseminated to be identified with republicans. Arguing that Milton derived his republican principles not primarily from Polybius but from Aristotle, Sallust, and Cicero, Dzelzainis emphasizes Milton's notion of an Aristotelian free commonwealth. As evidence, he points to *Of Education* (1644), a text modeled on Cicero's *De Officiis*, which represents Milton's "republican moment."[10] He proposes using the "Neo-Roman theory of liberty," a term coined by Quentin Skinner, that one is either free or a slave, to define republicanism, as it is espoused

---

[7] Margo Todd, *Christian Humanism and the Puritan Social Order* (Cambridge: Cambridge University Press, 1987).

[8] Zera S. Fink, *The Classical Republicans: An Essay in the Recovery of a Pattern of Thought in Seventeenth Century England* (Evanston: Northwestern University Press, 1945), 97.

[9] Janel Mueller, "Contextualizing Milton's Nascent Republicanism," in P. G. Stanwood, ed., *Of Poetry and Politics: New Essays on Milton and his World* (Binghamton: Medieval & Renaissance Texts and Studies, 1995), 263–82; Michael Mendle, *Dangerous Positions: Mixed Government, the Estates of the Realm, and the Making of "Answer to the xix propositions"* (University: University of Alabama Press, 1985).

[10] Martin Dzelzainis, "Milton's Classical Republicanism," in David Armitage, Armand Himy, and Quentin Skinner, eds., *Milton and Republicanism* (Cambridge: Cambridge University Press, 1995), 14, 16–17.

by both strict republicans and those willing to compromise with the king.[11]

Strictly defined, republicanism is antagonistic to kingship or even rule by a single person. While a mixed state stresses the balance of powers, republicanism rejects the monarchical element. Classical republicanism supports popular sovereignty, active participation in political life including involvement in making the law, and civic consciousness based on citizens' public virtues.[12] Liberty thus is closely linked to civic life and citizens' participation in furthering the common good. Indebted to classical Greek and Roman sources to conceive of the state as a *polis* and of subjects as citizens, classical republicanism is said not to appear in England till the 1650s because of the difficulties of nativizing such ideas in "an environment dominated by monarchical, legal, and theological concepts."[13] The notion that republicanism had little place in English political culture before the regicide, however, has been challenged. The most thoroughgoing is Markku Peltonen's argument that civic consciousness associated with Italian republicanism can be found in the English classical humanist tradition.[14] Reading English political treatises from between the mid-sixteenth and the mid-seventeenth centuries, Peltonen shows that English humanists saw themselves as reformers of the commonwealth: they discussed the merits of the mixed constitution, promoted the *vita activa*, and argued that virtue constituted true nobility. Besides the civic humanist and republican vocabulary of citizenship, he also finds explicit arguments for a republican form of government, for a government of meritocracy, and even for one in which the hereditary principle is abandoned. Peltonen establishes a strong tradition of humanist and republican thinking through both Elizabethan and Jacobean periods. While he identifies civic humanism as the basis of early modern republicanism in contradistinction to Walzer's argument about the role of puritanism, the evidence suggests that puritans also resorted to civic humanist language. Milton was a case in point.

Although Milton's reading of England as a mixed state does not adhere to the definition of a republic as a state not headed by a king and in which the

[11] Martin Dzelzainis, "Republicanism," in Thomas N. Corns, ed., *A Companion to Milton* (Oxford: Blackwell, 2001), 298, 301–2; Quentin Skinner, *Liberty before Liberalism* (Cambridge: Cambridge University Press, 1998), 55.

[12] M. M. Goldsmith, "Liberty, Luxury and the Pursuit of Happiness," in Anthony Pagden, ed., *The Languages of Political Theory in Early-Modern Europe* (Cambridge: Cambridge University Press, 1987), 225–51, particularly 226–30.

[13] J. G. A. Pocock, *The Machiavellian Moment: Florentine Political Thought and the Atlantic Republican Tradition* (Princeton: Princeton University Press, 1975), 334.

[14] Markku Peltonen, *Classical Humanism and Republicanism in English Political Thought, 1570–1640* (Cambridge: Cambridge University Press, 1995).

hereditary principle did not determine succession, the antiprelatical tracts reveal his admiration for classical republics. The republican emphases on the public good, nobility based on merit rather than birth, and particularly liberty are evident. Protesting the avarice of bishops in *Of Reformation* (1641), Milton cries, "We know that *Monarchy* is made up of two parts, the Liberty of the subject, and the supremacie of the King . . . See what gentle, and benigne Fathers they [bishops] have beene to our liberty."[15] The subject's liberty, the first bulwark of the state, is fundamental even to monarchy since if it falls the bishops turn next to attack the king's authority. Given these concerns, it is a short step from the mixed government of the antiprelatical tracts to the antimonarchism of the regicide tracts. The antiprelatical tracts lay the groundwork for Milton's later explicit republicanism. Important to his concern with liberty is the definition of subjection. Milton's Commonplace Book entries on the topics of liberty and slavery from Justinian's *Institutes* distinguish between those who are free and those under the dominion of another, such that slaves and children are not free.[16] The definition of subjection centers around the household, making it foundational to the state. In the *Doctrine and Discipline of Divorce*, Milton aligns the cause of divorce with the cause of Parliament in seeking the reformation of the state: "He who marries, intends as little to conspire his own ruine, as he that swears Allegiance: and as a whole people is in proportion to an ill Government, so is one man to an ill marriage."[17] With family standing in analogical relation to the state, new configurations of family – in particular, Milton's republican troping of family – make possible new forms of government.

When arguing against Episcopacy, Milton turns not only to the distinction between freemen and slaves, but also to the distinction between adults and children, where the second pair substitutes for the first. In *The Reason of Church-government* (1642), the rule of bishops is enslavement to Old Testament law: "How then the ripe age of the Gospell should be put to schoole againe, and learn to governe her selfe from the infancy of the Law, the stronger to imitate the weaker, the freeman to follow the captive, the learned to be lesson'd by the rude, will be a hard undertaking to evince" (*CPW* I, 763). The contrasting pairs all point to the same distinction between liberty and slavery, a distinction often couched in terms of

---

[15] Don M. Wolfe, ed., *Complete Prose Works of John Milton*, vol. I, 1624–1642 (New Haven: Yale University Press, 1953), 592. Further references to the antiprelatical tracts are from this edition and cited parenthetically by short title (*CPW* I) and page number.

[16] Wolfe, ed., *CPW* I, 410–11, 470–71.

[17] Sirluck, ed., *CPW* II, 229. Further references are from this edition and cited parenthetically as *CPW* II.

childhood versus adulthood in the antiprelatical tracts. While still a family, Milton's church is not rigidly hierarchical with an authoritarian bishop as patriarch. Even the ultimate father of all Christians, God himself, is no "schoolmaister of perishable rites, but a most indulgent father governing his Church as a family of sons in their discreet age" (*CPW* 1, 837). As father, God enacts only "the sweetest and mildest manner of paternal discipline" (*CPW* 1, 837). The emphasis is on familial affection. As a family, Christian community cannot tolerate slavery: "the government of the Gospell being economicall and paternall, that is, of such a family where there be no servants, but all sons in obedience, not in servility" (*CPW* 1, 848). Milton's sons are adults, obedient to their father but not servile. Such sons are not under the power of the father, as children and servants are; they are free, not slaves.

With his emphasis on sons, Milton's language of freedom is gendered. Liberty is associated with manliness. When castigating the slavish minds of prelates in the last antiprelatical tract, *An Apology Against a Pamphlet* (1642), Milton refers to the period of the Old Testament Law as the Egyptian slavery of the Jews while "the Gospell is our manhood, and the ministery should bee the manhood of the Gospell" (*CPW* 1, 950). Similarly, the bishops, Milton argues, "effeminate us all at home" and "despoile us both of *manhood* and *grace* at once" (*CPW* 1, 588). Associating New Testament grace with manhood, Milton aligns Christian grace with a masculine republican liberty. His fear of effeminizing slavery is evident in his rejection of the trope of church as mother, favored by defenders of Episcopacy. Responding to an attack by the unknown author of *A Modest Confutation of a Slanderous and Scurrilous Libell, Entituled, Animadversions etc.* (1642), Milton scorns his opponent's address to the church as "a certain rhetoriz'd woman whom he calls mother" (*CPW* 1, 877).[18] In *An Apology Against a Pamphlet* (1642), he suggests instead speaking to the church as "a number of faithfull brethren and sons, and not to make a cloudy transmigration of sexes," as did the church fathers, instead of "leaving the track of common adresse, to runne up, and tread the aire in metaphoricall compellations" (*CPW* 1, 877). Beautifully encapsulating Milton's disgust with the Episcopacy's disciplinary use of the maternal metaphor, the passage points to the gap between metaphor and reality. Through gender confusion created by the maternal metaphor, the defenders of Episcopacy attempt to turn Christian men into women and to make them dependent and servile. Citing scriptural precedent for

---

[18] Milton believed, erroneously, that the author of *A Modest Confutation* was Joseph Hall and one of his sons.

addressing the church as a community of men, Milton offers instead the vision of the church as a fraternity. Gendering his Christian fraternity male and imagining them as adult sons, Milton emphasizes the free status of Christians.

Milton contrasts Christian liberty and Episcopal tyranny by gendering the one male and the other female. Within this logic, he attacks Episcopacy in terms of stereotypical female sins, notably adultery and sexual crimes. In *Animadversions*, he fears the Pope, whose tyranny Protestants had shaken off, will again become Englishmen's despised father by copulating with the Church of England in an illicit affair, such that Christians are in danger of "sink[ing] under the slavery of a Female notion, the cloudy conception of a demy-Iland mother, and while we think to be obedient sonnes, should make ourselves rather the Bastards, or the Centaurs of their spirituall fornications" (*CPW* I, 728). The metaphor of the mother itself is dangerous because the bishops use it to deceive Christians into accepting forms of worship that put them in the thrall of Roman Catholicism. To be dutiful sons is to be the unnatural progeny, neither man nor beast, of a loathsome mixed marriage between Roman Catholicism and Protestantism. In *Of Reformation*, Milton pointedly uses a conventional emblem for marriage to reveal how bishops corrupt the proper relation of church and state: "I am not of opinion to thinke the Church a *Vine* in this respect, because, as they take it, she cannot subsist without clasping about the Elme of worldly strength, and felicity, as if the heavenly City could not support it selfe without the props and buttresses of secular Authoritie" (*CPW* I, 554).[19] He uses the marriage trope to underline the vicious inversion of relations between church and state. He objects to dependency, whether dependency on a benefice paid by the state or dependency on legal enforcement of scripture by secular law. If the church is dependent, it must be dependent on God. Otherwise, the church is guilty of adulterous relations with the world. Milton associates even incest with Episcopacy: in *Reason of Church Government*, he compares them to Amnon, the son of David, who raped his half-sister.[20] The metaphor takes a very literal turn here. The actual family is imperiled.

Instead of dependence, Milton conceives of the family as a community of brothers. *Of Reformation* argues for a return to the purity of the apostolic

---

[19] For Milton's use of the elm and the vine as symbols for husband and wife, see John Halkett, *Milton and the Idea of Matrimony: A Study of the Divorce Tracts and* Paradise Lost (New Haven: Yale University Press, 1970), 88–89, 104–05, 110–11. For the tradition of the elm and the vine as an emblem for marriage," see Peter Demetz, "The Elm and the Vine: Notes toward the History of a Marriage Topos," *PMLA* 73 (1958), 521–32.

[20] Wolfe, ed., *CPW* I, 851; II Samuel 13: 1–19.

church, in which bishops are elected by the community, elected "by the popular voyce, undiocest, unrevenu'd, unlorded" and rewarded with "nothing but brotherly equality, matchles temperance, frequent fasting, incessant prayer, and preaching, continual watchings, and labours in his Ministery" (*CPW* I, 548–49). In addition, the election is not even a promotion in rank. The bishop has no more than what he had before, which is brotherly equality. To return to an apostolic ministry, the church must become a Christian community of equals. In such a church, discipline is enforced by one's peers. Milton views this discipline as lovingly admonitory and familial, as in "the dear, and tender Discipline of a Father; the sociable, and loving reproof of a Brother; the bosome admonition of a Friend" (*Reformation*, *CPW* I, 570). Analogous to the discipline dealt out by family, Presbyterian church discipline is that of social pressure. More positively, this discipline connects members of the church in kinship. Milton's adjectives emphasize familial relationships based on affect rather than a hierarchy of power: discipline is enforced by the "sage and Christianly *Admonition*, brotherly *Love*, flaming *Charity*, and *Zeale*; and then according to the Effects, Paternal *Sorrow*, or Paternal *Joy*, milde *Severity*, melting *Compassion*" (*Reformation*, *CPW* I, 591).[21] The community is constituted by the emotional associations of the family. Familial admonition comes not just from the father, but also from brothers and friends, thus mitigating the potentially hierarchical nature of a fatherly reproof.

If Presbyterian discipline initially consists of familial counsel, essentially the pressure of social expectations, then the worst punishment possible is the reverse: it is excommunication, the threat of the complete withdrawal of affect and emotion, expulsion from the community. Excommunication allows the boundaries of community to be fairly elastic. As a family, its members are self-elected. Self-election is the model of the separatist churches, where Milton's sympathies lie. He speaks of the Gospel as a covenant, almost a contract, by which Christians join the community. By making Christians God's "adopted sons" (*Reason*, *CPW* I, 837), Milton denaturalizes the familial relationship between God and man. In so doing, he suggests the contingent nature of this tie. The denaturalizing of the family results from Milton's emphasis on choice. Created by association and ratified by

---

[21] Milton's language here sounds very close to that of the Quakers – see Chapter 7 below. The similarities may be attributed to the overlapping constellation of issues surrounding church government. But also the Quaker position (and the later Milton's) is a further radicalization of the Presbyterian stance toward church government. For the interconnections between *Paradise Regained* and Quaker texts, see David Loewenstein, "The Kingdom Within: Radical Religious Culture and the Politics of *Paradise Regained*," *Literature and History* 3 (1994), 63–89.

a covenant, his family is a voluntary association and not preexisting.[22] In the transition from community defined by obedience to the law of the Old Testament to a familial community of the New, God changes from a strict judge, remote and censorious, to a lenient father using only the gentlest discipline. Sons become adults capable of making their own decisions.

Milton's use of familial metaphors emphasizes lateral relations within the family (brotherhood) rather than vertical ones (father to son). Even in the divorce tracts whose subject is heterosexual marriage, he turns to brotherhood to depict ideal love. For all its valorization of marriage, *The Doctrine and Discipline of Divorce* (1644) offers as the best image of perfect and true (marital) love the twin brothers Eros and Anteros:

> And of matrimoniall love no doubt but that was chiefly meant, which by the ancient Sages was thus parabl'd, That Love, if he be not twin-born, yet hath a brother wondrous like him, call'd *Anteros*: whom while he seeks all about, his chance is to meet with many fals and faining Desires that wander singly up and down in his likenes. (*CPW* II, 254–55)

Although the gendering of the two true loves (both male) may suggest homosexual or homosocial bonding, it is "conflictual difference" rather than gender distinctions that matter so that "the carnally conflictual and individuated self [dissolves] into the perfect wholeness of ideal union."[23] This is especially so because the "fals and faining Desires" are counterfeit brothers. The difference between the false brothers and the twin brother is not gender, but who their mothers are. The divorce tracts go further than the antiprelatical tracts in insisting on a sameness of nature that can only be represented by twin brothers. Even a community of men is less than perfect love. When Eros "discerns that this is not his genuin brother, as he imagin'd, he has no longer the power to hold fellowship with such a personated mate" (*CPW* II, 255). The discovery that the brother is false weakens him such that he loses his divine power like the husband or citizen who loses his manhood. Revived by likeness, Eros recovers his power and

---

22 Arthur Barker notes, "Neither Milton nor the Smectymnuans proposed that this desirable unanimity should be achieved through pressure of authority from above in the Laudian manner. It was to be the spontaneous result of the voluntary co-operation of all good Christians associated in their respective congregations" (*Milton and the Puritan Dilemma 1641–1660* [Toronto: University of Toronto Press, 1942], 29). For Milton's shifting of authority from church hierarchy to the individual who has the right to make covenants with others, see Angela Esterhammer, "Meddling with Authority: Inspiration and Speech Acts in Milton's Prose," in Charles W. Durham and Kristin Pruitt McColgan, eds., *Spokesperson Milton: Voices in Contemporary Criticism* (Selinsgrove: Susquehanna University Press; London and Cranbury, NJ: Associated University Presses, 1994), 141–52.

23 Lana Cable, *Carnal Rhetoric: Milton's Iconoclasm and the Poetics of Desire* (Durham, N.C.: Duke University Press, 1995), 110.

strength only when he finds his true twin, who offers "the reflection of a coequal & *homogeneal* fire" (*CPW* II, 255). With the metaphor of twin brothers, we have come a long way from James's self-fashioning as father-king. If nothing else, the world of the perfect love of twins does not admit of such a figure as an authoritarian father.

REPUBLICAN LIBERTY

In the regicide tracts, Milton contends again with the hierarchical use of family tropes. To justify the church's authority, defenders of Episcopacy borrowed the royal language of divine right and the authoritarian interpretation of family metaphors. From debating Episcopacy to debating monarchy, Milton's repeated turning to the family metaphor testify both to its prevalence and its power to incite argument. In the antiprelatical tracts, his Presbyterian sympathies, in this early part of his career, led Milton to reconceptualize family as a brotherhood, much like the structure of Presbyterianism itself. In the regicide tracts where he directly confronts monarchy, the metaphor goes through an even more radical shift. Moreover, each response to royalist apology becomes increasingly anti-monarchical. While *Eikonoklastes* rejects only the applicability of the father-king analogy to Charles I rather than the analogy entirely, the *First Defence* argues for the superiority of a republic. In both, Milton returns to the points made in the antiprelatical tracts about slavery, the relation between father and child as an analogy for government, and the manhood of citizens. The antiprelatical tracts' humanist themes acquire in the regicide tracts a more explicit republican interpretation.

Eikonoklastes, published about seven months after the regicide – Thomason's dating is 6 October 1649 – has often been unfavorably compared to *Eikon Basilike*. Judged unpersuasive in combating the rhetoric of the *Eikon*, Milton's tract is criticized for the vehemence of its language.[24]

---

[24] Scholars tend to consider Milton's prose pamphlets the "achievements of the left hand," as Milton himself puts it: see Michael Lieb and John T. Shawcross, eds., *Achievements of the Left Hand: Essays on the Prose of John Milton* (Amherst: University of Massachusetts Press, 1974). William Riley Parker maintains that for Milton's contemporaries *Eikonoklastes* was a failure (*Milton's Contemporary Reputation: An Essay, Together with a Tentative List of Printed Allusions to Milton, 1641–1674, and Facsimile Productions of Five Contemporary Pamphlets Written in Answer to Milton* [Columbus: The Ohio State University Press, 1940], i. 361). Thomas Corns, however, quarrels with that assessment, pointing out that *Eikonoklastes* went through two editions in the first year, which were probably far larger than each of the clandestine printings of *Eikon Basilike*, and that today it is not a rare book despite the Restoration government's order to have copies of the book collected and destroyed. Corns's argument has its attractions, though it cannot be forgotten that the interregnum government also paid for the printings of *Eikonoklastes* and had a vested interest in its wide distribution

Eikonoklastes had to contend with the emotional impact of the regicide and with the assumption underlying all of *Eikon Basilike's* arguments – the analogy between state and family, which depends on a view of the family as a hierarchical institution. It does so by offering an alternative representation of the royalist family. Using sexual satire to discredit them, Milton suggests that paternal authority cannot be confused with masculine authority nor can claims of authority based on fatherhood be elided with claims on sex. He often includes only men when he speaks of political rights, but he does not make that claim based on their fatherhood. Bruce Boehrer castigates Milton for being unable to escape from family metaphors, which he considers ideologically royalist, but this interpretation assumes the family means only one thing.[25] As Lana Cable suggests, Milton attacks the "iconic structures in *Eikon Basilike* that so depended . . . on the affective elements of intimate family relations, on private emotions, and on select glimpses of the royal father-god's personal conduct."[26] Milton gives family metaphors republican meanings to counter the king's portrait of family relations. In the regicide tracts, he makes his brotherly community, the Christian voluntary association of the anti-prelatical tracts, a republican society.

Milton need not reject family metaphor entirely but simply one particular expression of it – the analogy between father and king. In *Eikonoklastes*, he disallows the use of the analogy only for this individual king. With actions not matching his rhetoric, Charles "could be no way esteem'd *the Father of his Countrey*, but the destroyer; nor had he ever before merited that former title" (*CPW* III, 543).[27] He self-aggrandizes through metaphors of the sun and comparisons to Christ. His embodiment of the familial metaphor makes grown men dependent children – and the kingdom "a great baby" (*CPW* III, 469) – when they are in fact mature citizens. By engrossing to himself the privileges of a father, the king takes away the rights of the people to have a part in governing the country. *Eikon Basilike's*

(*Uncloistered Virtue: English Political Literature, 1640–1660* [Oxford: Clarendon Press, 1992], 200). For *Eikonoklastes'* publication history, see J. Milton French, ed., *The Life Records of John Milton*, 5 vols. (New Brunswick: Rutgers University Press, 1949–58), IV: 322.

[25] Boehrer pronounces Milton's tracts derivative because he resorts to "family structure as the model for national government" ("Elementary Structures of Kingship: Milton, Regicide, and the Family," *Milton Studies* 23 [1987]: 112). Even Boehrer's fascinating work on incest prohibition as a strategy for royal self-promotion and self-defense, *Monarchy and Incest in Renaissance England: Literature, Culture, Kinship, and Kingship* (Philadelphia: University of Pennsylvania Press, 1992), pays insufficient attention to the ways in which the notion of family itself is contested and depicts the family as having a more or less stable meaning.

[26] Cable, *Carnal Rhetoric*, 150.

[27] Merritt Y. Hughes, ed., *Complete Prose Works of John Milton*, vol. III, 1648–1649 (New Haven: Yale University Press, 1962).

comparison of the king to the sun turns them into a dependent wife or servile women: "So that the Parliament, it seems, is but a Female, and without his [the king's] procreative reason, the Laws which they can produce are but windeggs" (*CPW* III, 467). When acts of Parliament are understood to result from the active force of a king, the metaphor renders Parliament passive and a mere auxiliary. Milton rejects this gendered relationship where a superior and active king rules over an inferior and feminized Parliament. Instead, because the law originates from Parliament, "it was a Parlament that first created Kings, and not onely made Laws before a King was in being, but those Laws especially, wherby he holds his Crown" (*CPW* III, 467). The king is the dependent child and Parliament his parent. Moreover, because a sign of the tyrant is "to dream of copulation with his Mother," the king is all the more tyrannical in asserting that Parliament, "which is his Mother, can neither conceive or bring forth *any autoritative Act* without his Masculine coition" (*CPW* III, 467). As the Yale editor of *Eikonoklastes* points out in the footnote, the young Nero was reputed to have desired sexual intercourse with his mother, Agrippina (*CPW* III, 467 n. 28). While Nero, in Milton's retelling, but dreams of incest, Charles commits it in full consciousness. Milton counters what he perceives as the king's literalizing or embodiment of the metaphor by literalizing it himself: he takes the king's metaphorical use of begetting and turns it into a sexual crime. *Eikonoklastes* too has its emotional appeal: *Eikon Basilike* elicits pity but the images in *Eikonoklastes* engender horror and indignation.

Milton's reinterpretations call into doubt metaphor's power to make reality. For him, a metaphor must have referentiality. By weaving together the king's metaphorical role as father of the country and his biological and natural role as father of his own children, *Eikon Basilike* opens the way for Milton to show how the real royal family is not its idealized representation and how the monarchy is nothing but "the ruins of one ejected Family" (*CPW* III, 493). Among other things, Charles is charged with patricide for protecting the Duke of Buckingham, suspected of murdering James I. Moreover, he is guilty of uxoriousness in his devotion to his Catholic wife, Henrietta Maria. Milton compares Charles not to Christ but to Mary Queen of Scots, "from whom he seems to have learnt, as it were by heart, or els by kind" (*CPW* III, 597). Like his grandmother, who was also executed, Charles, angry and arrogant, lacked Christ's patience and meekness. This family resemblance suggests that the Stuart family is naturally and constitutionally tyrannical. With acts of Stuart violence contaminating the country, Charles does not care about the effect of the war on English families, "who had lost Fathers, Brothers, Wives and Children"

(*CPW* III, 481). Despite his frequent turns to familial metaphors, Charles makes a travesty of family – both in his treatment of his father and in his treatment of his subjects. When Charles harps on his fatherhood, Milton argues instead that family influences are negative in state affairs. Insisting that royal family relations are private not public matters, he dismisses Charles's praises of his wife because what is important is that she was a bad subject. By including the letter from Charles to the Prince of Wales, *Eikon Basilike* asserts the interchangeability of the roles of father and king. Milton, however, makes Charles's duty as father private. But he also argues, perhaps inconsistently, that men who are ruled by women at home make poor governors, as when he criticizes the king for uxoriousness. His argument is negative. Private virtue cannot be public, but private vices lead to public ones.

Having dislodged Charles from the role of father of the country, Milton confers the title upon Parliament. The people gather daily at Westminster to give Parliament the support "due by nature both from whom it was offer'd, and to whom; as due as to thir Parents; . . . who were then best Fathers of the Common-wealth" (*CPW* III, 393). Although a dependent relationship, it arises out of Parliament's actions and merit, not the birthright claimed by the king. Milton replaces the king in the metaphor with the proper object, the correct tenor for the vehicle, which he retains. In dismantling the fiction of the king's fatherhood, whereby natural and metaphorical fatherhood are confused, Milton keeps the family metaphor metaphorical. Victoria Kahn argues that in the *Tenure of Kings and Magistrates* Milton "concludes that monarchy itself is a metaphor for which there is no literal, earthly referent," for "Milton stresses what Hobbes labours to conceal: that political contract involves only a metaphorical transfer, since power remains fundamentally with the people."[28] In *Eikonoklastes*, the title "father of the country" too can only be metaphorical. Having to be earned, the title must have reference to public action, not to private, household relations.

Because Charles tried to make the family metaphor literal, he turned the people into slaves. In fact, the family relation between king and people can only be metaphorical because the king must rule according to law. Steven Zwicker suggests that Milton overturns social hierarchy in *Eikonoklastes*: abusing his audience as vulgar, Milton broadens the term "to combat the elevation of king and court, their condemning of sectaries and schismatics as social rabble, and their derogation of political activism as the ingratitude

[28] Victoria Kahn, "The Metaphorical Contract in Milton's *Tenure of Kings and Magistrates*," in Armitage, Himy, and Skinner, eds., *Milton and Republicanism*, 83, 98.

of the barbarous hordes."[29] When Milton overturns social hierarchy to raise the people above the court, he puts Parliament above the king and overthrows the political hierarchy as well: "the Parlament sit in that body, not *as his Subjects* but as his Superiors, call'd, not by him but by the Law" (*CPW* III, 463). Once the people are considered mature and independent and the commonwealth is defined as self-sufficient, the monarch becomes redundant. Once Milton insists on the metaphoricity of the monarchy, it leads inexorably to its dissolution. The family metaphor, as the king uses it, has no meaningful referent. There is only a fiction of a link between the literal and the metaphorical. On the one hand, Milton probes at the truth of the real royal family; on the other hand, he demonstrates that the family works as a metaphor for Parliament.

Milton would again explode royalist myth by a judicious combination of exposing the literal and insisting on the metaphorical in his *Pro populo anglicano defensio*. The first *Defence* was Milton's reply, as Latin secretary to the English Commonwealth, to Claudius Salmasius's *Defensio regia* (1649). While *Eikon Basilike* was meant to garner support from the English people, *Defensio regia* was intended to rouse continental European monarchies against the new English government. *Defensio regia* soon became available in eight Latin editions, in multiple issues, in three Dutch translations, and one French.[30] The debate was rather like the combat between David and Goliath. Salmasius had an international scholarly reputation second only to Grotius, who was dead by then, while Milton was an unknown name. Milton's *Defence* made his reputation in Europe, for it thoroughly devastated Salmasius's tract, revealing the older man's fame for learning to be fraudulent. In the first *Defence*, Milton takes the royalist literalizing of family metaphors further, making the private lives of the king and his court subject to public scrutiny. He attacks Salmasius for uxoriousness, contending that Salmasius is a hen-pecked husband who imposes tyranny on others while "at home serve[s] out a most disgraceful and hardly masculine slavery."[31] Milton scrutinizes too the king's relations to the queen to find a negative causal relation between the king's home life and his public acts: "And so it was at home that he first began to be a bad king" (*Defence*, 240). While royalist family metaphors also posit such a causal relation, Milton

[29] Steven N. Zwicker, *Lines of Authority: Politics and English Literary Culture, 1649–1689* (Ithaca and London: Cornell University Press, 1993), 48, 49.

[30] See F. F. Madan, "A Revised Bibliography of Salmasius's *Defensio regia* and Milton's *Pro populo anglicano defensio*," *The Library*, 5th ser., 9 (1954), 101–21.

[31] Martin Dzelzainis, ed., *Political Writings*, trans. Claire Gruzelier (Cambridge: Cambridge University Press, 1991), 193. Further references to *A Defence of the People of England* are from this edition and cited parenthetically.

takes private acts far more seriously and he uses metaphors more scrupu-
lously. Treating comparison as identity, royalists simply call the king "father
of the country" whether the metaphor is appropriate or whether the king
deserves the title: "And when you have called kings fathers of their country,
you believe that you have persuaded people at once by this metaphor: that
whatever I would admit about a father, I would straightaway grant to be
true of a king" (*Defence*, 68). Once Milton insists that the metaphor must
have referentiality, the royalist metaphor implodes from its own emptiness:
Charles was "not a father of his country, but its destroyer" (*Defence*, 69).
The father may only rule his family absolutely because he begets and supports his dependants. Denying that the king resembles the father, Milton
also denies the king an absolute rule.

Milton's reinterpretation of the father-king analogy arises from his understanding of natural law. Structured largely as a legal argument, the first
Defence begins by searching in the Old Testament for evidence of Jewish
law and practices supporting tyrannicide, then in the gospels and in the history of the early church before culminating in an exposition of natural law
in chapter 5, about midway through the work.[32] While Salmasius resorts to
natural law to defend an absolutist divine-right monarchy, Milton argues
that natural law supports instead the people's right. Their differences are
part of a larger context of debates over natural law in the seventeenth
century. Seventeenth-century ideas of natural law largely derived from
Sir Thomas Aquinas's thirteenth-century amalgamation of political Augus-
tinianism that claimed the only just political society is the church and
Aristotle's notion that political societies are natural.[33] While Augustini-
ans asserted that only the pope wielded just political power, Aristotelians
claimed political authority and autonomy for the secular power with
the consequence of reducing the clergy's powers. Christianizing Aristotle, Aquinas argues that God gave everyone reason, making it possible even
for heathens to know right from wrong. To follow the promptings of reason
is to follow natural law, which is also God's law. Consisting of self-evident
precepts, natural law cannot be contravened by positive law. In the seventeenth century, however, the Thomistic formulation was rethought by
Hugo Grotius. The nature of Grotius's relation to Aquinas is still being
debated. While some scholars emphasize the continuity between scholastic

---

[32] For a survey of Milton's use of natural law in his prose and poetry, see R. S. White, *Natural Law in English Renaissance Literature* (Cambridge: Cambridge University Press, 1996), chapter 9, "Milton and Natural Law," 216–42.

[33] J. P. Sommerville, *Royalists and Patriots: Politics and Ideology in England, 1603–1640*, 2nd edn (London and New York: Addison Wesley Longman, 1999), 13–18.

natural law and Grotius's and other early modern Protestant natural law, others like Richard Tuck see a break in the tradition, reading seventeenth-century natural law thinkers as part of the "new humanism" based on philosophical skepticism.[34] Taking the stance that innovations occurred within a framework of continuities in moral thought, Knud Haakonssen notes that Grotius departed from the traditional model by finding three meanings of natural right as opposed to two – that it is a moral faculty inherent in persons and that it is an objective *lex*.[35] Grotius's third meaning conceives of it any action that does not injure others' property. Thus, for Grotius, natural law ensures the right for self-preservation and, by not allowing the rights of others to be infringed, makes society possible. Haakonssen argues that while scholastics believe natural law does not compel obedience, Grotius separates natural law from Christianity such that "people unaided by religion can use their perfect – and even imperfect – rights to establish the contractual and quasi-contractual obligations upon which social life rests."[36] Grotius's sociable theory of natural law, which "stressed individuality in the area of rights, but communality in the area of obligation," was borrowed by John Selden, who, though a consistent advocate for the liberty of the subject, went further than Grotius in making contracts unbreakable and thus further toward the argument for absolutism.[37] The different interpretations meant that natural law and its manifestation as a social contract theory – Grotius's particular modification – could be used to support absolutist as well as constitutionalist views.

In the 1640s, the debate between the king and Parliament led to a novel use of natural law in English political thought, one that Milton employs in the first *Defence*. Royalists argued that the laws of the land invested sovereignty in the king with Parliament simply for counsel. Confronted with accusations that it was breaking known laws, Parliament resorted to the natural law argument that subjects may disobey the letter of the law if it is against their natural rights.[38] In his *Observations upon Some of His Majesties Late Answers and Expresses* (1642), Henry Parker locates parliamentary power in the social contract: although people elect governors because they are social by nature, "power is but secondary and derivative in Princes, the fountaine

[34] Richard Tuck, *Philosophy and Government, 1572–1651* (Cambridge: Cambridge University Press, 1993), and *Natural Rights Theories: Their Origin and Development* (Cambridge: Cambridge University Press, 1979).
[35] Knud Haakonssen, *Natural Law and Moral Philosophy: From Grotius to the Scottish Enlightenment* (Cambridge: Cambridge University Press, 1996), 26–30.
[36] *Ibid.*, 29.   [37] Tuck, *Natural Rights Theories*, 97.
[38] For Parliament's adoption of natural law ideas, see Ernest Sirluck, "Introduction," *CPW* II, 12–25.

and efficient cause is the people."[39] According to Parker, the people can convey their power to the king or to Parliament, but they will not tolerate arbitrary government. Because the king is tyrannical, the statutes proving his sovereignty are invalidated by the more fundamental law of nature that *salus populi suprema lex*, that the people's safety is paramount. Parliamentary apologists rejected the royalist claim that monarchy was founded in unfallen nature, saying that all governments were founded in fallen nature. Nonetheless, the people retain something of the primary natural law written in human hearts before the fall, termed the secondary law of nature. There must be government or people will perish, but God does not intend their destruction; hence, "the secondary law of nature is the law of God as well as the law of necessity."[40] This law of necessity, or secondary natural law, entails the people's self-preservation, even from kings.

Ernst Sirluck argues that Milton borrows from parliamentary use of natural law to make the case for divorce, that marriage is a contract that can be broken when it is injurious to the parties concerned.[41] Milton also adopts social contract theory as inflected by parliamentary natural law ideas in the first *Defence*. The last half of his *Defence* alternates between attacks on Salmasius's character and further elaboration of the implications of the natural law argument, with an emphasis on the "ascending" theory of political organization, in which the king is a creation of the people's "will and votes" (*Defence*, 127).[42] The first *Defence* contains familiar elements of the parliamentarian case supporting this contractual view of the relation between king and subject: they revolve around justification from fundamental laws, often taken to be natural law and reason, but also by reference to the ancient constitution and medieval precedents such as the oft-quoted Bracton and Fleta as well as the laws of Edward the Confessor.[43] Milton, like others, insists on the legislative function of Parliament. Citing the Latin tag, *quas vulgas elegerit*, he says, "the part of the people which swore, swore not only

---

[39] Henry Parker, *Observations upon Some of His Majesties Late Answers and Expresses* (London, 1642), 2.
[40] Sirluck, "Introduction," *CPW* II, 132. [41] *Ibid.*, 52, 153–58.
[42] For a survey of the "ascending" theory, see John Sanderson, *'But the People's Creatures': The Philosophical Basis of the English Civil War* (Manchester: Manchester University Press, 1989).
[43] The seminal account of the ancient constitution is J. G. A. Pocock's *Ancient Constitution and the Feudal Law: A Study of English Historical Thought in the Seventeenth Century: A Reissue with a Retrospect* (Cambridge: Cambridge University Press, 1957, 1987). See also J. W. Gough, *Fundamental Law in English Constitutional History* (Oxford: Clarendon Press, 1955); Richard Tuck, *Natural Rights Theories*; Glenn Burgess, *The Politics of the Ancient Constitution: An Introduction to English Political Thought, 1603–1642* (University Park: Pennsylvania State University Press, 1993); and Sommerville, *Royalists and Patriots*. For the radical use of Edward the Confessor, see Janelle Greenberg, "The Confessor's Laws and the Radical Face of the Ancient Constitution," *English Historical Review* 104 (1989), 611–37, and *The Radical Face of the Ancient Constitution: St. Edward's "Laws" in Early Modern Political Thought* (Cambridge: Cambridge University Press, 2001).

to the king but to the kingdom and laws, by which the king was created, and indeed to the king only so far as he should observe the laws 'which the common people', that is, the community or the house of commons, 'shall choose'" (*Defence*, 247). Reading *elegerit* as the future tense, Milton participates in the contemporary development that defines legal sovereignty as one shared by king, lords, and commons, and that denies the king dispensing power.[44] In chapter 5, he refutes Salmasius's natural law argument for monarchy – that natural law not only urges the formation of societies but also selects the governors – by turning to the parliamentary natural law argument that "the right of the people is older than the right of the king" (*Defence*, 134). Like the parliamentarians, Milton equates natural law with God's law: "the law of God agrees exactly with the law of nature" (*Defence*, 149).[45] This point was not necessarily controversial as some divine-right clerics thought of natural law as part of divine law.[46] But he also bridges a possible gap between Mosaic law and law applicable in the new Christian dispensation by assuming God's essential constancy.[47] His equation of divine law and natural law locates power in the people rather than in the king. Assuming England to be a "free state" (*Defence*, 78), Milton argues that God's law gave the people the power to decide on the form of their commonwealth: "the king exists on account of the people: therefore the people are stronger than and superior to the king"; as an inferior, the king has no right to "damage the people, the superior, or keep them in slavery" (*Defence*, 150).

Based on social contract, Milton's natural law argument rejects Salmasius's claim that monarchy is based on a divine model, which naturalized the analogy of king and father. Milton proposes instead a new genealogy: "A father and a king are very different things. A father has begotten us; but a king has not made us, but rather we the king. Nature gave a father to people, the people themselves gave themselves a king; so people do not exist because of a king, but a king exists because of the people" (*Defence*, 68). Canvassing a large number of examples from classical history, scripture and the early church fathers, he argues, "the right of the people is older than the

---

[44] Corinne Comstock Weston and Janelle Renfrow Greenberg trace this development back, ironically, to Charles I's own description of mixed government in the Answer to the Nineteen Propositions of 18 June 1642 (*Subjects and Sovereigns: The Grand Controversy over Legal Sovereignty in Stuart England* [Cambridge: Cambridge University Press, 1981], 3, 35–38).

[45] The Latin reads: "legem Dei cum lege naturæ optimè consentire" (Clinton W. Keyes, ed., *The Works of John Milton*, vol. VII [New York: Columbia University Press, 1932], 266).

[46] Sirluck, "Introduction," *CPW* II, 29.

[47] Arthur Barker traces an evolution in Milton's thought, starting with the second edition of *The Doctrine and Discipline of Divorce* and with *Tetrachordon*, that conflates the law of nature with the gospel ("Christian Liberty in Milton's Divorce Pamphlets," *MLR* 35 [1940], 153–61).

right of the king" (*Defence*, 134). The institution of monarchy is a human invention, not natural. Because people made kings, they can be viewed as parent to kings. Reversing the royalist family hierarchy completely, Milton's reworking of the family metaphor has changed considerably since the antiprelatical tracts. There he only shifts a hierarchical relation into a lateral one (the community of brothers). In the *Defensio*, Milton turns the royalist hierarchy upside down so that the people are above kings. He compares the king to a child: "Hence quite often under our law the king is called an 'infant' and said not to possess his rights and dignities except in the manner of a child or ward" (*Defence*, 204). Milton greatly reduces the king's role to that of a figurehead, for everything is done by law. Later when he compares the king to no better than "a servant or agent of the people" (*Defence*, 216), Milton takes away from him even the patrimony that a child or ward would have. The king is left with no will of his own. The relation between royalism and republicanism is similarly transformed. When examined closely, Milton's contemptuous response to Salmasius's vindication of kingly prerogative on the basis of the familial analogy is only a modification of the royalist model: "But whereas you so often attribute to a king the ancient right of the head of the household, so that you may seek from there 'an example of the absolute power in kings', I have now frequently shown that it is totally different . . . Whence it is quite clear that in the very beginning of nations, paternal and hereditary government very soon gave way to virtue and the people's right" (*Defence*, 194–95). While he accepts the prior existence of the paternal model of government advanced by the royalists, Milton relegates it into the distant past, claiming that new forms soon replaced it.

This history is not a denial of Aristotle's distinction between a household and a nation in his *Politics*: "There he [Aristotle] says that they judge badly who think there is very little difference between a head of household and a king. 'For a kingdom is different from a household not only in number but in kind'" (*Defence*, 194–95).[48] Although Milton allows the family to remain foundational to the state, or at least the form of the very beginning of society, he embeds it deeper in the substructure of society, pushing it further back in time. These new forms, forms that have a distinctively republican cast in its emphasis on virtue and popular sovereignty, are preferred in Milton's scheme, their superiority deriving in part from the rapidity with which they succeeded the original. The implications of such a chronology that suggests, by argument from priority, that the paternal government favored by the

---

[48] The reference for the *Politics* is I, I (1252a).

royalists essentially gave birth to, is father of, republicanism can be adverse
to Milton's argument, not the least because seventeenth-century England
in its disputes over constitutional rights clung trenchantly to the idea of
an ancient constitution still in force in the shape of a common law whose
authority was secured by its customary character. A society that justified its
political claims by invoking a phrase such as "time out of mind" assumed
that historical precedence bore an incontrovertible logic. Yet this is not to
say that such a peculiar historical consciousness only yields stasis. Although
Milton is still forced to ascribe historical longevity to republican rights – he
says these rights quickly superseded paternal rule, which appear to have held
sway only very briefly – so that they too can claim authority from ancient
use, it is important that his historical explanation dismisses the claims of
priority. This dismissal reduces the power of the analogy by making paternal
rights appear the superannuated practice of a distant, presumably primitive,
age, whose very distance only betrays the obsolescence of the practice, the
brevity of which suggests an aborted experiment. It may not be obvious,
but such rebuttals do more than diminish the force of the analogy; they
do damage also to its expression. Milton gives a historical dimension to
a previously ahistorical analogy. Royalist apologists have so collapsed the
two parts of the analogy (king and father), have so erased differences and
emphasized correspondences, that they turn analogy into metaphor. The
new historical distance restores difference to the analogy to pry its elements
apart again.

   Historical awareness is not the only change. While Salmasius uses the
analogy between king and father to elucidate the nature of royal power,
Milton side-steps familial relations altogether to argue that royal power
has a republican origin. It is not the paternal role of the king that gives
him authority; rather, "virtue and the people's right . . . is the origin of
royal power, and the most natural reason and cause" (*Defence*, 195). Kingly
office arose out of a need for a judge to mediate between men and to
ensure the proper execution of laws. Milton's different understanding of
the kingly role is made possible by identifying the republican roots of kingship. Paternal government is not the same as monarchy. Rather, paternal
government gave way to a social compact that is republican in character:
"men first came together, not so that one might abuse them all, but so
that when one injured another, there should be law and a judge between
men" (*Defence*, 195). Monarchy necessarily comes after republican government. This dazzling maneuver does not remove the family as a model for
government but testifies rather to another, equally powerful, way of imagining the family: Milton shifts the emphasis in the family from one that is

organized according to vertical relations – father as head of household over wife, children, and servants – to one organized along horizontal lines – a brotherhood of men. Moreover, such a brotherhood can be more egalitarian than supposed. In *Eikonoklastes*, Milton argues that the outcome of the conflict between Presbyterians and Independents is determined by merit. When *Eikon Basilike* compares them to twins struggling in one womb, Milton points to the anecdote's Old Testament context to give it a different interpretation: "*Those twins* that strove *enclos'd in the womb* of *Rebeccah*, were the seed of *Abraham*; the younger undoubtedly gain'd the heav'nly birthright; the elder though supplanted in his Similie, shall yet no question find a better portion then *Esau* found, and farr above his uncircumcis'd Prelats" (*CPW* III, 562). Reminding his readers that God sanctioned Jacob's dominance over his elder brother Esau, Milton suggests that family hierarchy is flexible. The younger brother can gain ascendancy over the elder, if God wills it.

Even though it configures the family differently, republicanism too rests on the model of the family. But, with the comparison between father and king no longer the only or primary basis for metaphors of the family, the analogy becomes strained. Milton twists it even further when he begins comparing the king to the unthinkable – an infant, the opposite of a father. His retelling of the origin of kingship reveals the fissures in the analogy as used by royalists. In particular, kingship is a role and not a fixed identity: "while a father cannot stop being a father, a king can easily stop being either a father or a king" (*Defence*, 68). A father who kills is punished; even more so, a king who breaks the laws can be deposed. Metaphors must reflect reality and not manufacture something that does not exist. Under the pressure of republican claims, the comparison between king and father becomes distorted, making new analogical relations possible and allowing for resistance to tyrannical kings.

FATHERS AND CITIZENS

In dethroning the king, Milton's republicanism also dethrones the father. Yet, he does not do away with the father completely. Returning to the republican meaning of *pater patriae*, he reforms the figure of the father. Milton confers the title on good governors of the country instead of the father-king. Recognized on the basis of merit, his fathers form an aristocracy of virtue. Initially, Milton would identify such fathers with Parliament. As he became more disillusioned and more distrustful of the common people, his group of governors would shrink to an even smaller minority. On the eve of the Restoration, in *The Readie and Easie Way to Establish A Free Commonwealth* (1660), Milton makes the argument for an oligarchy to rule for life. In its final form, his republicanism rejects rule by a single person but also greatly emphasizes the aristocratic element over the democratic.

The republican reformation of the father can be found as early as the antiprelatical tracts. In *An Apology Against a Pamphlet*, Milton calls the members of Parliament fathers, arguing that they deserve the title for their service to English liberty: "Which hath gain'd them [Parliament] such an admiration from all good men, that now they heare it as their ord'nary surname, to be saluted the Fathers of their countrey; and sit as gods among daily Petitions and publick thanks flowing in upon them" (*CPW* 1, 926). Not only must the name of father be earned, it does not structure a hierarchical relation between Parliament and people. The fathers of the state do not grow arrogant from praise. Rather, Milton imagines the people's thanks shuttled back and forth: Parliament receives thanks only to return them again. That exchange establishes more equal relations between ruler and ruled, even while maintaining social hierarchies:

Insomuch that the meanest artizans and labourers, at other times also women, and often the younger sort of servants assembling with thier complaints, and that sometimes in a lesse humble guise then for petitioners, have gone with confidence, that neither their meannesse would be rejected, nor their simplicity contemn'd, nor yet their urgency distasted either by the dignity, wisdome, or moderation of that supreme Senate; nor did they depart unsatisfi'd. (*CPW* 1, 926)

Because of Parliament's *noblesse oblige*, the lower-class petitioners need not adopt a cringing servility. Instead, they approach their social superiors with confidence. There is a general celebratory tone in this passage. Milton revels in the fact that the meanest citizens and even women can enter the political arena and have their voices heard. All this is to the credit of the benevolence of Parliament, perhaps even to their *fatherly* benevolence. The state as family is still a hierarchical one, but hierarchy is mitigated by affectionate relations, so much so that hierarchy becomes somewhat leveled. It is neither simply a language of affect that serves only to conceal domination, nor is it that affect substitutes for such power relations and displaces hierarchy. Rather, affect interacts with a structure of hierarchical relations, resulting in a rapprochement between the governors and the governed such that hierarchy and equality easily merge.

The democratic potential is evident when such relations are counterposed to an authoritarian Episcopal hierarchy. But Milton's definition of citizens is never wholly democratic. Particularly as his view of his countrymen grew progressively darker, his judgment of their fitness to be citizens grew correspondingly dimmer. In *Areopagitica* (1644), he argues that to censor books is to distrust the "common people" and to "censure them for a giddy, vitious, and ungrounded people" (*CPW* II, 536). Instead they are "a Nation not slow and dull, but of quick, ingenious, and piercing spirit, acute to invent, suttle and sinewy to discours, not beneath the reach of any point the highest that human capacity can soar to" (*CPW* II, 551). London is "a City of refuge, the mansion house of liberty" (*CPW* II, 553–54) with citizens busy seeking after truth to bring about further reformation. Several years later, in *Eikonoklastes*, Milton would denounce the people as an "inconstant, irrational, and Image-doting rabble" (*CPW* III, 601). The depiction of manly citizens doing the work of truth in *Areopagitica* is as much prescriptive as it is anything else. In the first *Defence*, Milton would argue for the rule of the better sort even if they were the minority: "What if the majority in parliament should prefer to be slaves, and to offer the commonwealth for sale – should not the minority be allowed to prevent this and keep their liberty, if it lies in their power?" (*Defence*, 181–82). Perez Zagorin suggests that Milton's aristocracy encompasses those of independent means, the middling sort, but eschews the corrupt courtiers and the poor rabble.[49] Milton's rule of the virtuous minority, sometimes understood as an aristocracy of the saints, is thus not the populist republicanism of Niccolo Machiavelli but closer to the aristocratic one of Francesco Guicciardini.[50] As J. G. A. Pocock distinguishes them, Machiavelli democratizes his republic to argue for a popular government and a citizen army, while Guicciardini offers a Polybian-Venetian model of mixed government in which an aristocratic elite, a meritocracy, dominates. Machiavelli emphasizes military *virtù*; Guicciardini, rejecting the armed state, stresses political prudence in a civic context.[51]

Within this context of an increasingly restrictive notion of nobility of virtue, Milton sought to replace the king with the rule of fathers and householders. In *The Tenure of Kings and Magistrates* (1649), he argued for the people's right to depose their governor, couching the liberty of the people in terms of household management: a free people have "that power, which is the root and sourse of all liberty, to dispose and *oeconomize* in the Land

[49] Perez Zagorin, *A History of Political Thought in the English Revolution* (London: Routledge & Paul, 1954), 111–13.
[50] Paul Rahe, "The Classical Republicanism of John Milton," *History of Political Thought* 25.2 (2004), 243–75. On whether Milton's aristocracy is one of virtue or one of grace, see Arthur Barker, *Milton and the Puritan Dilemma*, 278–90, 308–26.
[51] Pocock, *Machiavellian Moment*, 219–71.

which God hath giv'n them, as Maisters of Family in thir own house and free inheritance" (*CPW* III, 237). By reinstating masters of households as proper governors, Milton displaces the father-king, disperses his authority, and multiplies fathers. Such fathers form a governing elite. Moreover, they are independent of the court. Instead of the king's creatures, the people are their own persons. In the first *Defence*, Milton rejects Salmasius's definition of nobility based on birth to offer one based on merit: "others who are their own ancestors by their hard work and virtue take the road to true nobility, and can be compared with any of the noblest at all" (*Defence*, 62). The virtuous nobles are self-made people. Their nobility is a purer kind, won from their own labor. They do not boastfully claim empty titles: "they prefer to be called 'sons of the earth' (at least it is their own) and to work energetically at home" (*Defence*, 62). Such self-made people must not be subjected to a slavish tyranny. While Salmasius grovels at the feet of his foreign lords, the people are their own masters. They are, independent, free citizens. Liberty, first Christian, then republican, is Milton's enduring concern, shaping his idea of family.

During the interregnum, however, not only did it become harder for Milton to be optimistic about the people's ability to govern themselves, it was also harder to trust the current governors. Milton would not repudiate rule by a single person until, in his last regicide tracts, after Oliver Cromwell's death. Before that he supported Cromwell. In a eulogy at the end of *Pro Populo Anglicano Defensio Secunda* (1654), Milton praised him as an exemplary regicide and republican. But by then, Cromwell had accepted the title of Lord Protector on 16 December 1653, making it harder for republicans to defend him. Moreover, ideal republican fatherhood was also harder to sustain. In stating the case again for a republic in the *Second Defence*, Milton struggles with the idea of Cromwell as *pater patriae*. While praising Cromwell as father of his country, he takes care to define the term to return to its republican roots. His praise of Cromwell is thus tinged with covert criticism.

Although not the only one praised in the *Second Defence* – others were Lord Fairfax and Henry Vane – Cromwell is singled out as the remaining hope of England, particularly with Fairfax's retirement into private life, and is hailed as the undisputed ruler of England.[52] Milton's delineation of Cromwell's role as ruler urges him to keep to republican principles. Insisting on Cromwell's equality with those he rules, he depicts Cromwell

---

[52] Robert W. Ayers, ed., *Complete Prose Works of John Milton*, vol. VII, 1659–1660, rev. edn (New Haven: Yale University Press, 1980).

as "the greatest and most illustrious citizen" (*CPW* IV, 672). It is in the context of citizenship that Milton names Cromwell "father of your country" (*CPW* IV, 672). Don Wolfe, the Yale editor of the *Second Defence*, points out the republican connotations of the term: "He equates Cromwell with Cicero, the first Roman to be called *pater patriae*, who was so named by the Senate after his destruction of the conspiracy of Catiline in 63 BC. The title was later bestowed upon Julius Caesar and Augustus" (*CPW* IV, 672 n. 508). The term was first a republican rather than an imperial title. While James I named himself, like the Roman emperors, *pater patriae*, Milton so names Cromwell in the very different context of a republic. The highest praise in a republic, to be named *pater patriae*, is to be a citizen who has done great patriotic deeds – indeed the greatest deed of a citizen is to liberate one's country – rather than an absolute king. By praising Cromwell for rejecting the title of king, Milton simultaneously admonishes him not to be tempted by the crown. But Cromwell has taken on a title and privileges resembling a king's. Milton makes the best of things. He attempts to assimilate the Lord Protectorship into republicanism, suggesting that the title is akin to the republican title of *pater patriae*, "a certain title very like that of father of your country" (*CPW* IV, 672). It is not an elevation or honor, however, but simply political expedience. Milton advocates a republican fatherhood, turning the protector into a citizen of the republic. He even suggests that the title diminishes Cromwell's achievements: "You suffered and allowed yourself, not indeed to be borne aloft, but to come down so many degrees from the heights and be forced into a definite rank, so to speak, for the public good" (*CPW* IV, 672). Finally, Milton attempts to restrain Cromwellian fatherhood, potentially expansive in its powers, by referring to another family metaphor: he reminds Cromwell of his "mother, your native land" (*CPW* IV, 673). Cromwell, though ruler, is under a greater authority – the country itself. To abandon republican principles of liberty is to be a disobedient son. Republican fatherhood is most true when it remembers it is about being a son.

By the end of the decade, even that limited optimism could no longer be sustained. The Restoration would dash Milton's hopes for a fraternal republic of peers uninfected by the disease of rank. His utopian vision of a society of equal brothers could not finally bear close scrutiny. Indeed, some of the proposals of the tracts were articulated in the face of a reality increasingly distant from his ideals. Written in the final throes of the commonwealth, the last tracts revealed his increasing disillusionment with his countrymen. This disillusionment led him to defend liberty on all fronts. His last tracts not only defended the regicide but also argued for church reformation. Publishing *Considerations Touching the Likeliest Means to Remove Hirelings Out of the Church* (1659) as a companion to *A Treatise of Civil Power* (1659), Milton saw civil liberty and religious freedom as closely related issues. In *Hirelings*, Milton treats family and church as distinct entities. Arguing against tithes, he distinguishes between what is owed to a priest and what to a "father, or the first born of each familie" (*CPW* vii, 286).[53] Tithes were paid by the father's "own children and servants, who had not wherewithal to pay him, but of his own" (*CPW* vii, 286). While tithes are part of a well-regulated family, they corrupt the church. Milton even does away with the priestly caste by declaring the people "kings and priests" (*CPW* vii, 286) with Christ. The argument for independence is a major theme in the last regicide tract as well.

The Readie and Easie Way to Establish a Free Commonwealth appeared on the eve of Charles II's return, the first edition in March 1660 and the second in early April, as a last-ditch effort to save the commonwealth. The *Way* favors perpetuating the Rump, a Parliament far from representative, "judging that most voices ought not alwaies to prevail where main matters are in question."[54] This argument for an oligarchy, whose members serve for life, makes it clearer than ever the thoroughly aristocratic nature of Milton's republicanism.[55] Yet, he continues to idealize his aristocracy of virtue through comparisons to the affectionate family. The governors of this free commonwealth are public servants and brothers to their fellow citizens: "they who are greatest, are perpetual servants and drudges to the public at thir own cost and charges, neglect their own affairs; yet are not elevated above thir brethren; live soberly in thir families, walk the streets as other men, may be spoken to freely, familiarly, friendly, without adoration" (*CPW* vii, 425). It is also a Christian concept of greatness in its emphasis on service and the public good. Attempting to reduce differences of rank between republican governor-fathers and citizens, Milton retains the notion of the commonwealth as a fraternity.

Milton's loss of faith in the political judgment of his countrymen measures his desperation. It also indicates how much his imagined community of brother-citizens has shrunk. Falling back on tactics perfected

[53] Don M. Wolfe, ed. *Complete Prose Works of John Milton*, vol. iv, part 1 (New Haven: Yale University Press, 1966), 671–72. Further references to the *Second Defence* are from this edition and cited parenthetically.

[54] *The Readie and Easie Way (Second Edition)* in Robert W. Ayers, ed., *Complete Prose Works of John Milton*, vol. vii, rev. edn (New Haven: Yale University Press, 1980), 415. Further references are from this edition and cited parenthetically.

[55] For Milton's aristocratic contractarianism, see Michael P. Zuckert, *Natural Rights and the New Republicanism* (Princeton: Princeton University Press, 1994), chapter 3.

in *Eikonoklastes* of depicting the monarchy in the worst light possible, Milton denounces the court for intemperate luxury and undue influence by Catholic queens. He fears that rule by a single person would reduce England once again to a state of dependence. Restoring the monarchy, he argues, would turn Englishmen, though able to "manage nobly thir own affairs themselves," into "more like boyes under age then men" (*CPW* VII, 427). Milton's worst fears came true. For a time he was forced into hiding. His arrest was ordered on 16 June 1660. Copies of his antimonarchical tracts were burned by the hangman in August. But, perhaps with Andrew Marvell's intervention, the Act of Oblivion of 29 August did not name Milton as one of the unforgiven. Finally arrested in October, he was pardoned and released on 15 December. He came very close to losing his life. Even with the pardon, he continued to fear assassination by someone who might think he had escaped lightly.[56] While he was to leave aside controversial writings, in his great poetic works of the Restoration, including *Paradise Lost, Paradise Regained,* and *Samson Agonistes,* Milton would continue his meditation on Christian fraternity and republican liberty by exploring family relationships and their political significance.

[56] William Riley Parker, *Milton: A Biography,* ed. Gordon Campbell, 2nd edn, 2 vols. (Oxford: Clarendon Press, 1996), 1:562, 576–77.

CHAPTER 3

Hobbes and the absent family

In his *Observations Concerning the Originall of Government, Upon Mr Hobs 'Leviathan,' Mr Milton against Salmasius, H. Grotius 'De Jure Belli'* (1652), the theorist of patriarchalism Sir Robert Filmer writes,

With no small content I read Mr Hobbes' book *De Cive*, and his *Leviathan*, about the rights of sovereignty, which no man, that I know, hath so amply and judiciously handled. I consent with him about the rights of exercising government, but I cannot agree to his means of acquiring it. It may seem strange I should praise his building and yet mislike his foundation, but so it is.[1]

Suggesting that Hobbes would do better to adopt a patriarchal basis for government, Filmer wishes Hobbes

would consider whether his building would not stand firmer upon the principles of *regnum patrimoniale* [a paternal kingdom], as he calls it, both according to Scripture and reason – since he confesseth the "father being before the institution of a commonwealth" was originally an "absolute' sovereign" "with power of life and death", and that "a great family, as to the rights of sovereignty is a little monarchy."[2]

Grouping Hobbes with Milton and Hugo Grotius, Filmer disapproves of the means of Hobbes's political theory though not the ends. All three authors were in some way contractualist theorists.[3] But in his opening remarks Filmer registers some genuine bafflement as well. It is not just that he is puzzled that Hobbes declines to build civil society on a patriarchalist foundation when Hobbes, like Filmer, aims at an absolutist state. It is also that Filmer finds it strange that Hobbes should fail to argue for patriarchal government when patriarchalist assertions are readily detected in *Leviathan*.

---

[1] Sir Robert Filmer, *Patriarcha and Other Writings*, ed. Johann P. Sommerville (Cambridge: Cambridge University Press, 1991), 184–85.

[2] *Ibid.*, 185.

[3] Richard Tuck suggests that Hobbes is heir to Grotius ("Grotius and Selden," in J. H. Burns and Mark Goldie, eds., *The Cambridge History of Political Thought, 1450–1700* [Cambridge: Cambridge University Press, 1991], 522).

76

Hobbes's inclusion of the paternal state in his discussion would seem to lend itself to the argument that paternity forms the origin of society and offers fundamental justification for rule.

Filmer is not alone in trying to reshape Hobbes into the mold of a patriarchalist. The patriarchalist residue of Hobbes's political philosophy has attracted the attention of modern commentators as well, with a notable lack of consensus about its significance.[4] Trying to disentangle his dependence on patriarchal assumptions from his innovations, a number of critics find Hobbes revising patriarchalism. Gordon Schochet argues that while Hobbes accepts the sovereignty of fathers in families in the state of nature – as well as the sovereignty of fathers in families where it does not impinge on that of the civil power – Hobbes differed from his contemporaries in deriving such power from consent, not generation.[5] Richard Chapman claims that Hobbes subverts patriarchal attitudes because he "saw the family as a diminutive state, as *Leviathan* writ small," though the distinction that Chapman makes is difficult to maintain since the analogy went both ways in the seventeenth century.[6] Finding Hobbes "a patriarchalist who rejects paternal right" in her influential feminist reading, Carole Pateman separates marriage from the family to argue that the Hobbesian family originated in conquest, which means "*sex-right or conjugal right must necessarily precede*

---

[4] For arguments against Hobbes as a patriarchalist, see Howard Warrender, *The Political Philosophy of Hobbes: His Theory of Obligation* (Oxford: Clarendon Press, 1957); Peter Laslett, "Introduction" to John Locke, *Two Treatises of Government* (Cambridge: Cambridge University Press, 1960); Quentin Skinner, "Hobbes on Sovereignty: An Unknown Discussion," *Political Studies* 13 (1965), 213–18; and John Zvesper, "Hobbes' Individualistic Analysis of the Family," *Politics* 5 (1985). For arguments that patriarchalism is central to Hobbes's philosophy, see Leo Strauss, *The Political Philosophy of Hobbes: Its Basis and its Genesis*, trans. Elsa M. Sinclair (Chicago: University of Chicago Press, 1952); Keith Thomas, "The Social Origins of Hobbes's Political Thought," in Keith C. Brown, ed., *Hobbes: Studies* (Cambridge, Mass.: Harvard University Press, 1965), 188–89; and R. W. K. Hinton, "Husbands, Fathers and Conquerors II," *Political Studies* 16 (1968), 55–67.

[5] Gordon J. Schochet, *Patriarchalism in Political Thought: The Authoritarian Family and Political Speculation and Attitudes Especially in Seventeenth-Century England* (New York: Basic Books, 1975), 241. Schochet is responding to the argument that Hobbes's description of the state of nature was a theoretical construct and not historical fact. The latter implies that the patriarchal family is the historical origin of society, while the former accounts for the presence of patriarchal elements in Hobbes without conflict between patriarchal theory and the prominently featured social contract. A. P. Martinich resorts to this argument when he discusses Filmer's criticism of Hobbes as a common contemporary confusion: "Filmer has confused the historical fact of patriarchy with the theoretical grounds or nature of government" (*Hobbes: A Biography* [Cambridge: Cambridge University Press, 1999], 261). Schochet argues, however, that the differences between the historical and the logical analyses of political authority diminish when it is observed that while fathers have absolute sovereignty within their families, the families themselves are in a state of nature (236–39).

[6] Richard Allen Chapman, "*Leviathan* Writ Small: Thomas Hobbes on the Family," *American Political Science Review* 69 (1975), 77.

the right of fatherhood. The genesis of political dominion lies in Adam's sex-right, *not* in his fatherhood."[7]

The disagreement among Hobbes's modern commentators mirrors Filmer's confusion. Mixing contract theory with patriarchalism, Hobbes's view on the relation between state and family can seem bewilderingly contradictory.[8] While Filmer and others have pointed to passages in *Leviathan* that indicate a patriarchalist mindset, we can also find other passages to contradict them. In the chapter on the intellectual capacity of man, Hobbes suggests that family and state cannot be compared: "To govern well a family, and a kingdome, are not different degrees of Prudence; but different sorts of businesse" (8.34).[9] If seventeenth-century patriarchalism in political thought is theory about how state and family are analogous, Hobbes does not seem to share that view. In another passage, he refers to native Americans as people living in a "brutish" state of nature, having no government "except the government of small Families" (13.63). So the government of families, in this passage, is no substitute for civil government of the sort that Hobbes is anxious to maintain. He compares the two only to reject the comparison.

The difficulty of positioning Hobbes in relation to patriarchalism stems from its overly narrow definition. Family analogies so important in defining patriarchalism can be given meanings that a patriarchalist theorist like Filmer would never accept. While "the details of Hobbes's thinking owe much to traditional notions," Hobbes rejects the central tenets of patriarchalism by deriving paternal power from the consent of children and from

---

[7] Carole Pateman, "'God Hath Ordained to Man a Helper': Hobbes, Patriarchy and Conjugal Right," in Mary Lyndon Shanley and Carole Pateman, eds., *Feminist Interpretations and Political Theory* (Cambridge: Polity Press with Basil Blackwell, 1991), 54, 57 (italics hers). See also Pateman, *The Sexual Contract* (Stanford: Stanford University Press, 1988). Pateman's "conjectural history" of male dominance posits that motherhood puts women with an infant to defend at a disadvantage. But would men not be equally disadvantaged by their dominion over women and children? Furthermore, Hobbes does not, as Pateman supposes, assume women are "always subject to men through (the marriage) contract" (55). In chapter 20, Hobbes notes two exceptions: Amazons that contract with neighboring men to have children and a female monarch marrying a subject both retain dominion.

[8] Accounts of Hobbes's social contract include C. B. Macpherson, *The Political Theory of Possessive Individualism: Hobbes to Locke* (Oxford: Clarendon Press, 1962); David Gauthier, *The Logic of Leviathan: The Moral and Political Theory of Thomas Hobbes* (Oxford: Clarendon Press, 1969) and *Morals by Agreement* (Oxford: Clarendon Press, 1986); Jean Hampton, *Hobbes and the Social Contract Tradition* (Cambridge: Cambridge University Press, 1986); Gregory Kavka, *Hobbesian Moral and Political Theory* (Princeton: Princeton University Press, 1986); and Jody S. Kraus, *The Limits of Hobbesian Contractarianism* (Cambridge: Cambridge University Press, 1993).

[9] Thomas Hobbes, *Leviathan*, ed. Richard Tuck (Cambridge: Cambridge University Press, 1991). References to *Leviathan* are from this edition and given parenthetically by chapter and original page number from the first 1651 edition.

the consent of the mother.[10] He reconfigures family metaphors in *Leviathan* to weaken and to displace the family analogy. What is most surprising is not the absence of familial ties in Hobbes's state of nature, it is the absence, for the most part, of the family in Hobbes's account of civil society. He reinterprets family metaphors in a number of ways. Hobbes reconceptualizes the meaning of a paternal state, and so disputes with the patriarchalist (Filmerian) understanding of monarchy. He defuses the power of the metaphor – wresting the family from the state – by displacing the family metaphor with that of the body politic, and so rhetorically stages the disappearance of the family metaphor. Hobbes dramatizes a confrontation between two of the most pervasive metaphors for polity in the early modern period: the family and the human body. In reducing the relevance of the family metaphor for the state, he remakes the family into the image of his Leviathan state. In attempting to divorce absolutism from its philosophical dependence on the family, Hobbes first has to confront patriarchalism.

HOBBES AND PATRIARCHALISM

Hobbes's use of family metaphors sometimes seems unreflective and conventional. He compares ignorant men to "little children, that have no other rule of good and evill manners, but the correction they receive from their Parents, and Masters" (11.50). This conception of the family supposes a hierarchical relation on the basis of knowledge. Because the ignorant are like children, they must be ruled in an absolute manner. Family metaphors still evoke traditional roles. Hobbes compares the rational man to the master of a family doing household accounts, prudently checking the accounting of each bill. Likewise, readers must check the arguments of authors: "so also in Reasoning of all other things, he that takes up conclusions on the trust of Authors, and doth not fetch them from the first Items in every Reckoning, (which are the significations of names settled by definitions), loses his labour; and does not know any thing; but onely beleeveth" (5.19). In Hobbes's lesson on reading, the figure of the active, perspicacious, and skeptical reader is compared to the master of household because both are traditional positions of privilege. It may also suggest that the implied audience of *Leviathan* are privileged householders, fathers of families.

Although fathers of families (as figures for men of substance) are the implied audience of *Leviathan*, Hobbes does not strictly retain the

[10] Johann P. Sommerville, *Thomas Hobbes: Political Ideas in Historical Context* (New York: St. Martin's Press, 1992), 74.

traditional privileges of fathers and of family hierarchy. His understanding of primogeniture – very important in maintaining the privileges of family hierarchy – fails to uphold the idea of inborn right. Instead, there is a large element of chance in his conception of primogeniture, which he categorizes as a kind of lottery. When property cannot be divided, it must be obtained by lot, of which there are two kinds – arbitrary and natural: "Arbitrary, is that which is agreed on by the Competitors: Naturall, is either *Primogeniture* (which the Greek calls κληρονομία [Rom. *klēronomia*], which signifies, *Given by Lot;*) or *First Seisure*" (15.78). Although primogeniture is natural lot rather than arbitrary, the term natural is used only to distinguish the means by which one comes to property. The first-born is comparable to one who obtains property by being the first to possess it: "And therefore those things which cannot be enjoyed in common, nor divided, ought to be adjudged to the First Possessor; and in some cases to the First-Borne, as acquired by Lot" (15.78). That primogeniture is by natural lot does not mean that it is natural right. The two categories of arbitrary and natural lot are still subsumed under the overarching category of lot. Furthermore, Hobbes equates inheritance with ownership through force. While arbitrary lot is decided among "Competitors," primogeniture is no less a competition; it is *"First Seisure"* in which the ablest wins. The effect of comparing primogeniture to arbitrary lot is to demystify birthright and so to demystify also patriarchalist justifications.

Hobbes undermines not just primogeniture but also the absolute power of fathers. While children are required to obey parents, upon gaining maturity they are no longer under parental authority but must simply respect and honor their parents in gratitude. Even the patriarchalist account of society Hobbes would have children taught in fact undoes its own patriarchalist moral: "To which end they [children] are to be taught, that originally the Father of every man was also his Sovereign Lord, with power over him of life and death; and that the Fathers of families, when by instituting a Common-wealth, they resigned that absolute Power, yet it was never intended, they should lose the honour due unto them for their education" (30.178). In Hobbes's retelling, the patriarchalist story is modified by a coda. Subsequent to the rule of fathers is the institution of commonwealths that ends absolute paternal power. The newly instituted commonwealth would be absolute, given what Hobbes has said so far about sovereignty, but it is no longer paternal. In the end, Hobbes retains for fathers only honor, justifying it by reference to the fifth commandment (30.178).

When Hobbes imagines colonies as children of a commonweath, he is able to envision a similarly independent relationship between colony and metropolis. Colonies that remain dependent are merely provinces. But if they are independent,

> they are . . . a Common-wealth of themselves, discharged of their subjection to their Sovereign that sent them, . . . in which case the Common-wealth from which they went was called their Metropolis, or Mother, and requires no more of them, then Fathers require of the Children, whom they emancipate, and make free from their domestique government, which is Honour, and Friendship. (24.131)

While the parent–child relationship remains in name, the relationship can evolve. Like the child who only owes honor to his father, the former colony is simply required to maintain friendly relations with its parent. Although hierarchical, family roles are not fixed. While they are not overturned or reversed, there is nonetheless a shift in the relation when parent gives up power over child. The location of power is fundamental to Hobbes's understanding of both state and family, and thus also to his response to patriarchalism.

Although he may sometimes compare families to monarchies, Hobbes explicitly denies the central basis of power in patriarchalist thought: the paternity, real or metaphorical, of the sovereign. Gordon Schochet argues, "Although his identification of primitive paternal authority with political power was in keeping with the writings of many of his contemporaries, Hobbes was unique in attempting to derive the father's power over his children from their consents."[11] Hobbes's departure from the patriarchalist theorists is greater than Schochet supposes. *Leviathan* constitutes an attack on patriarchal theories of the state. Hobbes describes what he calls "dominion by generation" or paternal dominion in terms that are completely at odds with conventional understanding.[12] Although Filmer declares that the king's power is in his paternity, traceable back to Adam, Hobbes finds dominion by generation patently not one acquired through begetting a child: "The right of Dominion by Generation, is that, which the Parent hath over his Children; and is called PATERNALL. And is not so derived from the Generation, as if therefore the Parent had Dominion over his Child because he begat him; but from the Childs Consent, either expresse, or by other sufficient arguments declared" (20.102). Insisting that power is not derived from generation, Hobbes retains the name but does away with the old meaning. His assertions in the beginning of *Leviathan* that

---

[11] Schochet, *Patriarchalism*, 241.
[12] Richard Chapman suggests that in this claim Hobbes goes further than other patriarchalist theorists of the period ("*Leviathan* Writ Small").

misunderstandings and sloppy thinking happen because of the failure to begin from precise definitions underwrite a vast overhauling of key terms.[13]

In order to justify his redefinition of paternal government as derived from consent, Hobbes points out that there are two parties involved in giving birth to a child: "For as to the Generation, God hath ordained to man a helper; and there be alwayes two that are equally Parents" (20.102). Again, he turns traditional language on its head. Calling the woman a "helper" and alluding to divine assignment of gender roles, Hobbes invites his readers to expect dominion over the child automatically given to the father. Yet, this dominion is given to the woman in the state of nature because Hobbes establishes sovereignty on the basis of the power to kill: "the Infant is first in the power of the Mother" (20.103), who can either "nourish, or expose it" (20.103). She has primary power over the child because of the absence of law, particularly laws of marriage. If she exposes the child and he is rescued by another, then "Dominion is in him that nourisheth it" (20.103). The child is assumed to have given consent if he allows his life to be preserved. In making this argument, Hobbes seems surprisingly free from assumptions about male superiority. While far from arguing for women's equality in society, he does argue for gender equality in the state of nature: "For there is not always that difference of strength, or prudence between the man and the woman, as that the right can be determined without War" (20.102). In civil society, men have legal advantage "because for the most part Common-wealths have been erected by the Fathers, not by the Mothers of families" (20.102–03). Hobbes does not, however, explain why men determine laws instead of women when they are not inherently superior.

By deemphasizing the importance of fathering a child, Hobbes attacks patriarchalist thought at its root. He points out that men share the generation of children with women only to dismiss the notion that who the parents are matters. Whoever preserves the life of the child commands its obedience. The relation between subject and sovereign is no longer familial. By dismissing the importance of generation, whether fatherhood or motherhood, Hobbes evades the problem of gender. Moving even further away from conventional understandings of paternal government, Hobbes argues that the right of succession in such a government is the same as the right

---

[13] This rhetorical strategy is Hobbes's method of proof: Victoria Silver says, "[Hobbes's] mode of expression operates at once as a rhetorical strategy, designed to win his reader's belief, and as an arbiter of truth in his discussion: for the form of argument, whether or not expression and idea cohere to make a rational statement, dictates its self-evidence"; denying words have a range of meanings, Hobbes insists on his single definition ("The Fiction of Self-Evidence in Hobbes's *Leviathan*," *ELH* 55 [1988], 371).

of succession in monarchy, as he has discussed it in chapter 19. Because he does not repeat or elaborate on this right of succession in the chapter on paternal dominion, the startling nature of this assertion is somewhat lost. Chapter 19 on monarchical government argues that the right of succession depends on the monarch's will:

> For the word Heire does not of it selfe imply the Children, or nearest Kindred of a man; but whomsoever a man shall any way declare, he would have to succeed him in his Estate. If therefore a Monarch declare expresly, that such a man shall be his Heire, either by Word or Writing, then is that man immediately after the decease of his Predecessor, Invested in the right of being Monarch. (19.100).

With no necessary familial connection, anyone can be named heir. A king can dissolve his kingdom even with sons to inherit: "though Nature may declare who are his Sons, and who are the nerest of his Kin; yet it dependeth on his own will . . . who shall be his Heyr. If therefore he will have no Heyre, there is no Soveraignty, nor Subjection" (21.114). Having disposed of the issue of generation, Hobbes turns the paternal state into a mirror image of the monarchical state with only minuscule differences between the two: "In summe, the Rights and Consequences of both *Paternall* and *Despoticall* Dominion, are the very same with those of a Soveraign by Institution; and for the same reasons" (20.104). Indeed, such assertions minimize differences between the various states to render them the same.

While Hobbes's various types of states mimic each other, the family is distinguished from the state such that he pulls the two terms of the analogy apart. The state, unlike the family, can defend itself against external attack: "But yet a Family is not properly a Common-wealth; unlesse it be of that power by its own number, or by other opportunities, as not to be subdued without the hazard of war" (20.105). Hobbes also stresses difference rather than likeness of the father-king analogy. He refuses to compare fathers to kings but claims "Kings are Fathers of Families" (42.296). This is literalism on his part: kings often are fathers, but few fathers are kings. With both commonwealths and kings, their defining characteristic is power.

Power is still Hobbes's emphasis when interpreting scripture to claim obedience for kings. Right after the passage in which he distinguishes between family and state, Hobbes uses scripture for the first time to argue for the rights of kings, pointing to several examples of absolutism in scripture, including the people's obedience to Moses and to King Saul. Hobbes interprets as scriptural justification for absolutism Samuel's warning to the people that if they should have the king they want then the king would have the right to their children, their servants, their fields, and their flocks:

"This is absolute power, and summed up in the last words, you shall be
his servants" (20.105). Rather than reading the passage as Samuel's attempt
to dissuade the Israelites from demanding a king, he considers it an argument for the absolute power of kings, turning the expectation of obedience
that Samuel uses as a threat into a command. The necessity of obedience,
rather than any elaboration on familial relations, prompts his inclusion of
Paul's injunction to children to obey parents. Included under the category
of "obedience of servants" (20.105), Paul's injunction is preceded by his
other command that servants obey their masters in all things. Hobbes's
absolutism, "that the Commands of them that have the right to command,
are not by their Subjects to be censured, nor disputed" (20.106), is not
grounded in a paternal theory of government as he conflates children with
servants, parents with masters. For him, there are only rulers and the ruled.
His different types of rule simply reproduce sameness and uniformity. Thus,
dominion is large and always the same, based on obedience to power: "So
that it appeareth plainly, to my understanding, both from Reason, and
Scripture, that the Sovereign Power, whether placed in One Man, as in
Monarchy, or in one Assembly of men, as in Popular, and Aristocraticall
Common-wealths, is as great, as possibly men can be imagined to make it"
(20.106–07). Hobbes's political theory is so thoroughly grounded in power
that he rejects the paternal explanation even for God's authority: "To those
therefore whose Power is irresistible, the dominion of all men adhaereth
naturally by their excellence of Power; and consequently it is from that
Power, that the Kingdome over men, and the Right of Afflicting men at
his pleasure, belongeth Naturally to God Almighty; not as Creator, and
Gracious; but as Omnipotent" (31.187). Hobbes's explanation, for men as
well as for God, is always power. Just as men's authority comes not from
their paternity, God's authority comes not from his role as creator but
from his omnipotence. This is circular logic: God is powerful because he is
all-powerful. By making this argument, Hobbes essentially eliminates the
paternal basis of authority from the equation.

Hobbes's paternal dominion is a chimera. Perhaps included because it is
an important category of political thinking in the period, the paternal state
is finally excluded from his conception of civil society. More accurately, the
paternal state is expelled – in order to circumvent the power of patriarchal
ideas, Hobbes allows the paternal state space in *Leviathan* only to eject
it. In the chapter on paternal dominion, he empties the term of its usual
meaning and substitutes for it something very different. By the end of his
analysis there is nothing recognizably paternal in what he calls a paternal
state. The paternal state more or less evaporates before the reader's eyes.
Only the name is retained.

FROM FAMILY ANALOGY TO BODY POLITIC

The disappearance of the paternal state is also effected in the larger structure of *Leviathan*. Hobbes conceptually expels the paternal state from his philosophy of civil society by displacing the family analogy with the analogy of the body politic. This expulsion is accomplished in two ways: Hobbes reimagines the meaning of the family analogy in such a way as to reduce its explanatory power; and he elevates the analogy of the body politic to such prominence as to overshadow a much enervated family metaphor. Hobbes's use of the body as an analogy has been much commented upon. Scholars too have long noted his novel reinvention of that body as mechanical. Leonard Barkan suggests that the analogy between the body and the state continued in a new form in Hobbes's *Leviathan* and that by then the body politic as a metaphor had decayed.[14] Quentin Skinner comments that the mechanical nature of the Hobbesian body "underpin[s] his claim that commonwealths can in no sense be regarded as God-given creations or natural occurences."[15] In his magisterial study, Skinner shows that *Leviathan* marks Hobbes's return to rhetoric, which he had repudiated in his earlier works, *The Elements* and *De Cive*. In part, my argument supports the claim that Hobbes's commonwealths are not natural or divinely sanctioned. By not making commonwealths natural, Hobbes undermines patriarchalist justifications from nature. While Hobbes may be returning to rhetoric in *Leviathan*, his displacement of one conventional metaphor for polity by another equally long-standing metaphor suggests an ironic stance toward rhetoric.

The central myth of patriarchalism is God's giving to Adam dominion over the world. Patriarchalism furthermore justifies the sovereignty of kings as fathers by maintaining that Adam as the original father was also king over his children, who comprised all the world. In the opening pages of *Patriarcha*, Filmer claims that Genesis is proof that "creation made man prince of his posterity. And indeed not only Adam but the succeeding patriarchs had, by right of fatherhood, royal authority over their children."[16] His contention that fathers have monarchical power over their children is made by analogy to Adam's example: "For as Adam was lord of his children, so

---

[14] Leonard Barkan, *Nature's Work of Art: The Human Body as Image of the World* (New Haven: Yale University Press, 1975), 113–15. See also David George Hale, *The Body Politic: A Political Metaphor in Renaissance English Literautre* (The Hague: Mouton, 1971), especially chapter 5, "Leviathan at Whitehall."

[15] Quentin Skinner, *Reason and Rhetoric in the Philosophy of Hobbes* (Cambridge: Cambridge University Press, 1996), 387.

[16] Filmer, *Patriarcha*, 6.

his children under him had a command and power over their own children, but still with subordination to the first parent, who is lord paramount
over his children's children to all generations, as being the grandfather of
his people."[17] Adam's status as first father who wields dominion forms the
bedrock of patriarchal political theory.

In contrast, Hobbes neglects Adam both in his exploration of monarchical authority and in his discussion of paternal power. When he considers
the paternal state, he turns instead to Abraham as his example of a patriarch.
Describing the kingdom of God in chapter 35 of *Leviathan*, Hobbes discusses Adam and Abraham in turn. Emphasizing Abraham's fatherly role,
he treats Abraham as ruler of a paternal kingdom. But Adam is a "peculiar"
or special subject of God, reigning over all as well as more directly over
specific groups of people and receiving commands from God "by a Voice,
as one man speaketh to another" (35.216). Significantly, the fate of Adam's
children is not tied to his. His posterity are punished for their own sins,
not for his: "And afterwards God punished his [Adam's] posterity, for their
vices, all but eight persons, with an universall deluge" (35.216). Adam is not
a patriarch ruling over a familial state.

Hobbes's interpretation of Abraham differs markedly. Covenants or contracts made between God and Abraham bind his posterity as well: the Old
Testament "containeth a Contract between God and Abraham; by which
Abraham obligeth himself, and his posterity, in a peculiar manner to be subject to Gods positive Law" (35.217). Abraham's acceptance of God's positive
law, the explicit laws of the state, rather than just natural law that all must
obey, obligates his children as well because Abraham is head of a patriarchal
kingdom. This emphasis on positive law marks Hobbes's rejection of the
natural law argument as used by parliamentary writers. Defining natural
law as the right to self-preservation (14.64), Hobbes nonetheless does not
allow natural law to overturn positive laws made by governing powers.
While the ultimate ruler is God, as father Abraham has sovereignty over his
children; and, in covenanting with God, Abraham turns that sovereignty
into a civil state, whose laws are unbreakable:

And though the name of *King* be not yet given to God, nor of *Kingdome* to
Abraham and his seed; yet the thing is the same; namely, an Institution by pact, of
Gods peculiar Soveraignty over the seed of Abraham; which in the renewing of the
same Covenant by Moses, at Mount Sinai, is expressly called a peculiar *Kingdome
of God* over the Jews: and it is of Abraham (not of Moses) St. Paul saith (*Rom.* 4.11.)
that he is the *Father of the Faithfull.* (35.217)

[17] *Ibid.*, 6–7.

Although original father, Adam does not institute a paternal state. Abraham, however, leads as father the faithful in God's kingdom. Moses's covenant with God simply renews Abraham's original covenant. Making Abraham the archetypal father-ruler, Hobbes denies that original sovereign power resides in Adam, thus displacing Adam from the place of prominence that patriarchalist theorists give him.[18]

Chapter 40, on the organization of the kingdom of God, elaborates further on the role of Abraham as patriarch. Abraham's status as the first father to rule over a political kingdom and his contract with God also bind his descendants: "The Father of the Faithfull, and first in the Kingdome of God by Covenant, was *Abraham*. For with him was the Covenant first made; wherein he obliged himself, and his seed after him, to acknowledge and obey the commands of God" (40.249). Earlier, Abraham's children are said to be subject to him absolutely because there is no other earthly king. They obey the laws he establishes "in vertue of the obedience they owed to their Parents; who (if they be Subject to no other earthly power, as here in the case of *Abraham*) have Soveraign power over their children, and servants" (26.149). The condition Hobbes sets – parents can only be sovereign if they are not ruled by others – is a crucial modification of patriarchal theory. Sovereignty is not justified on the basis of fatherhood, nor is the subjection of children to parents analogous to the subjection of citizens to kings. If there is a king, Hobbes says, the relation between children and parents will necessarily be altered by both children's and parents' primary relation to the king.

In overlooking Adam to favor Abraham as the example of paternal sovereignty, Hobbes rejects patriarchalism's most important myth. Since he was the first man, Adam's case can be universalized, as the patriarchalist theorists have done. The example of Abraham, as a figure who appears much later in biblical history, cannot be as easily generalized. In fact, Hobbes constructs Abraham's kingdom as a historically specific nation with a particular political constitution and not as model for all commonwealths. Although a patriarch, Abraham does not have Adam's status of being father to all mankind. Thus substituting Abraham for Adam as a model of a patriarch, Hobbes greatly reduces the significance of the family analogy. The paternal state becomes but one of several possible models of government.

---

[18] Later the Whig political theorist Algernon Sidney would contest Filmer's *Patriarcha* by imagining Abraham and the Israelites forming a community of equal brothers: "We cannot find a more perfect picture of freemen living together than Abraham and Lot"; among their descendants "there was no lord, slave, or vassal; no strife was to be among them: they were brethren" (*Discourses on Government* [1698], 3 vols. [New York: Richard Lee, 1805], ii:20, ch. 2, section 5).

The distinction Hobbes makes between Adam and Abraham and his use of Abraham to counter and to displace the patriarchalist (and Filmerian) use of Adam as symbol of paternal authority are perhaps clearer in *De Cive* (1642). As Hobbes's first exposition of his political ideas, written for an international audience of intellectuals, *De Cive* is far less rhetorical than *Leviathan*.[19] As his attempt at a science of politics – as opposed to a humanist approach – *De Cive* is organized as a series of propositions. Chapter 16 on God's kingdom discusses Adam in the second proposition only to dismiss the claim that Adam instituted the kingdom of God. The first proposition asserts that Abraham is the founding father of God's kingdom: "And from him [Abraham] *the Kingdom of God by agreement* took its origin."[20] The second proposition construes Adam's supposed patriarchal rule as one based on contract: "It is true that at the beginning of the world God's rule over *Adam* and *Eve* was not only natural but also by *agreement*; from which it appears that any obedience other than that which natural reason dictated should be given only by agreement, i.e. from men's own consent" (*De Cive*, 188). Even so, this contract was short-lived: "But as this *agreement* was immediately made void, and was never renewed, the origins of the Kingdom of God . . . [have] to be found elsewhere" (*De Cive*, 188). The origin that Hobbes finds is, of course, Abraham. The brief digression on Adam establishes that by breaking contract (eating the forbidden fruit) he forfeits all claim.

For all that Abraham is the origin of God's kingdom, Hobbes puts more stress on Abraham's role as sovereign than his role as father. The relation between Abraham and his people is that of a prince and his subjects:

For although God was their king both by *nature* and by the *Agreement* with *Abraham*, they nevertheless owed him only natural obedience and natural worship, as his subjects, but the religious worship which *Abraham* had instituted they owed him as subjects of *Abraham, Isaac* or *Jacob*, their natural Princes. For the only *Word of God* that they had received was the natural word of right reason, and there was no *agreement* between God and themselves except in so far as their wills were included in the will of *Abraham*, as their Prince. (*De Cive*, 191).

Owing Abraham obedience as prince, the people subsume their individual wills under that of their sovereign, such that they are party to any agreement he makes. Abraham's paternal state differs little from the Hobbesian Leviathan state. What is astounding about Hobbes's reasoning is that the

---

[19] Skinner, *Reason and Rhetoric*, chs. 7 and 8.
[20] Thomas Hobbes, *On the Citizen*, ed. and trans. Richard Tuck and Michael Silverthorne (Cambridge: Cambridge University Press, 1998), 188. Further references to *De Cive* are from this edition and cited parenthetically.

people's religious practice is not something they owe to God as their king (though God is that because they accept him as their special king). Rather, they must worship God in the manner Abraham prescribes because they are Abraham's subjects. Thus Hobbes maintains the right of earthly kings to determine the form of religious worship. Even in his discussion of a state formed in a direct covenant with God, Hobbes favors giving all power, including religious, to the civil authority, no matter if they are heathen princes, thus lending weight to arguments about his atheism.[21] (In my next section, I discuss how Hobbes's Christian commonwealth is no different from his civil Leviathan state.) Having displaced Adam with Abraham in *Leviathan*, Hobbes uses the example of Abraham's paternal state to argue for the obedience of subjects to kings, rather than their obedience to fathers or father-kings. Chapter 40 of *Leviathan*, like chapter 16 of *De Cive*, argues that kings have a right to determine religious matters: "From whence may be concluded this first point, that they to whom God hath not spoken immediately, are to receive the positive commandements of God, from their Soveraign; as the family and seed of Abraham did from Abraham their Father, and Lord, and Civill Soveraign" (40.249). From the example of Abraham's family, Hobbes comes to the rather surprising conclusion that subjects must obey sovereigns in the matter of religion, surprising because he does so without resorting to metaphorizing the relation between subjects and sovereigns as familial.

Hobbes derives from Abraham's position as father-king a conclusion quite different from that of patriarchalists like Filmer. Despite the analogy between a king and Abraham as head of his family, most of the discussion focuses on Abraham's role as king of his family: "For hee [the sovereign] hath the same place in the Common-wealth, that Abraham had in his own Family" (40.250). Abraham's family-nation is unusual in that he is the only earthly sovereign. This comparison is less an analogy than it first appears. While Filmer attributes power to kings by analogy to Adam's authority as father, Hobbes bases the power of kings on the equivalence of their position to that of Abraham as king. That Abraham is also a father of the nation he rules obscures the comparison Hobbes actually makes – between king and king.

[21] For seventeenth-century (antagonistic) reaction to Hobbes, including accusations of atheism, see John Bowle, *Hobbes and his Critics: A Study in Seventeenth Century Constitutionalism* (New York: Oxford University Press, 1952); and Samuel I. Mintz, *The Hunting of Leviathan: Seventeenth-Century Reactions to the Materialism and Moral Philosophy of Thomas Hobbes* (Cambridge: University Press, 1962).

Tracing the succession of kingship from Abraham to Isaac and Jacob and then to Moses, Hobbes notes that Moses's authority to govern is not based on inheritance, since during the Israelites' enslavement in Egypt the covenant with God was not in force. From that premise Hobbes reasons that Moses succeeds to the kingship of Abraham by consent: "His [Moses's] authority therefore, as the authority of all other Princes, must be grounded on the Consent of the People, and their Promise to obey him" (40.250). While Abraham's kingdom may have begun as a paternal state, it is no longer so in its later manifestation. When Moses leads the renewed kingdom of God, it is a commonwealth formed from the people's consent. Its foundation is contractual. Moses is no father to the people because he is no son to Abraham. But like Abraham he is king. And all later kings can be compared to Moses as well as to Abraham as kings. By highlighting the break in Abraham's line of descent, Hobbes very neatly excises the biological link between the kingdom of God under Abraham and that under Moses, thus eliminating justification through paternity. It is not important that the king be father to the people, but that he be father of the commonwealth, that is to say he creates it: "For whosoever ordereth, and establisheth the Policy, as first founder of a Common-wealth (be it Monarchy, Aristocracy, or Democracy) must needs have Soveraign Power over the people all the while he is doing of it" (40.251). It cannot be too strongly emphasized that Hobbes does not use paternal metaphors when speaking of the creation of a commonwealth.

In *Leviathan*, Hobbes also erodes the power of the family metaphor by making it subsidiary to his primary metaphor of the body politic. Part of his strategy is to introduce the family metaphor quite late. Abraham as an example of a father-king appears only in the second half of *Leviathan*, well after the body politic as metaphor has been thoroughly established. There is a brief mention of Abraham's relation to his descendants in chapter 26, but the extended discussion is in chapter 40, toward the end of section 3. Even chapter 26 comes toward the end of section 2. Both are chapters from the last half of *Leviathan*, comprising four sections (of which section 4 is the shortest with a mere four chapters) and forty-seven chapters altogether. When the family analogy is treated, it is discussed as the specific case of Abraham, and, given its placement in *Leviathan*, must be read in the context of the metaphor of the body, the dominant mode of reading the state in *Leviathan*.

The famous opening paragraph establishes the body as the governing metaphor of *Leviathan*:

NATURE (the Art whereby God hath made and governes the World) is by the *Art* of man, as in many other things, so in this also imitated, that it can make an Artificial Animal. For seeing life is but a motion of Limbs, the begining whereof is in some principall part within; why may we not say, that all *Automata* (Engines that move themselves by spings and wheeles as doth a watch) have an artificiall life? For what is the *Heart*, but a *Spring*; and the *Nerves*, but so many *Strings*; and the *Joynts*, but so many *Wheeles*, giving motion to the whole Body, such as was intended by the Artificer? *Art* goes yet further, imitating that Rationall and most excellent worke of Nature, *Man*. For by Art is created that great LEVIATHAN called a COMMON-WEALTH, or STATE, (in latine CIVITAS) which is but an Artificiall Man. (Introduction.1)

By placing the metaphor of the body politic at the very start of the work, Hobbes intends it to determine the reading of the Leviathan state. Indeed, the title already suggests such a reading: the biblical Leviathan is a mythical monster of the sea, literally a gigantic body threatening to swallow all up. Likewise, Hobbes's Leviathan state contains all within itself, contending only with other Leviathan states. This reading is supported by the iconography of the frontispiece, in which innumerable tiny figures form the body of a giant crowned man with sword and scepter looking on a landscape with a city in the foreground.[22] Citizens are contained within the body of the sovereign, having given up their wills to him.

Positioning the body metaphor such that his readers read *Leviathan* through this lens, Hobbes also teaches them how to interpret the body metaphor in order to control its meaning. He restricts the meaning that can be elaborated from the metaphor by funneling the family trope through another analogy. The body is a very particular one in Hobbes: the artificial, mechanical body. The body-state analogy is itself mediated by the analogy linking body and machine. Hobbes first suggests that machines are like bodies, comparing the different parts of a body with the parts of a machine. The pretext for the comparison is the motion observed in both. Only after he likens bodies to machines does he compare the state to man. But this is an artificial man. With the first analogy, Hobbes creates a new thing – a mechanical man – which he makes one of the terms in the second analogy. Embedded in the analogy linking body and state is an analogy linking body and machine. He uses a traditional metaphor for the state to smuggle in an unconventional mechanistic metaphor.

---

[22] Keith C. Brown, "The Artist of the *Leviathan* Title-Page," *British Library Journal* 4 (1978), 24–36; and M. M. Goldsmith, "Picturing Hobbes's Politics?: The Illustrations to *Philosophicall Rudiments*," *Journal of the Warburg and Courtauld Institutes* 44 (1981), 232–37.

Hobbes's comparison of the state to mechanical clockwork anticipates his argument for absolute obedience to the sovereign. If his analogy of the mechanical body is compared to the traditional analogy of the body, it is far more possible to imagine revolt in the traditional body. Typical accounts of the body politic identify either the head or the heart as the central organ of the body, depending on whether Aristotelian (heart at the center) or Galenic (head/brain at the top) physiology is assumed. Both ways of organizing the body nonetheless produce a structure affirming social hierarchies, where the feet support the head, or the stomach feeds the heart, but like the hierarchy of the social body, the hierarchy of the natural body can be unsettled by willful members rebelling against their traditional place. Often the parts of the body are personified and so imputed wills of their own. A member like the belly can be imagined to assert that will, revolting against hierarchy, by withholding food from the rest of the body.[23] Hobbes's machine is like life in that it has motion. But the machine is free from such recalcitrant and dangerous expressions of will.

The mechanized body defamiliarizes the old analogy of the body politic so that Hobbes can make precise and new analogies between parts of body and parts of state: the artificial man is

of greater stature and strength than the Naturall, for whose protection and defence it was intended; and in which, the *Soveraignty* is an Artificiall *Soul*, as giving life and motion to the whole body; The *Magistrates*, and other *Officers* of Judicature and Execution, artificiall *Joynts*; *Reward* and *Punishment* (by which fastned to the seate of the Soveraignty, every joynt and member is moved to performe his duty) are the *Nerves*, that do the same in the Body Naturall; The *Wealth* and *Riches* of all the particular members, are the *Strength*; *Salus Populi* (the *peoples safety*) its *Businesse*; *Counsellors*, by whom all things needfull for it to know, are suggested unto it, are the *Memory*; *Equity* and *Lawes*, an artificiall *Reason* and *Will*; *Concord*, *Health*; *Sedition*, *Sicknesse*; and *Civill war*, *Death*. Lastly, the *Pacts* and *Covenants*, by which the parts of this Body Politique were first made, set together, and united, resemble that *Fiat*, or the *Let us make man*, pronounced by God in the Creation. (Introduction.1)

What is remarkable about this extended analogy of the body politic is how Hobbes declines to employ certain parts of the body prominent in the

---

[23] For instance, Menenius Agrippa's fable of the belly in Shakespeare's *Coriolanus*. See Annabel Patterson, *Fables of Power: Aesopian Writing and Political History* (Durham, N.C.: Duke University Press, 1991), ch. 4, "Body Fables." For contradictory interpretations of the analogy of the body politic (including the unstable hierarchy of the body where the head vies with the heart for sovereignty, depending on the physiology one follows), see Michael Schoenfeldt, "Reading Bodies," in Steven Zwicker and Kevin Sharpe, eds., *Reading, Society and Politics in Early Modern England* (Cambridge: Cambridge University Press, 2003), 215–43.

history of the analogy. These parts include the head, the heart, and the stomach. Instead Hobbes highlights the soul, the joints, and the nerves. These are strange choices if we compare them with the body parts of other early modern renderings of the analogy.[24] Hobbes focuses on minor parts of the body that are not imagined to have a voice in the traditional uses of the body analogy. Moreover, the rest of his comparison seems to focus on abstract properties of the body rather than on its material parts: thus, strength, business, memory, reason and will, health, sickness, and death, instead of, for instance, "The kingly-crowned head, the vigilant eye, / The counsellor heart, the arm our soldier, / Our steed the leg, the tongue our trumpeter."[25] While the soul is easily imagined as an animating spirit, joints and nerves lend themselves to far less lofty positions. Joints and nerves simply keep the body going; they are difficult to metaphorize as parts that have will or make decisions. Indeed, will itself is imagined as a property of the body that can be compared to a particular part of state – laws. Importantly, will here is single, not the multiple conflicting wills of the fable of the belly. In other words, Hobbes's choice of body parts is significant in construing the kind of role the analogous parts of state may play. That role is of a conformist and obedient subordinate to the singular will of the gigantic body of Leviathan. Only bit parts are available here.

The organization of a body where there is one leader (the soul) and a multitude of unthinking followers (the body) would structure the reading of the rest of *Leviathan*. Hobbes's state of nature and his Leviathan commonwealth are logical consequences of such a hierarchy that has only two levels. Given the analogy of the artificial body, it follows that people not ordered into a commonwealth are imagined to be in state of war. They can be likened to uncoordinated, disordered body parts that are mutually destructive. Hobbes calls them a "Multitude" (17.87). When collected together in a commonwealth, this multitude necessarily forms the nerves and joints – the material part – of the body while the sovereign is the soul who is its animating force. Hobbes argues that men need to establish a common power in order to prevent the warring state in nature and the way to do this is "to conferre all their power and strength upon one Man, or upon

---

[24] Granted, in *Coriolanus*, Menenius' speaking belly, claiming that it sends food to all from the highest to the lowliest, includes the "strongest nerves and the small inferior veins" (1.1.138) in its constituency (William Shakespeare, *The Riverside Shakespeare*, ed. G. Blakemore Evans *et al.*, 2nd edn [Boston, Mass.: Houghton Mifflin, 1997]). My point, however, is that Hobbes highlights nerves over more prominent parts of the body.

[25] *Coriolanus* 1.1.115–17.

one Assembly of men, that may reduce all their Wills, by plurality of voices, unto one Will" (17.87). In describing the formation of a commonwealth, he actually describes the creation of a person:

[All must] submit their Wills, every one to his [the sovereign's] Will, and their Judgements, to his Judgment. This is more than Consent, or Concord; it is a reall Unitie of them all, in one and the same Person . . . This done, the Multitude so united in one Person, is called a COMMON-WEALTH, in latine CIVITAS. This is the Generation of that great LEVIATHAN, or rather (to speake more reverently) of that *Mortall God*, to which wee owe under the *Immortal God*, our peace and defence. (17.87)

To establish a commonwealth, people must give up their wills and convert themselves into pliant automata. The warring men of Hobbes's state of nature bear little resemblance to the disciplined material body parts of the analogy. But once they are formed into the commonwealth they are turned into absolute submission. Without that there is no commonwealth. Thus, civil war is for Hobbes death of the body. This analogy is easily comprehended in the Hobbesian state of nature: it is both civil war and the death of the body politic. Hobbes's conception of the Leviathan state – and the Leviathan body – mediates his reading of the family. It enables, for instance, his interpretation of Abraham's paternal state, emphasizing subjects' obedience and the subsuming of their wills to that of Abraham. Hobbes's particular reading of the body analogy presents Abraham as king rather than as father. When we come to chapter 40 on Abraham, we would already have absorbed much of Hobbes's ideas about how a state functions so that the kind of paternal state he describes – which lacks the familial ties of love and affection – does not seem strange.

Revising both family and body metaphors, Hobbes turns the body into a machine with only two levels of hierarchy, instead of the complicated relations of the parts of the natural body in more conventional uses of the analogy. This Hobbesian body provides the ground for reenvisioning the family as similarly organized: the sovereign and his subjects. Made in the image of the Leviathan state, Hobbes's family is not recognizable; it is without father, mother, elder and younger brothers, sisters, or servants, or any subtle gradations of hierarchy. Given parental authority based on the power to kill, nor do family bonds exist in Hobbes. His family is flattened out just as there is no network of relations in his artificial body. Rather, human relations are always only relations between sovereign and subject. Both his family and his state are institutions in which subordinates are bound by fear to the master.

Hobbes uses the analogy of the body to displace the family metaphor fundamental to patriarchalist theories of state, killing off the family analogy with the trope of the body. Nor does he preserve the body metaphor; turning it into a machine, he drains life away from the body. Using one metaphor to overturn the other, Hobbes turns metaphor against itself. His manipulation of metaphor – his linking and unlinking of body and family – suggests that his return to rhetoric is not entirely straightforward. After all, early in *Leviathan*, Hobbes excludes the use of metaphor in argument and in searching for truth because metaphors "openly professe deceipt" (8.34). Hobbes's return to rhetoric may be worth a second look, for even as he uses rhetorical tools such as metaphor he ironizes them. In the case of the family metaphor, he finally repudiates it.

THE CIVIL STATE OF CHRISTIAN COMMUNITY

The structure of *Leviathan* has given rise to some controversy. Unable to agree on how the two halves of *Leviathan* fit together, given that the first two sections on man and civil society and the second two sections on Christianity and Christian community appear so different, scholars debate whether Hobbes's views on Christianity were sincere or ironic.[26] Arguing that Hobbes reconciled biblical revelation with the philosophy of natural rights, Paul D. Cooke suggests that "Hobbes's intention in treating the Bible as he did . . . was to sustain the form of Christianity while changing its actual substance for such readers, and this intention required the greatest care, manifested as a kind of duplicity, or, . . . a conspiracy against Christianity."[27] My analysis of Hobbes's use of the family analogy shows him to be a wily manipulator of definitions, changing the substance of things and yet calling them by their old names. This section extends Cooke's insight to show how Hobbes's Christian commonwealth is finally not much different from the Leviathan state. Hobbes is primarily concerned with establishing the absolute power of the sovereign, only this time he calls the sovereign a Christian prince.

The last half of *Leviathan* establishes the Christian sovereign as the supreme interpreter of religion. Hobbes wants to create a hierarchy where

---

[26] A. P. Martinich, *The Two Gods of* Leviathan: *Thomas Hobbes on Religion and Politics* (Cambridge: Cambridge University Press, 1992) argues for Hobbes as an orthodox Christian. Other theistic critics include Eldon Eisenach, *Two Worlds of Liberalism: Religion and Politics in Hobbes, Locke, and Mill* (Chicago: University of Chicago Press, 1981); and S. A. Lloyd, *Ideals as Interests in Hobbes's* Leviathan: *The Power of Mind over Matter* (Cambridge: Cambridge University Press, 1992).

[27] Paul D. Cooke, *Hobbes and Christianity: Reassessing the Bible in* Leviathan (Lanham, M.D.: Rowman & Littlefield, 1996), 18.

civil authority is superior to religious authority. Since the English monarch is already understood to be head of the national church, his answer is to combine in the figure of the sovereign both civil and spiritual authorities. Although this need not be a controversial claim, Hobbes is doing something quite new in that he insists that interpretation of the scripture be the right of the king only. He insists more absolutely than anyone has before that "Christian Soveraignes are in their owne Dominions the supreme Pastors" (42.305). Moreover, Hobbes compares kings to fathers to counter clerical claims for spiritual fatherhood: kings are fathers but divines are merely "Schoolmasters to Christianity" (42.296). He even reverts to the family metaphor to justify the monarch's role as head of the church:

> Soveraigns are supreme Teachers (in generall) by their Office; and therefore oblige themselves (by their Baptisme) to teach the Doctrine of Christ: And when they suffer others to teach their people, they doe it at the perill of their own souls; for it is at the hands of the Heads of Families that God will require the account of the instruction of his Children and Servants. It is of Abraham himself, not of a hireling, that God saith (*Gen.* 18.19) *I know him that he will command his Children, and his houshold after him, that they keep the way of the Lord, and do justice and judgement.* (42.305)

Urging sovereigns not to leave religious instruction to clergy, Hobbes envisions a far more active role for them than simply being titular head. While heads of families must instruct their household, the example he chooses, Abraham, is both father and king. In Hobbes's commonwealth, heads of families cannot controvert the sovereign's official doctrines. Abraham usefully combines in one person the various roles of sovereign, father, and head priest. He is all the more useful because his authority does not derive from his paternity.

Hobbes also interprets the analogy of the body politic to support his claim for the sovereign's role as head of the state religion. His rewriting of the body politic in terms of the new sciences has attracted much commentary. But perhaps his most daring revision of the trope is to make the sovereign the soul of the artificial man. Unlike other automata, the artificial man possesses a soul, albeit artificial, to distinguish it from an animal or mere machine, and in it "the *Soveraignty* is an Artificiall *Soul*, as giving life and motion to the whole body" (Introduction.1). Furthermore, "The Soveraignty is the Soule of the Common-wealth; which once departed from the Body, the members doe no more receive their motion from it" (21.114). In making the sovereign the soul, Hobbes challenges the political organization and hierarchy underwritten by the body analogy as elaborated by

John of Salisbury in *Policraticus* (1159). The earliest extended exposition of political theory in the middle ages and the only significant political treatise before the rediscovery of Aristotle in the thirteenth century, *Policraticus* also represents the first full development of the body analogy. In this first mature version of the body analogy, John of Salisbury identifies clergy as the soul of the body politic:

> Those things which establish and implant in us the practice of religion, and transmit to us the worship of God . . . fill the place of the soul in the body of the commonwealth. And therefore those who preside over the practice of religion should be looked up to and venerated as the soul of the body. For who doubts that the ministers of God's holiness are His representatives? Furthermore, since the soul is, as it were, the prince of the body, and has rulership over the whole thereof, so those whom our author calls the prefects of religion preside over the entire body.[28]

Like Hobbes, John of Salisbury makes the soul the reigning part of the body, but unlike Hobbes, he associates clergy with the soul and thus gives sovereignty to the church.

In a fairly elaborate formulation of the body analogy likening various parts of the body – from head to feet – to different members of the polity, John of Salisbury conforms more or less to a hierarchy based on social class linked to a hierarchy of the body ordered vertically. Officials and soldiers, for instance, are hands while husbandmen are feet. Judges and governors, who are their social superiors, are placed still higher and compared to eyes, ears, and the tongue. The monarch is the head:

> The place of the head in the body of the commonwealth is filled by the prince, who is subject only to God and to those who exercise His office and represent Him on earth, even as in the human body the head is quickened and governed by the soul.[29]

Subject to priests, John of Salisbury's monarch is not the absolute sovereign of *Leviathan*. In this John departs from social hierarchy, making a sharp distinction between spiritual and temporal realms. This distinction is one Hobbes denies when he makes the sovereign chief priest. When Hobbes's use of the body analogy is read in the context of this history, his particular innovation becomes clearer. It also explains the last half of *Leviathan*, which justifies his substitution of the monarch for the priest as the soul of the commonwealth.

---

[28] John of Salisbury, *The Statesman's Book of John of Salisbury*, trans. John Dickinson (New York: A. A. Knopf, 1927), 64.
[29] *Ibid.*, 65.

To justify this displacement, Hobbes made the monarch also a priest. Thus, while he allows the pope to be a king and pastor in his own domain, he rejects the claim that the pope has authority anywhere else. Priestly celibacy was contrived, he says, to prevent kings from becoming priests and assuming both civil and spiritual authority: "the Deniall of Marriage to Priests, serveth to assure this Power of the Pope over Kings. For if a King be a Priest, he cannot Marry, and transmit his Kingdome to his Posterity; If he be not a Priest then the Pope pretendeth this Authority Ecclesiasticall over him, and over his people" (47.383). The pope's claim to spiritual authority results in the king losing his kingdom. If the king should practice celibacy, he also loses his kingdom because he would not have sons to inherit. At the end of *Leviathan*, Hobbes scornfully points out the moral failings of clergy by maliciously comparing priests and fairies. One term of comparison is the single state of both: "The *Fairies* marry not; but there be amongst them Incubi, that have copulation with flesh and bloud. The *Priests* also marry not" (47.387). Although Hobbes stops short of making the comparison between incubi and sexually voracious priests, his meaning is quite clear.

Marriage (and by extension, family) serves the corrupt purpose of the church in its bid for supremacy. In the last half of *Leviathan*, Hobbes revises some of the central family metaphors of Christianity to diminish their importance when they vindicate the power of the church and limit monarchical power. For instance, the father–son relation between God and Christ becomes less central to God's identity. The name of father denotes a specific function such that God "were not called by the name of Father, till such time as he sent into the world his Son Jesus Christ" (40.255). God's paternal role is confined to his relation to Christ. The marriage metaphor, describing God's relation to the church, is diminished by Hobbes's rereading, which presents marriage and procreation as products of the fall. Within the logic of this metaphor, priests are superior to laymen because in keeping celibate they commit themselves to a marriage with God. Laymen's loyalty to God is suspect because they can be seduced by worldly relationships with their wives. Hobbes cites Revelation 2.1 and 10 to suggest that St. John's vision shows that the eternal dwelling place for the saved would be earth, that "the new Jerusalem, the Paradise of God, at the coming again of Christ, should come down to Gods people from Heaven, and not they goe up to it from Earth" (38.239). He also cites the gospel of Matthew to show that eternal life would be without marriage: "Again, that saying of our Saviour (*Mat.* 22.30.) *that in the Resurrection they neither marry, nor are given in marriage, but are as the Angels of God in heaven*, is a description of an Eternall Life, resembling that which we lost in Adam in the point of Marriage" (38.239). Since the eternal government of Christ will be on earth, it is logical that procreation was not intended before the fall: "For if Immortals should have generated, as Mankind doth now; the Earth in a small time, would not have been able to afford them place to stand on" (38.239). The series of exegeses of key biblical texts allow Hobbes to make his argument for reducing the power of the clergy. As an institution of the fall, marriage cannot serve as an elevating metaphor for the clergy's special relationship to God. By devaluing procreation along with marriage, Hobbes strikes another blow at patriarchalist theories of state. Describing eternal life as being unlike the present, without marriage and without children, Hobbes chides those who would use family metaphors to compare earthly life to eternal life:

The Jews that asked our Saviour the question, whose wife the woman that had married many brothers, should be, in the resurrection, knew not what were the consequences of Life Eternall: and therefore our Saviour puts them in mind of this consequence of Immortality; that there shal be no Generation, and consequently no marriage, no more than there is Marriage, or generation among the Angels. (38.239)

Procreation is only an inferior form of eternal life – "the specificall eternity of generation" (44.345) – to be discarded when one has the real thing. Ironically, his account of eternal life resembles his account of the state of nature. Hobbes's state of nature imagines men "as if they had just emerged from the earth like mushrooms and grown up without any obligation to each other" (*De Cive*, 102). As in the state of nature, in eternal life there are no marriage, no children, and no family relations. In this aspect, the Leviathan state does not much differ from eternal life either. While the contemporary state of civil life in England demands procreation from the monarch to ensure continuation of the royal line, in his Leviathan state Hobbes provides a way for doing away with both marriage and procreation. In a state where the sovereign is free to name his heir, family metaphors have far less evocative power.

CONCLUSION

Justifying absolutist rule by consent, Hobbes differs from both absolutist patriarchalists and moderate royalists wanting a mixed monarchy, even though he was a royalist – he sought Charles II's patronage for the work – when he wrote *Leviathan*.[30] Hobbes's absolutism is marked by a total lack of tolerance for dissent such that he audaciously redefines conscience – understood in the period as private beliefs, the dictates of one's heart – as communal agreement:

When two, or more men, know of one and the same fact, they are said to be CONSCIOUS of it one to another; which is as much as to know it together. And because such are fittest witnesses of the facts of one another, or of a third; it was, and ever will be reputed a very Evill act, for any man to speak against his *Conscience*; or to corrupt, or force another so to do: Insomuch that the plea of Conscience, has been always hearkened unto very diligently in all times. Afterwards, men made use of the same word metaphorically, for the knowledge of their own secret facts, and secret thoughts; and therefore it is Rhetorically said, that the Conscience is a thousand witnesses. And last of all, men, vehemently in love with their own new opinions, (though never so absurd,) and obstinately bent to maintain them, gave those their opinions also that reverenced name of Conscience, as if they would have it seem unlawfull, to change or speak against them; and so pretend to know they are true, when they know at most, but that they think so. (7.31)

Arguing that the current meaning of conscience is corrupted and merely a deceptive metaphorical use, Hobbes dismisses the claims of private conscience – claims made by a remarkable range of religious dissenters in the century, from John Lilburne before the Revolution to John Bunyan in the Restoration – to uphold truths declared by the community. In his state, however, this community has no separate voice and simply affirms the declarations of the sovereign, to whom they have surrendered their wills. For Hobbes, community requires absolute obedience, leaving no room for disputation: "He therefore that breaketh his Covenant, and consequently declareth that he thinks he may with reason do so, cannot be received into any Society, that unite themselves for Peace and Defence" (15.73). Those who do not obey do not belong.

The Hobbesian state has only one power – the sovereign – with no intermediate levels of authority. The Hobbesian family similarly lacks elaboration, a lack that could perhaps be traced back to Hobbes's own bachelor existence as member of the great household of William Lord Cavendish, Earl of Devonshire.[31] Hobbes concentrates power in one person as the

---

[30] For Hobbes's relation to moderate royalists, see Glenn Burgess, "Contexts for the Writing and Publication of Hobbes's *Leviathan*," *History of Political Thought* 11 (1990), 675–702. For moderate royalism, see C. C. Weston, "The Theory of Mixed Monarchy under Charles I and after," *English Historical Review* 75 (1960), 426–33.

[31] Richard Tuck has remarked on the number of seventeenth-century theorists who were bachelors, disengaged from family ties, in the service of a noble (*Hobbes* [Oxford and New York: Oxford University Press, 1989], 3).

solution to the problem of competing loyalties, a problem that patriarchalism poses – when one's father, one's king, and one's priest are all authoritative patriarchs demanding obedience, where does one's primary loyalty lie? Such demands can sometimes come into conflict, as his analysis of the relation between church and civil state shows. Hobbes's elimination of intermediate levels of authority is related to his dislike of subcommunities, which he calls factions. Ministers, those educated in the universities, and the Independents are among those he castigates in *Behemoth* for being "seducers" of the people.[32] Even the government of families in America is considered primitive, akin to the state of war. Concentrating power in the monarch, he is content to banish the family.

Hobbes's concentration of power in one body derives from his fear of popular politics, which determined also the place of *Leviathan*'s composition. He had earlier composed a treatise on the absolute power of the sovereign, *The Elements of Law*, which circulated in manuscript, and which "occasioned much talk of the Author; and had not His Majesty dissolved the Parliament, it had brought him into danger of his life."[33] The increasingly volatile situation in the Long Parliament with calls for limits on the king's power and attacks on claims for absolute monarchy, which would include Hobbes's *Elements*, made him decide to go abroad in 1640. *Leviathan* was composed in Paris nearly a decade later (Hobbes probably began the work in the fall of 1649 and had it printed in 1651) when the number of royalist exiles in Paris had increased after the king lost the war. The fundamental argument of *Leviathan* was not much different from that of *The Elements of Law*, but the explicitly pro-royalist trappings had been pruned such that Hobbes would be able to claim that *Leviathan* discusses sovereignty *per se* and not necessarily only monarchical sovereignty. He later claimed a loyalist position, explaining that he wrote *Leviathan* on behalf of "those many and faithful Servants and Subjects of His Majesty" who had been forced to compound for their lands, and that "They that had done their utmost endeavour to perform their obligation to the King, had done all that they could be obliged unto; and were consequently at liberty to seek the safety of their Lives and Livelihood wheresoever, and without Treachery."[34] Such an argument had been interpreted as a defense of the Commonwealth

---

[32] Thomas Hobbes, *Behemoth; or The Long Parliament*, ed. Ferdinand Tönnies (Chicago: Chicago University Press, 1990), 2.
[33] Thomas Hobbes, *Mr Hobbes Considered in his Loyalty, Religion, Reputation, and Manners. By way of a Letter to Dr Wallis* (London, 1662), 5. My account of the conditions of the composition of *Leviathan* depends on Noel Malcolm, "A Summary Biography of Hobbes," in Tom Sorell, ed., *The Cambridge Companion to Hobbes* (Cambridge: Cambridge University Press, 1996), 13–44.
[34] Hobbes, *Mr Hobbes Considered*, 20.

government. Certainly, Hobbes had wanted to return to England, and perhaps *Leviathan*, which he labored to publish in London, would ingratiate him with England's new rulers. Yet, while Hobbes may not define sovereignty as only monarchical, the sovereignty described in *Leviathan* is still unrepentantly absolute. However we interpret Hobbes's relation to royalism at the time of his return to England in December of 1651, the position he takes in *Leviathan* is far from a republican one.

CHAPTER 4

Cromwellian fatherhood and its discontents

On Friday 3 September 1658 Oliver Cromwell died unexpectedly at White-hall. Although he had been ill, his illness was not believed to be mortal.[1] But on the night of 17 August he was once again bedridden with severe pains and on 24 August Secretary John Thurloe reported to Henry Cromwell that his father had fallen into fits. Even by then, Thurloe, one of Cromwell's inner circle, reported that "the doctors do not conceive there is any danger to his life."[2] No provision had yet been made for the succession and ministers were still confidently thanking God for his recovery when on 2 September the Council of State attempted to have Cromwell name his successor. By then Cromwell was largely comatose, unable to speak, and the attempt failed. The Council members claimed they put his eldest son Richard's name to him and Cromwell gave a sign of assent, either a nod or a whispered yes. When Cromwell finally died, Richard was immediately proclaimed protector.

Not the most rational choice for a successor, Richard was perceived as less capable – certainly he was less experienced in public affairs – than his brother Henry, at the time Lord Deputy of Ireland. A contemporary observer, the puritan Lucy Hutchinson, wrote that Cromwell's "army and court [substituted] his eldest son, Richard, in his room, who was a meek, temperate, and quiet man, but had not a spirit fit to succeed his father, or to manage such a perplexed government."[3] There were also other, abler men, including Cromwell's son-in-law, Charles Fleetwood, who some believed was Cromwell's nominee in a private document drawn up before he was installed as protector. Contemporary accounts of the succession vary greatly.

[1] W. C. Abbott, ed., *The Writings and Speeches of Oliver Cromwell*, 4 vols. (Cambridge, Mass.: Harvard University Press, 1937–47), IV:859, n. 225; cited in Antonia Fraser, *Cromwell, The Lord Protector* (New York: Dell, 1975), 765, n. 23.
[2] John Thurloe, *A Collection of the State Papers of J. T. To which is prefixed the life of Mr Thurloe by Thomas Birch*, 7 vols. (London, 1742), VII:354.
[3] Lucy Hutchinson, *Memoirs of the Life of Colonel Hutchinson With a Fragment of Autobiography*, ed. N. H. Keeble (London: Everyman, 1995), 261.

In a letter to Henry, Thurloe claimed Oliver "was pleased before his death to declare my Lord Richard successor."[4] On the contrary, Edmund Ludlow and Bishop Burnet, the one obstinately republican, the other stubbornly royalist, believed that the Council chose Richard to maintain their own power.[5]

Whatever the truth was, the whole proceeding acquired the aspect of a monarchical succession by primogeniture. Ludlow insinuated that Cromwell intended to establish a hereditary monarchy but that he was "unwilling to discover his intention to leave the succession to his son, lest thereby he should, in case of recovery, disoblige others, whom he had put in expectation of that power."[6] If it was the work of his advisors, by selecting the eldest son they thought it wiser to maintain primogeniture, an act consistent with their urging Cromwell to accept the crown. In his study of the Protectorate court, documenting the ways and progress of Cromwell's adoption of regal authority, Roy Sherwood argues that if he had lived, Cromwell would have eventually become king.[7] Among other things, Cromwell made Richard a Privy Councillor, just as James I did with Charles as the new heir.[8] When in 1657 Parliament replaced the title "king" with "protector" in the Humble Petition and Advice, Lady Elizabeth Conway wrote that Parliament had "settled the government which they proffered under the style of kingship to one as absolutely regal and hereditary, only altering the name to Protector."[9] If, as Christopher Hill says, "Oliver remained ambiguous to

[4] Thurloe, *A Collection of the State Papers*, VII:372.
[5] Burnet writes, "Richard, the eldest, though declared protector in pursuance of a nomination pretended to be made by him, the truth of which was much questioned, was not at all bred to business, nor indeed capable of it" (*Burnet's History of My Own Time. A New Edition based on that of M. J. Routh, D. D.*, ed. Osmund Airy, 2 vols. [Oxford: Clarendon Press, 1897–1900], 1:147). Ludlow suggests that Cromwell's Council and army wanted a puppet leader: "So that having tasted of sovereignty under the shadow of their late master, they resolved against the restitution of the Parliament" and proclaimed Richard protector "in hopes that he, who by following his pleasure had rendred himself unfit for publick business, would not fail to place the administration of the government in the hands of those who were most powerful in the army" (*The Memoirs of Edmund Ludlow, Lieutenant-General of the Horse in the Army of the Commonwealth of England, 1625–1672*, ed. C. H. Firth, 2 vols. [Oxford: Clarendon Press, 1894], II:46). For contrasting views on whether Cromwell nominated Richard, see Earl M. Hause, "The Nomination of Richard Cromwell," *The Historian* 27 (1965), 185–209, and *Tumble-Down Dick; The Fall of the House of Cromwell* (New York: Exposition Press, 1972), ch. 2; and Austin Woolrych, "Milton and Cromwell," in Michael Lieb and Thomas Shawcross, eds., *Achievements of the Left Hand: Essays on the Prose of John Milton* (Amherst: University of Massachusetts Press, 1974), 202–08.
[6] Ludlow, *Memoirs*, II:44.
[7] Roy Sherwood, *Oliver Cromwell: King in All but Name, 1653–1658* (New York: St. Martin's Press, 1997), 1. See also Sherwood, *The Court of Oliver Cromwell* (London: Croom Helm; Totowa, NJ: Rowman & Littlefield, 1977).
[8] Sherwood, *Oliver Cromwell*, 120.
[9] Thurloe, *A Collection of the State Papers*, VI: 15; SP 18/113, fol. 220. Cited in Sherwood, *Oliver Cromwell*, 92, and in Sherwood, *The Court of Oliver Cromwell*, 160.

the last in his attitude to the hereditary principle," some contemporaries interpreted events as signs of the return of monarchy in another guise.[10] There may be reason to think Cromwell intended for Richard to succeed since from the period of his investiture he started drawing Richard into the public eye while keeping Henry in Ireland.[11]

The title and form of Cromwell's position are important. If Cromwell were made king, his heirs would have the right to inherit the throne. The question was whether the country was to have a hereditary monarchy, a presumed outcome should Cromwell take the title of king, or a protector instead, and if so, was that position to be nominative or elective? The problem of succession would haunt the Republic and the Protectorate as Richard's nomination suggested that the Protectorate was modeling itself on a hereditary monarchy. Richard was even referred to as Richard the Fourth by a member of his Parliament.[12] Richard's succession was all the more revealing of the hold that traditional notions of family had on people, given the terms of the Humble Petition and Advice. In it the protector has the right to nominate his successor during his lifetime. The scope of Cromwell's power was perhaps larger than that of the king he replaced, for in a hereditary monarchy the succession automatically fell on the eldest child. A nominated ruler need not select only from blood heirs; theoretically the fittest person can be chosen. In the early 1650s, Hobbes had shown in *Leviathan* that an absolute monarchy could discard primogeniture by becoming a nominative monarchy, with an absolute king who chooses his successor. With Richard's nomination, England failed to take advantage of the flexibility of a nominative protectorship and lost the opportunity to experiment with a Hobbesian king. The Protectorate fell back into traditional notions of family.

While the 1650s began with a great deal of expectation for the English Republic, it ended with a quasi-monarchy and finally in 1660 with the return of the Stuarts. Along the way, both the English Republic and the Protectorate had to grapple with the powerful idea of *pater patriae*, particularly resonant for an interregnum government held together by Cromwell's single person. With no good alternative found for the monarchy, the English

---

[10] Christopher Hill, *God's Englishman: Oliver Cromwell and the English Revolution* (New York: Dial Press, 1970), 191.

[11] Antonia Fraser believes Cromwell's silence on the matter of the succession may not be significant given his conservatism in family affairs (*Cromwell*, 768).

[12] An entry in Thomas Burton's diary notes: "*Mr. Redding*, in his speech to the Committee, called the Lord Protector Richard the Fourth" (*Diary of Thomas Burton, Esq., Member in the Parliaments of Oliver and Richard Cromwell, From 1656 to 1659*, ed. John Towill Rutt, 4 vols. [London: H. Colburn, 1828], III:65).

clung to the customary structure of rule by a single person and the two houses of Parliament. Political fatherhood did not disappear with the regicide. The question was how to apply it first to a republic and then to a protectorate. In the 1650s, authors as diverse as Gerrard Winstanley, John Milton, James Harrington, and William Baxter returned again to the idea of *pater patriae*. In envisioning a new form of government they felt compelled to reenvision fatherhood, as if they were closely linked. The English were fascinated by the single person as head of state, whether it be the martyred King Charles or the Protector Oliver.

The debate over Cromwellian fatherhood in the interregnum culminated in the succession question. What did Cromwell's literal fatherhood mean politically? Because Richard was an unpromising eldest son, abdicating only several months after coming into power, Cromwell's fatherhood became a weak point that royalists could satirize. By the Restoration the Protectorate had paved the way for the return of monarchy at least in this one respect: it revived the notion of *pater patriae* and the importance of fatherly political authority.

REFORMING CROMWELL: WINSTANLEY, SEXBY, AND HARRINGTON

As Oliver moved closer to becoming a monarch in the guise of a protector, the term *pater patriae* became more applicable. Yet, such a use of the trope, burdened, as it were, by royalist associations, would be anathema to republicans. As the new government grew to be as authoritarian as the old – the Levellers and others were disgruntled with the limited reforms of the parliamentarians as early as 1648 and 1649 – supporters of a free commonwealth had to find ways to rehabilitate the idea of *pater patriae*. One common strategy was to apply the term to Parliament instead, reemphasizing commitment to a republic. In the early 1650s, it was still possible to imagine a benign father figure who would keep to republican principles, as did Milton in his *Second Defence* or as would Gerrard Winstanley, leader of the Digger movement. As the interregnum decade wore on, idealizing Cromwell proved more difficult for republicans like Edward Sexby and James Harrington. After Cromwell purged the Rump in April 1653 and dismissed Barebone's Parliament that December to take the title of Lord Protector, republican opposition greatly intensified and representations of Cromwell grew satirical or even hostile.

In their early calls for economic reform, Diggers berated landowners as oppressive elder brothers and called themselves and those they championed younger brothers. In *A New-Yeers Gift* (1649), Gerrard Winstanley protested the closing up of the commons in familial language: "Surely the Earth was never made by God, that the Younger brother should not live in the Earth, unless he would work for, and pay his Elder brother Rent for the Earth: No; this Slavery came in by Conquest, and it is part of the Kingly power; and England cannot be a Free Common-wealth; till this *Bondage* be taken away" (372–73). Linking primogeniture to monarchical power, Winstanley's condemnation of the propertied class was all the more pointed: if the commonwealth is a family, the rich were stealing from kin. When the Digger experiment failed – only after a few weeks, they were driven out by local landowners from their commune on St. George's Hill at Cobham and again from Surrey, where they relocated – Winstanley's rhetoric shifted. The millenarian cast of his earlier writings changed abruptly to the emphasis on institutions in *The Law of Freedom* (1652), his last published work, in which "the state was the key instrument of social discipline and harmony."[13] While *The Law of Freedom* may be written out of defeat, it nonetheless offers an alternative, more equitable model of society.

The dedication to Cromwell compares him to Moses, praising him for the divine honor of ejecting a tyrannical king though warning that he will not complete his task until the Commoners have free possession of land and liberty. Cromwell must complete the reformation he had begun. George Shulman argues, "As the exodus story shows Moses authorizing each tribe to appoint elders, who later become the rulers of Israel, so Winstanley imagines Cromwell initiating a process of self-governance and rendering himself superfluous."[14] Advocating elections every year for new members of Parliament, the ruling power, Winstanley envisions it as a constantly changing body so that the role of father or elder is not concentrated in a few persons. Provided the state is built on the right foundation, Cromwell is not crucial. But while he remains in power, he should be an exemplary father.

Winstanley's radical plan for economic reform is situated within a familial theory of the origin of society, albeit a revised account. In *The Law of Freedom*, he accepts that rule, or what he calls "magistracy" (sovereignty transformed into a popular form since the ejection of the king), began in the

---

[13] J. C. Davis, *Utopia and the Ideal Society: A Study of English Utopian Writing 1516–1700* (Cambridge: Cambridge University Press, 1981), 170. See also Perez Zagorin, *A History of Political Thought in the English Revolution* (London: Routledge and Kegan Paul, 1954), chapter 4; T. Wilson Hayes, *Winstanley the Digger: A Literary Analysis of Radical Ideas in the English Revolution* (Cambridge, Mass.: Harvard University Press, 1979), 246; George M. Shulman, *Radicalism and Reverence: The Political Thought of Gerrard Winstanley* (Berkeley: University of California Press, 1989), part 4.

[14] Shulman, *Radicalism and Reverence*, 224.

Adamic family: "The Original Root of Magistracy is *common Preservation*, and it rose up first in a private Family: for suppose there were but one Family in the World, as is conceived, Father *Adams* Family, wherein were many persons" (536). Although the first ruler, Adam is called "Governor" rather than king: "Therein *Adam* was the first Governor or Officer in the Earth, because as he was the first Father, so he was the most wise in contriving, and the most strong for labor, and so the fittest to be the chief *Governor*" (536). Adam's role as leader is justified not by reference to his paternity but by merit: because he is wise and strong, he is best fit for the position. Winstanley's non-elitist politics regard Adam's ability to perform "labor" as fundamental to rule.

Winstanley should not be conflated with conservative patriarchalists like Filmer.[15] For him, Adam is subject to law, not absolute: "The Law of Necessity, that the Earth should be planted for the common preservation and peace of his houshold, was the righteous Rule and Law to *Adam*, and this Law was so clearly written in the hearts of his people, that they all consented quietly to any counsel he gave them for that end" (536). The law that governs the governor is a form of natural law found in the hearts of the people. Instead of the will of the ruler, the people embody the law: "Therefore not *Adams* Will onely, but the Will of his People likewise, and the Law of common Preservation, Peace and Freedom, was the righteous Law that governed both *Adam* and his houshould [*sic*]" (536). Moreover, the people choose their leaders: "The necessity of the children that sprang from him [the Father] doth say, Father, do thou teach us how to plant the Earth, that we may live, and we will obey. By this choyce, they make him not onely a Father, but a Master and Ruler. And out of this root springs up all Magistrates and Officers" (538). Significantly, Winstanley calls necessity choice. While apparently close to Hobbes's absolutist argument that children are subject to fathers because of their weakness, he emphasizes not the Hobbesian father's power to kill but the father's nurturing role. Although the father ranks higher than children, among children there should be no differences of rank. Idealizing the family, Winstanley envisions a more equitable society without turning his world completely upside down. While retaining some form of hierarchy (fathers govern children), he tries to level family hierarchy (no differences among siblings) and therefore also social hierarchy. No arbitrary or absolute ruler, Winstanley's governor is yet an authoritative figure opposed to monarchical power and to social rank. *Pater patriae* is rejuvenated as a republican concept, in which fatherhood is characteristic

---

[15] As does Gordon J. Schochet, *Patriarchalism in Political Thought: The Authoritarian Family and Political Speculation and Attitudes Especially in Seventeenth-Century England* (New York: Basic Books, 1975), 161–62.

of the good citizen rather than the absolute monarch. The connotations of Winstanley's *pater patriae* necessarily differ from James I's, given his vastly different social location. Writing from a position of relative powerlessness, Winstanley sees himself as a younger brother, identifying his own position as lacking authority. Using the idealized picture of a loving father to call for reform and to demand justice, he offers paternal love as a way to structure relations between the governors and the governed.

As Cromwell's political power grew, however, his fatherly image looked rather less benign. While radical groups had opposed Cromwell well before the Protectorate, after the Protectorate various factions – Levellers, republicans, Fifth Monarchists, and Quakers – began to form loose coalitions.[16] Radicals even sought temporary alliances with royalists to topple Cromwell. Edward Sexby and James Harrington reject Cromwellian fatherhood outright. Beyond *pater patriae*, they reject the family itself as an analogy for the state. Recognizing that the metaphor is leading the country back into monarchy, Sexby and Harrington want the father dead. In her study of how family narratives structure the political sphere, Lynn Hunt uses Freud's term "family romance" to describe the French Revolution's violent disruption of the old patriarchal political order as an acting-out of the unconscious fantasy of replacing their political parents, the king and queen.[17] In the English Revolution, fantasies of killing the father were applied not to the king but to Cromwell as Lord Protector, as English republicanism only came to be explicitly expressed after the fact of regicide.

At one time a bedfellow of Cromwell and a soldier in his army, Edward Sexby, a Leveller disillusioned with Cromwell, started conspiring to assassinate him soon after he was made Lord Protector.[18] Working with Levellers, disgruntled soldiers, excluded parliamentarians, Baptists and Fifth

---

[16] On republican resistance to the Protectorate, see J. G. A. Pocock, ed., *The Political Works of James Harrington* (Cambridge: Cambridge University Press, 1977), 36–42; David Norbrook, *Writing the English Republic: Poetry, Rhetoric and Politics, 1627–1660* (Cambridge: Cambridge University Press, 1999), 299–325.

[17] Lynn Hunt, *The Family Romance of the French Revolution* (Berkeley: University of California Press, 1992).

[18] According to Edward Hyde, Sexby boasted to royalists of being in Cromwell's confidence: "He had been, in the beginning, a common soldier of Cromwell's troop, and afterwards was one of those Agitators who were made use of to control the Parliament; and had so great an interest in Cromwell that he was frequently his bedfellow, a familiarity he frequently admitted those to whom he employed in any great trust, and with whom he could not so freely converse as in those hours. He was very perfect in the history of Cromwell's dissimulations, and would describe his artifices to the life" (Edward Hyde, Earl of Clarendon, *The History of the Rebellion and Civil Wars in England begun in the year 1641*, ed. W. Dunn Macray, 6 vols. [Oxford: Clarendon Press, 1888], xv.133, cited by James Holstun, *Ehud's Dagger: Class Struggle in the English Revolution* [London and New York: Verso, 2000], 313, n. 44). For Sexby's life and career, see Holstun, *Ehud's Dagger*, chapter 8, and "Ehud's Dagger: Patronage, Tyrannicide, and *Killing No Murder*," *Cultural Critique* 22 (1992), 99–142.

Monarchists, Sexby participated in the failed 1654 "Overton Plot."[19] Soon
Sexby was intriguing with royalists and Catholics.[20] Under the pseudonym
William Allen, one of many he adopted, Sexby wrote *Killing Noe Murder*, a
spirited justification of tyrannicide with a fascinating mix of republican ire
and irony. At once indignant and satirical, it argues that Cromwell displays
the traits of a tyrant as described by authorities such as Plato, Aristotle, Tac-
itus, Machiavelli, and Grotius. For examples of tyrannicide, the tract turns
to scripture, including Moses' murder of the Egyptian, Samson's slaughter
of the Philistines, Jehoiada's assassination of Athaliah, and Ehud's killing
of the tyrant Eglon with a concealed dagger. Sexby argues, "The example of Ehud shews us the naturall and almost the only remedie against a
Tyrant, and the way to free an opprest people from the slavery of an insult-
ing Moabite, tis done by prayers and teares, with the help of a Dagger,
by . . . crying to the Lord, and the left hand of an Ehud."[21] Characteristic
of Sexby's acerbic wit, this passage surprises by yoking dissimilar things
together, in this case the seemingly passive act of imploring God with the
violent aggression of murder. Like Ehud's act of coming before Eglon with
a concealed weapon, which he brandishes unexpectedly, Sexby's rhetoric
often uses the element of surprise.

The surprise attack is part of the larger shape of the tract. The opening
address to Cromwell initially gives it the appearance of a dedicatory letter
from a grateful client. But it quickly becomes evident that Sexby is satirizing
the patron–client relation: "To your Highness justly belongs the honour of
dying for the people, and it cannot choose but be an unspeakable consolation to you in the last moments of your life, to consider, with how much
benefit to the world you are like to leave it" (sig. A, 1). Using the language
of patronage and patriotism ironically, Sexby urges Cromwell to become a
martyr. Emphasizing justice for the people, he applies the word "justice"
ironically to Cromwell, who had given him time to write by forcing him
into exile. Paying Cromwell back in a grotesque rendering of the patronage relation, Sexby, a former client of Cromwell, suggests that Cromwell's
tyranny made mockery of the patron–client relation between him and the
people. James Holstun suggests much the same in his analysis of the tract
as a parody of the symbolic economy of patronage and a rejection of the

[19] Named after the former Major General Robert Overton, the plot involved seizing General Monck's
headquarters in Scotland. See the *Dictionary of National Biography* entry on Robert Overton; Maurice
Ashley, *John Wildman, Plotter and Postmaster: A Study of the English Republican Movement in the
Seventeenth Century* (London: J. Cape, 1947), 82–94; and Barbara Taft, "The Humble Petition of
Several Colonels of the Army," *Huntington Library Quarterly* 42 (1978), 15–41.
[20] Holstun, *Ehud's Dagger*, 316–17.
[21] Sexby, *Killing Noe Murder* (London, 1654), sig. Bv, 9. Further references are given parenthetically.

filiative fiction of patriarchal monarchy, which Sexby replaces with "radical republican affiliations" and "an affiliative genealogy of anti-tyrannical writers in place of the patriarchal dynasty."[22] Family relations are akin to patronage because they are both filiative, binding participants in a relation of mutual duties and obligations with set, hierarchical roles. In patriarchalism, these relations merge as what would be considered patronage relations are imagined as familial ones. This is precisely how Sexby has identified the Cromwellian state. He satirizes patronage relations that have been converted into family relations, debunking family in all its forms as a political model and exposing the hollowness of Cromwell's pretensions as *pater patriae*. Cromwell will be truly father of his country only when he dies: "All this we hope from your Highnes happie expiration, who are the true Father of your Countrie for while you live we can call nothing ours, and it is from your death that we hope for our inheritances" (sig. Av, 2). Rather than a picture of benevolent government, Sexby presents patriarchal government as one where an oppressive father hoards the goods and keeps it from his heirs who are all too ready to inherit. The family romance turns out to be a tragicomedy of heirs waiting for a rich, miserly relative to die. Sexby makes the analogy only to sever the presumed link between family and state. They are disparate, even opposite, things: "to be under a Tyrant is, not to be a commonwealth; but a great Family, consisting of master & Slaves" (sig. B2v, 12). Sexby was no social radical, acknowledging fathers as the ultimate authority in the household: "To Fathers within their private Families nature hath given a Supreme power" (sig. A2v, 4). But rulers do not have fatherly power in the state. Power comes from God "or the Peoples consent" (sig. A2v, 4). A state modeled on the family fosters a master–slave relation between its rulers and its people. Moreover, even as Cromwell turns the state into a "great family," he destroys families. His wars left "mothers . . . childlesse . . . children Fatherlesse" and "many a woman husbandlesse, many a father childlesse" (sig. Bv, 10).

In demystifying the term *pater patriae*, Sexby uses it only once. Tellingly, he uses it to refer to Cicero in a passage about Roman tyrannicide. Not only do Romans believe it lawful to kill a tyrant, Plutarch even calls it lawful to kill someone who merely aspired to tyranny. Discussing the conspiracy against Julius Caesar, Sexby calls the conspirators heroic, noting that Caesar himself thought Brutus a worthy successor. Even if Cicero was not part of the conspiracy, he, "who had the title of *Pater Patriae*" (sig. B, 9), was honored to be thought part of it. Since Cicero first had the title *pater*

---

[22] Holstun, "Ehud's Dagger: Patronage, Tyrannicide, and *Killing No Murder*," 125.

patriae, his praise of tyrannicide is important in defining the term. Using it to refer only to Cicero – in the prefatorial letter, he mentions the titles Cromwell usurps but does not actually use the words *pater patriae* – Sexby emphasizes the term's republican roots. Nonetheless, Sexby's roundabout phrasing suggests an uneasiness with the term. Rather than simply calling Cicero *pater patriae*, he notes that Cicero has the title. This uneasiness reappears in Sexby's translation of the term as "deliverer of his Countrie" (sig. Bv, 10). Instead of translating it literally, he returns to the fundamental meaning of the term. Sexby circumvents the patriarchal politics of the Cromwellian regime to retain the honorable deed of saving one's country without using the suspect title. Instead, he uses the true meaning of the term to threaten Cromwell: "Ther's a great Rowle behinde, even of those that are in his own muster-Rowles, that are ambitious of the name of the Deliverers of their Countrey: and they know what the action is that will purchase it" (sig. B4v, 16).

The same year Sexby's *Killing Noe Murder* was published, between September and November 1656, James Harrington issued *The Commonwealth of Oceana*, perhaps intending to influence the September parliamentary elections. John Toland, who edited Harrington's collected works in 1699 and published them in 1700, included a manuscript, *The Examination of James Harrington*, in which Harrington claims that he wrote *Oceana* because Cromwell's power was illegitimate: "I did not write under a prince, I wrote under a usurper, Oliver . . . therefore I wrote not against the king's government . . . After Oliver the parliament said they were a commonwealth: I said they were not, and proved it."[23] Known only from Toland's edition, *The Examination* may have been a Restoration rehabilitation of Harrington's character. While Harrington proved congenial company for Charles I from May 1647 to New Year 1648–9 when he was under arrest by Parliament, it is doubtful that Toland and others like John Aubrey and Anthony Wood were correct to assert that *Oceana* was motivated by his personal devotion to the king, though it does seem clear that *Oceana* is a response to the growing power of the protector.[24] Harrington's doubts about Cromwellian fatherhood, however, differ from Sexby's. Rather more circumspect, he advocates not tyrannicide but self-annihilation. While Sexby's pamphlet is

[23] Pocock, ed., *The Political Works of James Harrington*, 859.
[24] J. G. A. Pocock, Harrington's modern editor, suggests that *Oceana* may be part of the opposition literature of 1656, arising out of the Amy's discontent with Cromwell's assumption of supreme military power ("Introduction," *ibid.*, 8–14). Discussing the similarities of *Oceana* and Henry Neville's *A Copy of a Letter from an Officer in the Army* (1656), Blair Worden too connects *Oceana* to Army malcontents ("Harrington's *Oceana*: Origins and Aftermath, 1651–1660," in David Wootton, ed., *Republicanism, Liberty, and Commercial Society, 1649–1776* [Stanford: Stanford University Press, 1994], 113–26).

unabashedly polemical, Harrington writes in a genre with a literary tradition, the utopia, allowing for indirect criticism. The abdication of Olphaus Megaletor, Harrington's fictional version of Cromwell, after he establishes Oceana as a commonwealth, gently suggests a metaphorical death, political suicide rather than murder. *Oceana* is both a blueprint for establishing a commonwealth and an advice manual for Cromwell's graceful exit.

Applying the term *pater patriae* to Olphaus only after abdication, Harrington dissociates the term from rulership. Only in the "Corollary" to *Oceana*, stylistically very different from the main text, does Harrington develop the fatherly image of Cromwell/Olphaus. When he abdicates, Olphaus is said to leave the senate bereft like orphans: "He [Olphaus] escaping left the senate with the tears in their eyes of children that had lost their father."[25] Nowhere before this moment has Olphaus been described as a father. Moreover, the titles of father and archon or prince given to Olphaus are strictly separated in the main parts of *Oceana*. In the "Corollary," Olphaus is dubbed *pater patriae* at his death, when the citizens set up a "colossus, mounted upon a brazen horse . . . in the piazza of the Pantheon" with the following inscription: "Grata Patria / Piae et perpetuae memoriae / D. D. / Olphaus Megaletor / Lord Archon and sole Legislator / of / OCEANA / Pater Patriae" (265–66). James Holstun astutely notes that the analogy between Olphaus and Lycurgus leads to Olphaus's redundancy once he puts republican orders into motion, and that the senate's reaction to Olphaus's abdication – the offer "as it were to lay violent hands on him" (246) – hints of the "competitive violence of Freud's primal horde."[26] Only with the father dead can the people, children to Olphaus/Cromwell's father figure, govern themselves. Reading the inscription as a taboo or prohibition, Holstun suggests that Olphaus finally becomes a mythic figure, not to be imitated. The titles of "Pater Patriae" and "sole Legislator" conferred upon Olphaus are unique to him, historical titles confined to the originary moment of the republic. Holstun argues, "Harrington encourages the Lord Protector to imitate first the tyrant, then the tyrannicide."[27] With the tyrant having self-annihilated, he can be commemorated as the legislator and as *pater patriae*, father of his country who literally founded it. With a perfect, stable commonwealth, there can be only one father or founder. Harrington

---

[25] Harrington, *The Commonwealth of Oceana; and, A System of Politics*, ed. J. G. A. Pocock (Cambridge: Cambridge University Press, 1992), 246. All references to *Oceana* are from this edition and cited parenthetically.

[26] James Holstun, *A Rational Millennium: Puritan Utopias of Seventeenth-Century England and America* (New York and Oxford: Oxford University Press, 1987), 229–30.

[27] *Ibid.*, 232.

endorses Olphaus' dictatorship because it is not to be repeated. Such a commonwealth needs no renewal; its founder can remain a shadowy figure of the past. The term *pater patriae* at the end of *Oceana* thus names a role meant to become obsolete.

While the inscription can act as a taboo, prohibiting any potential emulators of Olphaus/Cromwell, it cannot and does not contain the great tyrant himself. The "Corollary" is more equivocal about *pater patriae* as an honorific than Holstun suggests. Deeply ironic, it depicts both the abdication of Olphaus and his reinstatement. The familial language marks the dangers of Cromwellian fatherhood by projecting it into a mythic, unrecoverable past and by pointing to the collapse of the republic into the politics of family, a politics that the main parts of *Oceana* had so decisively rejected. The appearance of familial language in the "Corollary" is surprising because the main sections of *Oceana* – the introduction, the preliminaries, and the model – curtail its use. In particular, *Oceana* reinterprets fatherhood in very limited ways to circumscribe the role of father and to restrict paternal right. When commenting on the procedure to elect representatives from the elders of parishes, Harrington accepts paternal power as a legitimate form of authority but limits its political application. While acknowledging "paternal power" to be "in the right of nature" and that "the derivation of power from fathers of families [is] the natural root of a commonwealth," he argues that the establishment of such orders in the commonwealth was the ruin of Rome: "The distinction of the patrician as an hereditary order from the very institution, engrossing all the magistracies, was indeed the destruction of Rome; . . . By which it should seem that this order was no otherwise hereditary than as a man's estate, nor gave it any claim to magistracy" (80). Despite its patriarchal basis, Harrington's commonwealth does not naturalize power to include all fathers. Elections mean that not all fathers or elders exercise political power, a point emphasized by Harrington's example of Israel as the original model for commonwealths, in which "the patriarchs or princes of families . . . had the like right [i.e. of leading and judging] as to their families, but neither in these nor the former was there any hereditary right unto the Sanhedrim," that is the Israelite senate (139). Paternal power in the household does not automatically confer political power in Parliament, particularly since Harrington rejects the hereditary principle. In Oceana, there is no easy transference of paternal authority from the family to the state.

Although the natural aristocracy of Oceana possesses "*auctoritas patrum,* the authority of the fathers," the senate is chosen by election, not selected by hereditary right nor by great estate. The natural superiority of a third of society makes them counselors, who are to debate issues, but the majority chooses the country's course of action, though "they hang upon their [the aristocracy's] lips as children upon their fathers" (23). It is not a father–child relation where the father makes all the decisions: "the office of the senate is not to be commanders but counselors of the people" (23). Sharing governance, each performs the task most suited to talent. While it divides society into two, Harrington's aristocracy does not create a pyramidal structure with a single father figure at the top. Rather, he disperses the paternal function by multiplying fathers. They are a third of the community, or six of every twenty. But the other fourteen have their own sphere of authority. What is proposed by the senate and resolved by the people "is enacted *auctoritate patrum et jussu populi*, by the authority of the fathers and the power of the people, which concurring make a law" (24). Decisions of the state are made in a shared process, not the prerogative of senate fathers alone.

Borrowed from vocabulary common in republican Rome, Harrington's term "father" suggests neither the large scope of powers justified by patriarchalism nor the glorification of Cromwell. *Oceana* attempts to model a new commonwealth and to renovate the institution of family. By limiting the amount of an inheritance, forcing the division of large estates among all children – even daughters may inherit – *Oceana* abolishes primogeniture. Harrington gently satirizes greedy eldest sons with the character Philautus, an elder son who argues against the agrarian law that prevents excessive accumulation of property in one person: "The case of my lord Philautus was the most concerned in the whole nation; for he had four younger brothers, his father being yet living, unto whom he was heir of ten thousand pounds a year" (104). The more equitable distribution of property benefits the state by preventing any faction from acquiring too much power, since political authority is based on property, landed estates in particular. Given the way that Oceana's perfection depends on a careful balance, primogeniture causes families harm: "we . . . use our children as we do our puppies: take one, lay it in the lap, feed it with every good bit, and drown five! . . . And all this for his cruel ambition that would raise himself a pillar, a golden pillar for his monument, though he have children, his own reviving flesh and a kind of immortality" (109). Instead, nurturing all children profits both family and commonwealth, just as the flow of the river Nile into a delta, parting into several streams, "multiplies his fertile shores by distributing, yet keeping and improving, such as property and nutrition as is a prudent agrarian unto a well ordered commonwealth" (109). Primogeniture is in the interests of monarchy while supporting all members tends toward the formation of a commonwealth. Harrington even suggests doing away with

the practice of giving dowries, which encourages marriages based on economic calculations. Without dowries, children can have "more freedom of
their own affections" (112). The attacks on primogeniture and on dowries in
Oceana are attacks on paternal power. Where estates are distributed evenly,
there can be no patriarch, and where there are no dowries, fathers cannot
force marriages.

Having distinguished fathers from the people who choose them, it is
just as important to distinguish the role of prince or archon from that of
father, which Harrington does by reference to the popular analogy between
Cromwell and Moses. As the original republic and model for later republics,
ancient Israel becomes the model for Oceana. But Harrington downplays
the role of Old Testament patriarchs. For instance, the Sanhedrim, or senate,
is chosen by lot. Harrington depicts Moses as prince, not father: "Moses
for his time, and after him his successor, sat in the midst of it as prince
or archon, and at his left hand the orator or father of the senate" (27).
Contemporary parallels between Cromwell and Moses, as in the elegies
on Cromwell's death, portray Cromwell as a divinely sanctioned patriarch
of his people. Since Olphaus occupies the position of prince, Harrington
clearly alludes to this parallel. He even makes a direct comparison: Archon's
"meekness resembled that of Moses" (179). Harrington, however, strictly
separates the roles of prince and senate father so that Moses' authority does
not derive from his status as patriarch. In redefining Moses' role, Harrington
also redefines Cromwell's, distancing him from paternal authority. At the
end of "The Model of the Commonwealth of Oceana" when Olphaus
abdicates, he distances himself from the commonwealth he created, along
with the ruling "magistracy both of orators and legislators" (243), and the
commonwealth starts completely anew.

The commonwealth's newness is exemplified by the "Corollary"'s
opening story of the lawgiver Lycurgus. After putting his government in
order, Lycurgus makes his people promise to keep his laws without any
change until he returns from Delphos. When Apollo confirms that his
laws are perfect, Lycurgus commits suicide through starvation to prevent
his people from altering his laws; consequently, his city gains fame for
the excellence of its government. Making a parallel between Lycurgus and
Olphaus, the "Corollary" draws out what is implied by the abdications, particularly for Olphaus, and encourages Cromwell to stop acting the tyrant.
The language of fatherhood is, however, applied not only to Olphaus. The
senate is addressed as "your fatherhoods, most truly so called, as being the
loving parents of the people" (254). In the "Corollary" the title of father is
no longer simply a term for the orator. The "Corollary" makes it a metaphor

for the relation between senate and people that the main parts of *Oceana* avoid doing. Here both Olphaus and the senate are seen as father figures.

The "Corollary" raises the issue of Oceana's potential change from a republican to a paternal state. When Olphaus abdicates, the people almost immediately reinstate him: the gratitude of the people and their sadness at Olphaus' withdrawal into private life lead them to offer him "the dignity and office of Archon or protector of the commonwealth of Oceana . . . for the term of his natural life" (251). The description of his reinstatement is an ambiguous assessment of the role of a prince in a republic:

> But the senate, being informed by the signory that the Archon had accepted of his dignity and office, caused a third chair to be set for his highness, between those of the strategus and the orator in the house, the like at every council; to which he repaired, not of necessity, but at his pleasure, being the best, and . . . the greatest prince in the world; for in the pomp of his court he was not inferior unto any, and in the field he was followed with a force that was formidable unto all. (257)

While formerly taking a primarily legislative role, here the Archon's position is more monarchical. Quite understandably, there is unease about the kingly aspects of his office. The passage attempts to mitigate such monarchical associations by deriving Olphaus's greatness not from ambition but "from the root of the people" (257). Indeed, Archon would not have been as great if he had been ambitious, especially if the state was "monarchical" (257). The claim for Olphaus's good character, however, is odd, given the foundational assumption for Harrington's modeling of Oceana: "give us good orders, and they will make us good men" (64).

The "Corollary" depicts two possible futures. Oceana's prince, uncorrupted by ambition, could be the "sole legislator" who creates a perfect commonwealth. But the "Corollary" also registers anxiety about the prince who would not or could not truly abdicate. The language of fatherhood that appears in the "Corollary" reveals the dark underside of Cromwell as Lord Protector. Olphaus' funeral monument is similarly ambiguous. The Renaissance inherited the sculptural genre of the equestrian monument from late republican and imperial Rome. It was the prerogative of the *eques*, the aristocrat, in the late Republic but during the Empire the equestrian statue, particularly in bronze, became the symbol of imperial authority.[28] Thus the equestrian monument initially had a republican context but came to acquire monarchical significance. The question then is whether the statue for Olphaus celebrates the republic or is truly a symbol

---

[28] H. W. Janson, "The Equestrian Monument from Cangrande della Scala to Peter the Great," in *Sixteen Studies* (New York: H. N. Abrams, n.d. [1974?]), 159–88.

of his monarchy. The last lines of the plaque, also the last sentences of
the "Corollary" and thus of *Oceana* as a whole, are deeply ambivalent:
Olphaus/Cromwell is the one "Who, setting the Kingdoms of the Earth at
Liberty, / Took the Kingdom of the Heavens by Violence" (266). Cromwell
can do great good but also great harm.

The ambivalence of the "Corollary" makes for a striking contrast with
the apparent optimism of the main parts of *Oceana*. While the threat of
failure looms over the whole venture – Olphaus is not the only threat; figures like Philautus or Garrula objecting to the silent ballot, who oppose the
new orders, signal fissures in the new republic – it is held at bay by Olphaus'
overwhelming power. The commonwealth is only realized if Olphaus tyran-
nically forces it into being, and it only remains so if Olphaus is an impossi-
bly good man. Oceana is unsustainable, as utopias are often utopian in the
modern sense of the word. Harrington's critique of Cromwell is at the same
time less personal than Sexby's and more far-reaching because he recognizes
Cromwell's potential for good. Ultimately, both Sexby and Harrington are
pessimistic about the possibility of reforming Cromwell, only they imagine
his death differently.

"A CROMWELL IN AN HOURE A PRINCE WILL GROW": RICHARD THE PROTECTOR

Almost immediately, the public representation of Richard made much of his
identity as Oliver's son. The commemorative medal engraved by Thomas
Smith for Oliver's funeral features a design emphasizing the continuity
of Cromwellian rule. On the obverse is a profile bust of Oliver crowned
with laurel and in armor. The inverse shows a flourishing olive tree next
to a stump of a larger tree, apparently just cut down, with two shepherds
tending their flock in the background. The legend on the obverse reads:
"NON. DEFITIENT. OLIVA. SEP. 3. 1658."[29] As Henry William Henfrey
explains, "The date of Oliver's death follows this motto, which obviously
signifies that 'the olives (or Olivers) will not be wanting,' to continue the
government of the nation . . . The device is also a play on Cromwell's name
Oliver, representing him under the allegory of an olive tree. The motto
tells us that, although the great Oliver, the first Protector, is dead, other
Olivers (or other Cromwells, in the persons of his sons) will not be wanting
as the future Protectors of the Commonwealth."[30] Although one Oliver is

[29] The correct Latin should read: Non deficient olivae.
[30] Henry William Henfrey, *Numismata Cromwelliana: Or, the Medallic History of Oliver Cromwell*
    (London, 1877), 167.

cut down, another one rises in his place, and the government continues as smoothly, it is implied, as if the protector had not died. The allusion is unmistakably to the idea of the king's two bodies, and in particular, the immortal nature of his political body.

Richard's public image made constant reference to his father in hopes of transferring support from Oliver to the new protector. The funeral elegies written for Oliver and the congratulatory addresses to Richard show a keen awareness of the dynastic nature of the succession. Richard's status as son of Oliver was asserted as evidence of his virtue and fitness for the protectorship. The attempt was not to portray Richard as Oliver's double, given his lack of military experience. But the close family connection was highlighted in Richard's favor, even as the Protectorate was carefully distinguished from a hereditary monarchy. In the process, these public representations of Richard's succession altered the meaning of dynastic succession to conform to the new institution of the protectorship. Thus, father–son tropes were also accompanied by numerous allusions to Oliver and Richard as Moses and Joshua. Richard's spiritual inheritance from Oliver as a latter-day Moses, bringing England out of the Egyptian tyranny of a monarchy, was more important than his blood relation to Oliver. The circumstances of the succession meant that the praise of Richard Cromwell required balancing a fine line between spiritual sonhood and dynastic succession.

If the Protectorate was not a hereditary monarchy, Richard's fitness for the position had to be proven. In his funeral elegy, "A Poem upon the Death of O. C.," Andrew Marvell explored the issue of how one can tell whether a physical son is also a spiritual child, ending with a fairly lengthy section on Richard. In the last twenty lines, almost a caudal sonnet with a six-line tail, the tone shifts from despair to hope when moving from lamenting Oliver's death to celebrating the new protector. To the people, left so destitute that "Onely our sighs, perhaps, may thither reach [Oliver]" ("Poem," line 304), Richard is offered as the new hope of the nation.[31] But as the new hope and ruler, Richard is anti-climactic after Oliver. His are the "milder beams" ("Poem," line 7) rather than the unstoppable lightning that Oliver was in Marvell's "An Horatian Ode." Where Oliver is self-made, *sui generis*, who "thorough his own Side / His fiery way divide" ("Horatian Ode," lines 15–16), Richard is imitative, a follower rather than a leader, even a little

[31] Andrew Marvell, *The Poems and Letters of Andrew Marvell*, ed. H. M. Margoliouth, rev. Pierre Legouis and E. E. Duncan-Jones, 3rd edn, vol. 1: Poems (Oxford: Clarendon Press, 1971). All references to Marvell are from this edition and cited parenthetically by line number.

plodding: "And Richard yet, where his great parent led, / Beats on the rugged track" ("Poem," lines 305–06).

The elegy attempts to posit a parallel between the careers of father and son: "He, as his father, long was kept from sight / In private, to be view'd by better light" ("Poem," lines 309–10). But while "An Horatian Ode" marvels at Oliver's military and political accomplishments, and his lightning rise, despite a past life of privacy, "A Poem" cannot do the same for Richard. Tentatively expressing hope for similar successes from the son, the poem raises questions where, if it were a praise of Richard, it ought to be asserting his virtues. Rather than celebrating Richard's successful transition into public life, it wonders what would happen if he were to be exposed to public view: "But open'd once, what splendour does he throw?" ("Poem," line 311). Even the answer is mildly ambiguous: "A Cromwell in an houre a prince will grow" ("Poem," line 312). Either a Cromwell will become a prince or the young prince (Richard) will grow into a Cromwell. The first is an apt description of Oliver, but will Richard prove himself a Cromwell? That enigmatic line is followed by an assertion of Richard's fitness for his father's place but even such an assertion turns into a half question: "How he becomes that seat, how strongly streigns, / how gently winds at once the ruling reins?" ("Poem," lines 313–14).

In the end, Richard turns out to be most unlike Oliver. Oliver is linked to war and Richard to peace. In "An Horatian Ode," Oliver is lightning: "burning through the Air he went, / And Pallaces and Temples rent: / And *Caesars* head at last / Did through his Laurels blast" ("Horatian Ode," lines 21–24). In "A Poem" the forces of nature are again associated with Oliver. Although Oliver dies quietly, Nature groans in sympathetic response: "But oh what pangs that Death did Nature cost! / First the great *Thunder* was shot off, and sent / The Signal from the starry Battlement. / The *Winds* receive it, and its force out-do, / As practicing how they could thunder too" ("Poem," lines 112–16). Alive, a lightning force that tears old structures down, dying, Cromwell calls down a storm threatening a great flood: "Then heavy *Showres* the winged Tempests lead, / And pour the Deluge ore the *Chaos* head" ("Poem," lines 121–22). In contrast, Richard "by his milder beam assures" ("Poem," line 307) rather than threatens. He is associated not with a storm but the aftermath of one: "Heav'n to this choice prepar'd a diadem, / Richer than any eastern silk, or gemme; / A pearly rainbow, where the sun inchas'd / His brows, like an imperiall jewell grac'd" ("Poem," lines 315–18). The rainbow of peace becomes Richard's crown: "Cease now our griefs, calme peace succeeds a war, / Rainbows to storms, Richard to Oliver. / Tempt not his clemency to try his pow'r, / He threats no deluge, yet foretells a showre" ("Poem," lines 321–24). Richard is Oliver's child in the way that a rainbow is born out of a storm. As justification of Richard's kinship to Oliver, it is from unlikeness rather than likeness.

Other funeral elegies by less accomplished poets also make that turn to Richard in their conclusions. The anonymous *Upon the much Lamented Departure of the High and Mighty Prince, Oliver Lord Protector* ends by expressing hope in terms of family: "Wee wish that his Successour may excel, / and bee thee Sonne of great *Jerubbaal*."[32] The subjunctive "wish," however, denotes tension between desire and reality. Jerubbaal, meaning "contender with Baal," was the surname of the twelfth-century Israelite warrior Gideon, who turned down the kingship of Israel to preserve Israel's theocratic government.[33] If Oliver is a latter-day Gideon who rejected kingship, then to be the son of Gideon is to do the same. Because the succession was to all outward respects hereditary, the reference to Gideon may well be covertly rebuking the Protectorate or expressing fears that it was moving inexorably toward a full monarchy.

Thomas Davies's *The Tenth Worthy; or Several Anagrams in Latine, Welsh and English* goes much further in glorifying family ties than either Marvell's "A Poem" or *Upon the much Lamented Departure*.[34] Besides the anagrams of Oliver's name at the top of the broadsheet, following his poem Davies includes commendatory anagrams on the names of Richard and Dorothy Cromwell as well as on the names of Oliver's other children and their spouses, unabashedly celebrating Oliver's progeny. About the last sixth of the poem focuses on Richard, employing the metaphor of the olive tree of the funeral medal. Although the poem and the broadsheet as a whole devote considerable attention to Richard, he nonetheless remains secondary to Oliver. Despite being the "primest Branch" of the Cromwell family, he is only the "second Glory" of the nation. His future still has to be inferred from Oliver's past: "As by the Anagrams of both we see / What was the one, the other like to be." Because Richard lacks accomplishments, Davies devises anagrams to divine his future, finding evidence of virtue in signs rather than in deeds.

While the other two funeral elegies lack Marvell's subtlety in exploring the problem of succession, the largely formulaic congratulatory addresses to

---

[32] *Upon the much Lamented Departure of the High and Mighty Prince, Oliver Lord Protector of England, Scotland and Ireland, &c. A Funeral Elegie* (London, 1658).

[33] Judges 6:32; 8:29; 1 Samuel 12:11.

[34] Thomas Davies, *The Tenth Worthy; or, Several Anagrams in Latine, Welsh and English, upon the Name of that most highly Renowned Worthy or Worthies, Oliver, Late Lord Protector. Together with some Elegeical Verses upon his much lamented Death, who dyed in body Sept. 3. 1658. And also more Anagrams on his now Highness, and others of that most Noble and Puissant Family* (London, 1658).

Richard are even less subtle. Nonetheless, within the formula, the addresses must negotiate the fine line between celebrating dynastic succession and honoring the non-monarchic structure of the Protectorate. Like the elegies they look for evidence of Richard's spiritual sonhood. Collected from newspapers in the anonymous *A True Catalogue, Or, An Account of the several Places and most Eminent Persons in the three Nations* (1659), the addresses to Richard from various cities and counties use a set of common images and metaphors that speak to their concern over his suitability as heir. Lamenting their loss of Oliver, who is "so worthy a nursing father to his people," the addresses resort to familiar terms to describe him.[35] A number assert that the people "claim a share in his [Richard's] sorrow, and do say, that they also had lost a Father, the Father of their Countrey."[36] While the metaphor of the father of the country is neither new nor newly applied to Cromwell, the addresses have to find a place for Richard within the logic of the trope. On the one hand, he is the mourning son; on the other hand, in replacing his father, he has to become a father figure himself. Acknowledging his ancestry, the addresses see Richard as a "*branch* out of that *noble stem* that God hath made choice of for a *Scepter* to *Rule* these *Nations*, and one out of his loins succeed him in the government."[37] But biological family ties are insufficient; Richard needs also to be Oliver's spiritual son. The addresses urge him to "walk in his Fathers steps, in being a nursing Father to the Saints" or try to reassure readers that Richard will resemble his father: "they comfort themselves that God will repair his Royal Fathers absence by his presence, and have them think they have not lost, but exchanged him."[38]

With the country at a point of transition, the addresses cannot use the trope of *pater patriae* straightforwardly. They must confront the issue of the relation between the old and the new protector. Imagining Richard as Oliver's spiritual heir, they depict Oliver as a Moses and Richard as Joshua: "*taking away a Moses*, [God] *bestows on them a* Joshua. Though their Governour be removed, their Government remains, and their happiness under it."[39] Others make explicit the hope that Richard would be a spiritual

[35] *A True Catalogue, or, An Account of the several Places and most Eminent Persons in the three Nations, and elsewhere, where, and by whom, Richard Cromwell was Proclaimed Lord Protector of the Commonwealth of England, Scotland and Ireland* (London, 1659), Diurnal, Thursday 17 February 1658, Warwick County, 41.

[36] *Ibid.*, Diurnal, Monday 11 October 1658, Worcester County, 41.

[37] *Ibid.*, Diurnal, Thursday 23 September [1657], Officers of the Army in Ireland, 22.

[38] *Ibid.*, Diurnal, Thursday 18 November 1658, Berwick upon Tweed in Northumberland, and Diurnal, Monday 3 January [1659], Cumberland County, 49.

[39] *Ibid.*, Diurnal, Thursday 17 February 1658, Warwick County, 42.

son by referring to Elijah's mentorship of Elisha: "he [God] who hath raised his *Highness* [Richard] to sway the Scepter in his [Oliver's] stead, will cause both the *mantle and spirit of* their departed *Elijah, (even the chariots and horsemen in their Israel)* to rest upon his head, and heart, to guide and protect him in carrying on that blessed work of reformation so happily begun."[40] Indeed, the references to Elijah and Elisha are as numerous as the ones to Moses and Joshua. One particularly enthusiastic address combines both allusions with another to David and Solomon, a fortuitous reference since it offers an example of a nominative rather than a hereditary monarchy – though not his son, David succeeded Saul, bypassing Saul's eldest son.[41] The biblical references are so repetitive that the anti-Cromwellian author and compiler of the tract suggests that the addresses were "hatched at Court by the late Secretary *Thurloe,* and the old Malignant Pamphletter, . . . *Nedham.*"[42] The attempt to make Richard resemble his father can go to ridiculous, even blasphemous, lengths. The royalist Bishop Burnet reports an incident in which Cromwell's minister, Peter Sterry, implicitly compares Richard to God's divine son: "Sterry, praying for Richard, used these inde-cent words, next to blasphemy, *Make him the brightness of the father's glory, and the express image of his person.*"[43] In language straight out of Hebrews, Sterry broaches blasphemy by turning to that supreme father–son relation-ship, God and Christ. Perhaps the outrageousness of the claim was meant to compensate for how far Richard fell short of his father.

Richard was unfavorably compared to his younger brother as well as to his sister Bridget, who was said to have their father's spirit. But Elizabeth was Oliver's favorite child. The closeness of the dates of Elizabeth's and Oliver's deaths means that Richard would also be compared to his gentle sister, a comparison implicit in Marvell's "A Poem upon the Death of O. C." While "An Horation Ode" represents Oliver as a singular, even natural force, without family origins, "A Poem" is remarkably attentive to Cromwell's family relationships. Aside from the last twenty lines on Richard, the first section concentrates on Elizabeth, who is Oliver's kindred soul, "with Smiles serene and Words discreet / His hidden Soul at ev'ry turn could meet" (lines 41–42). The poem declares Elizabeth's closeness to Oliver while it can only surmise that Richard will resemble his father. Marvell uses the image of Oliver as the parent tree in relation to Elizabeth in an unexpected way. Instead of Richard the young olive tree replacing the old dead Oliver, Oliver is the grieving vine, who dies when his child dies: "If some dear

[40] *Ibid.*, Diurnal, Thursday 10 February [1657], Churches of Baptized Persons, 27.
[41] *Ibid.*, Diurnal, Monday 3 January 1658, Norwich, 29.
[42] *Ibid.*, 53.   [43] Burnet, *Burnet's History*, 1:148.

branch where it extends its life / Chance to be prun'd by an untimely knife, / The Parent-Tree unto the Grief succeeds, / And through the Wound its vital humour bleeds" (lines 93–96). Given the attention the poem lavishes on Elizabeth, the section on Richard can seem almost perfunctory. Hence, perhaps, the detached quality of the section on Richard, as if it were an afterthought. The section on Elizabeth, in contrast, is integral to the poem's depiction of Oliver's character. It may be suggestive that Marvell calls her "Eliza," recalling a prior English monarch, rather than the name by which she was commonly referred to, Betty. On balance, Richard seems far less his father's son than Elizabeth her father's child.

There are dangers in seeing family resemblance. Marvell's "A Poem" may end up praising Elizabeth over Richard. Sterry can slip into blasphemy. Richard may not turn out to be Joshua or Elisha. His term as protector lasted only months. After abdicating he had to hide in Westminster to avoid his creditors, and he ended up spending much of his life in exile. Striving to mold Richard in the image of his father, the various eulogies of Oliver and encomiums of Richard express equal parts of hope and fear.

GHOSTLY CROMWELLS: ANTI-CROMWELLIAN SATIRE

Cromwell continued to be abused in satirical tracts even after his death.[44] Once dead he was repeatedly resurrected in royalist satires to appear in hell or to walk on earth as a ghost. The ghostly presence of Cromwell in the pamphlet literature speaks to the persistent hold Oliver's memory had on the national imagination. While friends mourned his death, royalist enemies found that his long-wished-for death did not result immediately in the monarchy's return. To their disappointment, the transfer of power to Richard was uneventful. Efforts to discredit the new government had to continue. But even with the restoration of the monarchy, when there was less of a need for a pamphlet war, Cromwell remained a popular subject for royalist mockery.

Although in part a celebration of his death, these satires also indicate a psychic need to come to terms with the memory of a man who did the unthinkable in bringing down the monarchy and to render him harmless through satire. Many such satires associate Oliver (and his confederates) with hellishness and portray him getting punished in hell. From 1659 on, the trope of Cromwell in hell was a common one in royalist satires,

[44] For representations of Cromwell in the popular press through his career, see Laura Lunger Knoppers, *Constructing Cromwell: Ceremony, Portrait and Print, 1645–1661* (Cambridge: Cambridge University Press, 2000).

which represented Oliver as alternately monstrous and comical. The opening scene of *Hell's Higher Court of Justice* (April 1661), a monologue by the ghost of Machiavelli, plays on the common association of Cromwell with Machiavellian deception. Ultimately, the tracts reveal the monster to be toothless when Cromwell is powerless to command even his own redcoats in hell. Royalist satires vary in their presentation of the power-hungry Cromwell. Sometimes he is contrite about his past misdeeds. Other times he boastfully enumerates his crimes. In the latter case, the tone is often at odds with the description of his acts as wrongs. There are also instances where the ghost of Charles I makes an appearance. In *A Dialogue Betwixt the Ghosts of Charles I, Late King of England: and Oliver* (June 1659), for instance, Cromwell confesses his villainy to Charles I. He is even contrite, accusing himself of making "horrid and damnable contrivances."[45] In Marchamont Nedham's *A New Conference Between the Ghosts of King Charles and Oliver Cromwell* (June 1659),[46] on the other hand, the ghost of Oliver brazenly declares his wickedness to the ghost of Charles I. Either way, the satiric tracts serve as a catalog, and sometimes history, of Cromwell's rule.

After his death, royalist satires not only exploited the figure of Cromwell's ghost for their polemical purposes, but they also specifically attacked his fatherhood. For royalists, it is a mockery of the king as true father of the people; for republicans, Cromwell failed to reform fatherly political authority. The Protectorate's return to the traditional conception of fatherly political authority is evident in the conventional family tropes in a eulogy such as the funeral sermon for Cromwell in Ireland: Cromwell is *"Pater Patriae,* a common Father, carefull to protect and provide for all, especially for those of the Houshold of Faith," *"a Nursing Father, Isa.*49. 23. to carry them in his Bosome," and "such a Friend, such a Father."[47] This eulogy idealizes Cromwell as the traditional, monarchical *pater patriae*, and ultimate, albeit benevolent, authority. But the metaphor has to bear a double weight since Richard too has to demonstrate fatherly authority.

Richard's failure makes Oliver's fatherhood suspect, and the father–son relationship becomes an obvious target of attack by royalists. Deriding

---

45 *A Dialogue Betwixt the Ghosts of Charles I, Late King of England: and Oliver, The late Usurping Protector* (London, June 1659), 7.

46 Adam Wood [Marchamont Nedham], *A New Conference Between the Ghosts of King Charles and Oliver Cromwell* (London, 1659).

47 O. Whitbie, *Threni Hybernici: Or, Ireland Symphathising with England and Scotland, In a sad Lamentation for loss of their Josiah. Presented in a Sermon at Christ-Church in Dublin, before his Excellency the Lord Deputy, with divers of the Nobility, Gentry, and Commonalty, there Assembled, to Celebrate a Funerall Solemnity, upon the death of the late Lord Protector* (London, 1659), sig. B3, 5.

Cromwell's biological fatherhood, royalists call his political authority into question and cast doubt on the political authority of the Protectorate. Royalist satires judge the success of Cromwell's rule on its longevity, and they closely associate Oliver's rule with that of his son Richard. Oliver's rule is judged a failure because Richard is quickly overthrown. In Nedham's *A New Conference*, midway through Oliver's boastful account of his acts, Richard's Genius interrupts to tell him that Richard has lost everything. Charles gets the last laugh now that Oliver gets his just deserts. Strangely enough, Oliver is not overly perturbed by the news because he goes on to finish his speech about what he did to gain power, perhaps because the primary object of the tract is to recount his misdeeds. Nonetheless, it is striking that Oliver has little sympathy for Richard: "I ventured Body and Soul to get three Dominions, to leave him Lord of, and he would not sell his to keep them; he is not to be pitied."[48] Oliver's attitude suggests either that Richard is so inept that no parent could feel much sympathy or, more damningly, that Oliver himself lacks parental concern.

Royalist tracts often portray Richard as a simpleton, or at least politically naïve, a striking contrast to the wily Oliver of these tracts. In Nedham's *A New Conference*, Oliver calls Richard "my simple Son *Dick*, who hath not the spirit of Government upon him."[49] Oliver's Machiavellian machinations come to naught because Richard is unable to inherit the empire that he built. Stressing Richard's failure, royalist satires focus on the issue of succession from the perspective of the traditional hereditary monarchy. Without sons to inherit, Oliver is unable to sustain a lasting empire. The ineptitude of his sons, particularly Richard, causes the downfall of the Cromwellian Protectorate. In *The Case is Altered; or, Dreadful news from Hell* (August 1660), Oliver and his wife themselves criticize Richard, lamenting at length over Richard's incompetence. Joan says, "*he knew no more how to govern them then did a dog*"; Noll concurs, "he had more mind to his Dogs and his Haucks, then he had to be a Tyrannical Protector, like me."[50] Richard lacks Oliver's qualities, his "devilish parts" and "devilish braines."[51] The failure of this transfer of power originates in a failure to transfer Oliver's character to his sons. Rather than govern, Richard prefers to hunt – like a cavalier, a comparison often made in the popular press. Satires of Richard

---

[48] Wood, p. 7.   [49] *Ibid.*, 6.

[50] *The Case is Altered; or, Dreadful news from Hell. In a discourse between the ghost of this grand Traytor and Tyrant Oliver Cromwel and Sir reverence my Lady Joan his wife, at their late meeting neer the Scaffold on Tower-hill. With His Epitaph written in hell, on all the grand Traytors, now in the Tower* (London, August 1660), sig. A4v, 8.

[51] *Ibid.*, sig. A4–A4v, 7–8.

also question Cromwell's fatherhood, and from it turn to question Richard's manliness. In *Fourty Four Queries to the Life of Queen Dick* (June, 1659), query 1 asks, "Whether *Richard Cromwell* was *Oliver's* Sonne, or no?"[52] As is obvious from the title, the tract impugns Richard's manhood as well as (implicitly) Cromwell's. For his inability to keep the crown is troped as a sexual lack, and he is mocked as a "queen." Query 8 asks, "Whether *R.C.* might not get favour amongst the Ladies, though he hath lost himself amongst the People, if he had but his Fathers *Long Instrument*?"[53] The jokes about Richard's sexual competence are framed in ways that take his political incompetence for granted. Doubts about Cromwellian fatherhood easily slide into jokes about virility and sexual performance. Because the Protectorate fails from lack of a viable heir, the satires condemn the tyrant Cromwell as both biological and political father.

At the same time, satirical pamphlets mock Cromwell's followers' pretensions to rule in his stead. In Marchamont Nedham's *A New Meeting of Ghosts at Tyburn* (March 1661), Henry Ireton claims Cromwell as "Father *Cromwell*." As his "right hand" and "chief contriver of the Kings death," Ireton was rewarded with Cromwell's daughter and a governorship in Ireland, for Ireton "was your only beloved Son in Law in whom you trusted all your secret Mackinations and wicked Contrivances, and had not I been fetcht away before you, no doubt but I had succeeded you; and exceeded you (if possible) in all your Villanies."[54] The tract insinuates that Cromwell institutes a familial bond in recognition of a spiritual kinship, or perhaps more accurately, political alliance. The language, imitating scriptural language describing God's relation to Christ, mocks the sham of the Protectorate, which royalists see as a deceitful imitation of the real thing. Ireton is the fake son of a fake king. Royalist satires were fairly astute about how the Protectorate became stymied by traditional notions of lineal succession. They recognized Ireton as someone who took after Cromwell and would have made a better protector if he had not died prematurely. They also recognized Cromwell's (or his council's) choice of Richard to succeed as an attempt to preserve primogeniture. In *A Parly between the Ghosts of the Late Protector and the King of Sweden* (May 1660) Cromwell's foreign ally, the King of Sweden, berates him for leaving his sons in charge: "Twas the

[52] *Fourty Four Queries To the Life of Queen Dick. By one who will at any time work a Job of Journey-Work To serve his Countrey* (London, June 1659), sig. A2, 3.
[53] *Ibid.*, sig. A2v, 4.
[54] Nedham, *A New Meeting of Ghosts at Tyburn. Being a Discourse of Oliver Cromwell, John Bradshaw, Henry Ireton, Thomas Pride, Thomas Scot, Secretary to the Rump, Major Gen. Harrison & Hugh Peters the Divells Chaplain* (London, March 1661), sig. A2v, 4.

well chosen, not the lineal Succession brought *Rome* to its greatnesse."[55]
Making the position of Lord Protector hereditary causes the dissolution
of the Protectorate. Sweden is probably referring to Imperial Rome, where
the emperors appointed their own successor, but the lesson would apply
equally to republican Rome. The Protectorate fell because of too close an
adherence to traditional forms.

While many of these tracts focus on Cromwell's lackluster progeny, *The
World in a Maize, or, Olivers Ghost* (May 1659) makes the relationship
between Oliver and Richard the subject of satire. Staging a dialogue between
Oliver and Richard, it parodies *Hamlet*. Instead of calling Richard to avenge
his wrongs, Oliver's ghost cross-examines his son about his conduct in the
government he left him. In this tract, Richard appears to have some mettle,
honor, and a sense of justice. Although Oliver scolds Richard for lack of
ambition and for letting the army overthrow him, Richard in turn chastises
his father for causing the people misery in getting his illegal power through
force, boldly asserting he would have done things differently: "I would have
set the Saddle upon the right horse, mistake me not you ghost, if you be
my fathers Ghost, I know not ye or no."[56] The suggestion seems to be that
Richard would have restored the king, and certainly the ghost thinks he
means Charles Stuart. But it turns out Richard is speaking on behalf of
the army. The concern about soldiers' pay suggests that the tract may have
been written by a disaffected Cromwellian like Sexby who perhaps allied
with royalists. By highlighting the ambiguity of Richard's words, the tract
suggests republicans and royalists can find common cause. Richard even
sounds somewhat sarcastic, challenging his father to "bring [him] into a
primuinry,"[57] that is, to bring a writ of praemunire against him. The irony
is that bringing a writ of praemunire is exactly what Cromwell had done to
the king, challenging the supremacy of the crown by appealing to a foreign
court (in that the higher court of justice was a new institution) to judge
Charles I.

The anti-Cromwellian *World in a Maize* also gives a new twist to the well-
worn subject of doubts about Oliver's fathering of Richard. Richard, like
Hamlet, is uncertain whether the ghost is his father's ghost. Having asked
the ghost a riddle that he does not solve correctly, Richard concludes that the
ghost is a devil: "Thou lyest, thou art some Fiend sent from Hell to disturb

---

[55] *A Parly Between the Ghosts of the Late Protector, and the King of Sweden, At their Meeting in Hell*
(London, 1660), 8.
[56] *The World in a Maize, or, Olivers Ghost* (London, May 1659), sig. A2v–A3, 4–5.
[57] *Ibid.*, sig. A3, 5.

my thought, / Who altered the Government of the Common-wealth."[58] But of course the bitter joke is that Cromwell did alter the government of the commonwealth and was a devil at least to his enemies. This short tract ends with Richard singing verses to a popular tune: "*I have sung my Ghost away Sirs, / Who ayms at a Crown, / Shall tumble down / I care not who bears sway Sirs.*"[59] Like Richard, who claims to have sung the ghost away, the pamphlet means to exorcise the ghost of Oliver Cromwell. The concluding line of this verse suggests indifference about the form of government but the refrain hints at something else: "Still did they cry bonny boys, bonny mad boys, / We should be ruled by Reason / If Reason say we, / Shall bear the sway, / I hope 'will be counted no Treason."[60] Who are "we"? Are the "bonny boys" the army? If so, the character Richard is made to speak, even sing, on behalf of the body instrumental in overthrowing him. There is a certain vagueness in the tract's polemic: concerned with the practical question of how the soldiers were treated, it has little to say about larger issues and nothing at all about who should take Cromwell's place if his ghost is rejected as a false father.

The attacks on Cromwell as father were attempts to undermine the legitimacy of the Protectorate by damaging its self-representation. The corollary to the intense focus on Cromwell's fatherhood was Richard's own lack of fatherly authority. Richard became the victim of other people's schemes, in stark contrast to Oliver's authoritative *pater patriae*, who not only laid down the law but also remade it. Anti-Cromwellian satires exposed the truth of Richard's Protectorate government, which fell because of power struggles among the various factions: the father was dead and what was left was sibling rivalry. Cromwellian brothers failed to reestablish the kingdom.

[58] *Ibid.*, sig. A3v, 6.   [59] *Ibid.*, sig. A4v, 8.   [60] *Ibid.*, sig. A4v, 8.

PART II

Restoration imaginings

Interchapter: revolutionary legacies

With the failure of the republican experiment, Charles II returned to near-universal acclaim. Yet, there was little agreement on what a king was. The Long Parliament, which met from February to March 1660, failed to settle on the form of civil government. When Charles landed at Dover on 25 May 1660, he was bound only by the vague 4 April *Declaration of Breda* with constitutional issues left unresolved. The question of royal prerogative and its limits continued to trouble relations between king and Parliament. Promising to govern through Parliament, Charles nonetheless held absolutist views on monarchical prerogative. In order to become independent of Parliament, Charles made secret agreements with France in return for subsidies. Both sides were far more wary of each other since the late civil wars: the one fearful of arbitrary government and the other afraid of popular rebellions. Still, unlike his father and his brother James later, who were both deposed, Charles II was an astute politician able to side-step potential crises.

The religious question also continued to haunt the Restoration. Again with no more than the *Declaration of Breda* as guide, the established church was restored on less than firm ground. Charles promised toleration and forgiveness, declaring "a liberty to tender consciences, and that no man shall be disquieted or called in question for differences of opinion in matters of religion which do not disturb the peace of the kingdom," though his toleration of nonconformity came from his desire to protect Catholics like his brother James.[1] Parliament, filled with Anglicans, felt differently, especially after the panic of Thomas Venner's 1661 Fifth Monarchist uprising. The restored government passed a series of severely restrictive acts to force a uniform church and an absolute crown, including the Corporation Act of 1661 ejecting those who are not royalists from town councils

---

[1] Andrew Browning, ed. *English Historical Documents 1660–1714* (London: Eyre & Spottiswoode, 1966), 58.

and other corporations; the Act of Uniformity of 1662 requiring clergy to adhere to Anglican rituals and beliefs, including the use of the Book of Common Prayer; the Press Act, also of 1662, reestablishing censorship of printed matter; the Conventicle Act of 1664 forbidding assemblies of more than four; and the Five Mile Act of 1665 reinforcing the earlier Uniformity Act and forcing on teachers an oath of passive obedience. These acts, and others, which came to be known as the Clarendon code, sought to reestablish the old hierarchies by greatly curtailing religious and political freedom. Even Presbyterians became defined as religious dissenters and were lumped together with sects thought to be more subversive such as the Quakers.

The intertwined political and religious conflicts that led to civil war were rehearsed in the Restoration to be resolved only with the Glorious Revolution. With continued instability, Charles II's Restoration did not put an end to ideological uses of family metaphors. Jonathan Sawday argues that through the spring and summer of 1660 the Restoration came to be "transformed into a marriage ceremony with Charles in the role of the bridegroom, and England in the role of the bride – an iconography which carries with it triumphal scriptural echoes."[2] Charles was also piously greeted as father of his country, sometimes by the same poets who praised Cromwell as *pater patriae*. As the previous chapter suggests, the Cromwellian Protectorate initiated the return to traditional forms of family. Poets who praised Cromwell turned to praise Charles II in much the same terms: Edmund Waller reworked his *Panegyrick to my Lord Protector* into a poem to Charles, *To the King, upon his Majesties Happy Return*. David Norbrook notes, "It was difficult to restore a Stuart Augustanism without reviving memories of Cromwellian Augustanism."[3] Royalists readily turned to the figure of the father to depict monarchical power, greeting the king as the return of the rightful father, as in *To the Kings Most Excellent Majesty* (1664): he is a "lawful Steward" climbing "The Widowed Throne; and in this Orphan-land, / Restor'd the Father's Soveraign Command."[4] The poem celebrates the father-king in order to assert hereditary succession. The usurper ejected, the state can reconstitute itself once more as a proper family.

Even so, anti-patriarchalist, even anti-monarchist, uses of family metaphors did not disappear. The title of father of his country was also

---

[2] Jonathan Sawday, "Re-Writing a Revolution: History, Symbol, and Text in the Restoration," *The Seventeenth Century* 7 (1992), 181.

[3] David Norbrook, *Writing the English Republic: Poetry, Rhetoric and Politics, 1627–1660* (Cambridge: Cambridge University Press, 1999), 427.

[4] *To the Kings Most Excellent Majesty. The Humble Petitionary Poem of Edmond Dillon* (London, 1664), sig. A4.

used to mock Charles: "The truest *Pater Patriae* e're was yet, / For all, or most of's subjects, does beget."[5] Stuart patriarchalism traces a direct lineal descent from Adam to the present monarch. The satire shifts the literalizing of family metaphors into contemporary times to expose Charles's shameless fathering of bastards and the sexual license of the court. While Charles sired many children, of whom he acknowledged fourteen, none were by his queen. The royal marriage was a barren one. Moreover, Charles openly flaunted his numerous mistresses. His natural body would be so much in the public eye that political affairs would come to be intertwined in the public imagination with the sexual misconduct of the king himself.[6] The proliferation of "porno-political" literature signals the monarchy's crisis of representation. This crisis centers around the frail, mortal body of the king, a body embarrassed by the public execution of Charles I and Charles II's promiscuity.[7]

The debate over political patriarchalism reignited with particular vigor in the Exclusion Crisis when Ashley Cooper, Earl of Shaftesbury and his followers attempted to exclude the Catholic James, Duke of York, from the succession, promoting instead the king's illegitimate son, James Scott, the Duke of Monmouth. Family metaphors had particular resonance in what was essentially a family quarrel. Tory supporters of Charles reprinted Sir Robert Filmer's *Patriarcha* to uphold the king's absolute prerogative and to defend James's succession. In response, several Whigs wrote tracts disputing political patriarchalism, such as James Tyrell's *Patriarcha non monarcha* (1681). The debate was conducted not only in controversial pamphlets but also in literary genres. Presenting the king's case in *Absalom and Achitophel* (1681), Dryden, a client of the Duke of York, tried to influence the verdict of the grand jury called to indict Shaftesbury, who was sent to the Tower of London for high treason. In contrast, Nathaniel Lee's *Lucius Junius Brutus* (1681) portrays the overthrow of the tyrant Tarquin to make the republican argument for constitutional limits on monarchy. Together they demonstrate the continuing vitality of family metaphors in Restoration political discourse.

---

[5] *A Satyr upon the Mistresses*, in J. W. Ebsworth, ed., *The Roxburghe Ballads*, vol. v (Hertford: S. Austin & Sons, 1885), 130, lines 16–17.

[6] For the Restoration connection between politics and sex, see Steven N. Zwicker, "Virgins and Whores: The Politics of Sexual Misconduct in the 1660s," in Conal Condren and A. D. Cousins, eds., *The Political Identity of Andrew Marvell* (Aldershot: Scolar Press; Brookfield, Vt.: Gower Publishing, 1990), 85–110; and James Grantham Turner, *Libertines and Radicals in Early Modern London: Sexuality, Politics, and Literary Culture, 1630–1685* (Cambridge: Cambridge University Press, 2002).

[7] Paul Hammond, "The King's Two Bodies: Representations of Charles II," in Jeremy Black and Jeremy Gregory, eds., *Culture, Politics and Society in Britain, 1660–1800* (Manchester: Manchester University Press, 1991), 13–48.

Dryden's *Absalom and Achitophel* casts the actors of the Exclusion Crisis as characters in the biblical story of Absalom's rebellion against King David. Comparisons between Charles and David were common.[8] Moreover, an earlier Tory poem, *A Dialogue Between Nathan and Absalom* (1680) had linked Monmouth to Absalom.[9] Dryden portrays Charles II as a sexual father-king, whose fecundity expresses his generosity as king and as father: "Israel's monarch after Heaven's own heart, / His vigorous warmth did variously impart / To wives and slaves; and, wide as his command, / Scattered his Maker's image through the land" (lines 7–10).[10] Set in ancient Israel, the poem shields Charles from the charge of promiscuity by naturalizing it, making his polygamous alliances serve the public good. This past allows for an imagined space where the sexual father is graced by God, his fecundity an imitation of the heavenly Father's creative productiveness, and his sexual expansiveness piety itself. The institution of monogamy becomes instead the fallen state. Dryden slyly winks at Charles's promiscuousness, for, by pointing at Monmouth's bastard status to defend James's succession, he calls attention to Charles's failure to provide a legitimate heir.

Portraying David/Charles as benevolent and mild, Dryden highlights the unnaturalness of a son rebelling against his father. Yet Absalom/Monmouth is simply deluded by Achitophel/Shaftesbury's constitutionalist rhetoric. Absalom is at first doubtful: "And what pretense have I / To take up arms for public liberty? / My father governs with unquestioned right" (lines 315–17). True right is the king's and connected, even if allusively, to David's paternity. But Achitophel convinces him of the superiority of a constitutional or limited monarchy: "And nobler is a limited command, / Given by the love of all your native land, / Than a successive title, long and dark, / Drawn from the moldy rolls of Noah's ark" (lines 299–302). With hereditary succession associated with antiquated tradition, royal authority rests instead on the people's election. However, the people are "a headstrong, moody, murmuring race" (line 45). This unruly mob act without precedent, dangerously plotting "To raise up commonwealths and ruin kings" (line 84). Hence, Absalom cannot reign secure. Moreover, Achitophel's motives are impure. The cry for the people's liberty conceals his devious ambitions: "Not that he [Achitophel] wished his [Absalom's] greatness to create / . . . /

[8] R. F. Jones, "The Originality of *Absalom and Achitophel*," *Modern Language Notes* 46 (1931), 211–18.
[9] Howard H. Schless, "Dryden's *Absalom and Achitophel* and *A Dialogue between Nathan and Absalom*," *Philological Quarterly* 40 (1961), 139–43.
[10] John Dryden, *The Works of John Dryden*, vol. II: Poems, 1681–1684, ed. H. T. Swedenberg, Jr. (Berkeley: University of California Press, 1972). References are given parenthetically and cited by line numbers.

But, for he knew his title not allowed, / Would keep him still depending on the crowd, / That kingly power, thus ebbing out, might be / Drawn to the dregs of a democracy" (lines 222–27). Knowing that Absalom's rebellion is illegal, Achitophel aims at bringing down the state. Constitutional monarchy is only a step toward democracy. A covert republican, Achitophel raises the specter of civil war.

Despite his criticism of popular sovereignty, Dryden does not argue for monarchical authority from paternity. And this despite his making David's paternity fundamental to monarchical identity. Instead, the state is founded on a prior social contract: "If those who gave the scepter could not tie / By their own deed their own posterity, / How then could Adam bind his future race? / How could his forfeit on mankind take place?" (lines 769–72). While the people consented to be governed, this social contract is Hobbesian in making the transfer of power permanent. Its permanence safeguards private property: "For who can be secure of private right, / If sovereign sway may be dissolved by might?" (lines 779–80). On this point, Dryden's social contract differs significantly from that of his contemporary John Locke, whose *Two Treatises* (1681) promotes the Exclusion Bill on behalf of his patron the Earl of Shaftesbury.[11] Dryden's position is neither wholly contractual nor completely patriarchist. Fathers bind their posterity in a contract not of their own making. The king's role oscillates between father and monarch. Given the last word, David suddenly appears at the end, like a *deus ex machina*, to obliterate his opponents with a long speech. His godlike pronouncements, "by Heaven inspired" (936), gives the impression of an absolute father-king, whose wrath is mitigated by a paternal mercy: "So much the father did the king assuage" (line 942). Yet, Dryden may be ironizing David in his parallel between the Sanhedrin/Parliament's deceit and Jacob's: "True, they petition me to approve their choice; / But Esau's hands suit ill with Jacob's voice" (lines 981–82). Dryden perhaps intended an allusion that contradicts his narrator: violently yoking trope to the thing, he ignores its absurdity or abitrariness to throw himself "into the *fiction* of the divinity of order."[12] Harder to sustain in the Restoration, the political myth of the father-king is useful fiction that must somehow be maintained. Irony, particularly in the portrayal of David as sexual father, measures the gap between belief and doubt.

[11] For a comparison of Dryden and Locke in the Exclusion Crisis, see Steven N. Zwicker, *Lines of Authority: Politics and English Literary Culture, 1649–1689* (Ithaca: Cornell University Press, 1993), chapter 5, "Paternity, Patriarchy, and the 'Noise of Divine Right': *Absalom and Achitophel* and *Two Treatises of Government.*"

[12] David Gelineau, "Allusion, Legitimacy, and Succession: Milton's Hands Suit Ill with Dryden's Voice," *The Eighteenth Century: Theory and Interpretation* 35.1 (1994), 38.

While David's sexual virility is virtuous in Dryden, an excess of desire undoes monarchy in Nathaniel Lee's *Lucius Junius Brutus*. One of Dryden's collaborators – they wrote an adaptation of *Oedipus* (1678) and *The Duke of Guise* (1683) – Lee had an anti-monarchist past. His father, Dr. Richard Lee, was a Presbyterian minister, rector of Hatfield, who held preferments in the Commonwealth, but after the Restoration, as chaplain to General Monck, conformed to the Church of England. The play is a Whiggish dramatization of the rape of Lucretia (Lucrece in the play) from Livy, a *locus classicus* for republicanism, for Livy identifies her rape as the event triggering the tyrant Tarquin's overthrow.[13] Performed in 1680 and published in 1681, the play, with the subtitle *Father of His Country*, comments also on the Exclusion Crisis. Lee takes the classicizing mode of Stuart Augustanism and makes it republican.

Lee's Brutus is a committed republican even though as ruler his primary identification is as father. In recognition of his virtue, Brutus is hailed as "father and redeemer of thy country" (2.243).[14] This salutation emphasizes his role as "redeemer," linking him to republican Cicero rather than the imperial *pater patriae*. The people praise him as "Deliverer of lost Rome! Shield of the commonwealth and sword of justice! / Hail, scourge of tyrants, lash for lawless kings!" (3.1.39–41). Brutus liberates the people to give them "free government, / Where every man is master of his own, / Sole lord at home, and monarch of his house" (3.2.59–61). While a tyrannical king enslaves his people, a republican father makes them kings. Taking the people seriously, the play argues that the "people's law [is] . . . better than the arbitrary power of kings" (2.120–22). Although the people act like a mob, trying and punishing the king's courtiers, the courtiers well deserve their rough justice. One courtier, Fabritius, formerly the queen's coachman, is exposed as a destroyer of families. He purchases his knightly rank with such impious misdeeds as driving the queen's "chariot over her father's body" (2.79) and seducing citizens' wives and daughters for the king's sons. The monarchy itself destroys families. Brutus tells the people that Tarquin's deed is "a plot upon yourselves, your persons, families, and your relations; even to your wives, mothers, sisters, all your kindred" (1.186–88).

---

[13] For the argument that the play was not pro-Whig, see Antony Hammond, "The 'Greatest Action': Lee's *Lucius Junius Brutus*," in Antony Coleman and Antony Hammond, eds., *Poetry and Drama 1500–1700: Essays in Honour of Harold F. Brooks* (London: Methuen, 1981); and Victoria Hayne, "'All Language Then is Vile': The Theatrical Critique of Political Rhetoric in Nathaniel Lee's *Lucius Junius Brutus*," *ELH* 63 (1996), 337–65.

[14] Nathaniel Lee, *Lucius Junius Brutus*, ed. John Loftis (Lincoln: University of Nebraska Press, 1967). References are given parenthetically.

Like Dryden, Lee focuses on the relationship between father and son. While Brutus prepares to banish the Tarquins, his son Titus is in love with Teraminta, a Tarquin. Brutus's struggle for the liberty of Rome becomes also a struggle for his son's heart, a parallel that he makes explicit: he will "tug with Teraminta for thy heart / As I have done for Rome" (2.339–40). His concern for Titus makes him "Not Roman Brutus but a father now" (1.1.240). But Brutus' republican principles overrule his fatherly emotions. He banishes Collatinus, husband to his daughter Lucrece, because he cannot allow "The name of king . . . [to] light upon a Tarquin" (3.1.66). When his own son Tiberius is named "king of sacrifices" after Brutus denies it to Collatinus, he refuses to let Tiberius accept: he "would have none of Brutus' blood / Pretend to be a king" (3.1.152–53). Even the virtuous Titus is sacrificed to the republic. While Tiberius and Brutus' other sons turn out to be monarchists, Titus only subscribed to the king's party to save Teraminta's life. Learning this, Brutus forgives Titus but nonetheless proceeds with his execution to "show the difference betwixt the sway / Of partial tyrants and of a freeborn people" (5.2.43–44). Driven by duty, Brutus is emotionally controlled, even merciless. As father of his country, Lee's Brutus is the polar opposite of Dryden's David.

These works demonstrate the range possible in uses of family tropes. While the Restoration appeared to be a complete victory for the king, even pro-Stuart panegyrists revealed acute awareness of the "undeniably secular basis of and consequent limits to royal power" such that "Alongside celebrations of the benefits of monarchy, the debate over liberty continued."[15] Richard Greaves's three-volume study of radical dissent during the Stuart regime amply records the extent of the opposition: far from chastened into quietism, radical nonconformists simply went underground.[16] Traditional literary history, however, occludes the radical, republican, and nonconformist strands of the Restoration. It treats the period after 1660 as the beginning of the long eighteenth century as though the Restoration signified a complete break. Authors who shifted allegiances from Cromwell to Charles II, like Dryden, aided the writing of this history when they tried to bury their anti-monarchist past. In fact, authors, both royalists and radicals, who wrote in the 1650s continued to do so later, including

[15] Gerald M. MacLean, *Time's Witness: Historical Representation in English Poetry, 1603–1660* (Madison: University of Wisconsin Press, 1990), 264.
[16] Richard L. Greaves, *Deliver Us from Evil: The Radical Underground in Britain, 1660–1663* (New York: Oxford University Press, 1986), *Enemies under his Feet: Radicals and Nonconformists in Britain, 1664–1677* (Stanford: Stanford University Press, 1990), and *Secrets of the Kingdom: British Radicals from the Popish Plot to the Revolution of 1688–1689* (Stanford: Stanford University Press, 1992).

Abraham Cowley, Katherine Phillips, Margaret Cavendish, George Wither, Andrew Marvell, and, preeminently, John Milton.

This history highlights certain literary modes and elides others. In order to maintain the idea of the Restoration as a cultural break, traditional literary history locates Milton in an earlier Renaissance culture and obscures the fact that his major poetic works were written and published in the Restoration. Milton's biblical epics with their emphasis on sin and redemption – even his tragedy *Samson Agonistes* is based on scripture and has similar themes – did not fit the conventional image of Restoration literature as neoclassical, balanced, and cosmopolitan. What dominated was courtly taste, at once imperial in the public mode of Dryden, its foremost poet, and debauched in the coterie voice of the pornographic Earl of Rochester. The Restoration's other name, the Augustan age, suggests the influence of the writers of Augustus Caesar's reign – Virgil, Horace, and Ovid – and recalled Restoration England and Augustan Rome's analogous position of having emerged from civil wars. The celebration of Charles II as Augustus repudiated puritan literary culture, despite its continuing vitality. Neil Keeble's seminal work uncovering the vast body of nonconformist writings suggests that puritanism's "political defeat was the condition of cultural achievement."[17] This rich cultural achievement indicates a continuing, if evolving, puritan culture between the first half and the second half of the seventeenth century.

Reading Milton or John Bunyan as part of Restoration culture makes visible a broader literary culture of dissent. Instead of simply withdrawing, dissenters in the radical underground continued to agitate, to write, and to pray for their beliefs. Nonconformist writings have been viewed as expressions of quiescence and political withdrawal into a "paradise within," as some critics of Milton suggest.[18] Other critics, however, argue for Milton's and other dissenters' continued political engagement.[19] Returning *Paradise Lost* to its original revolutionary context (two-fifths of the epic were composed before the return of the king), David Norbrook denies that the poem is

[17] N. H. Keeble, *The Literary Culture of Nonconformity in Later Seventeenth-Century England* (Athens: University of Georgia Press, 1987), 22.

[18] Blair Worden, "Milton's Republicanism and the Tyranny of Heaven," in Gisela Bock, Quentin Skinner, and Maurizio Viroli, eds., *Machiavelli and Republicanism* (Cambridge: Cambridge University Press, 1990), 244; Mary Ann Radzinowicz, *Toward* Samson Agonistes: *The Growth of Milton's Mind* (Princeton: Princeton University Press, 1978), 108.

[19] Christopher Hill, *Milton and the English Revolution* (New York: Viking Press, 1977), and *The Experience of Defeat: Milton and Some Contemporaries* (New York: Viking Press, 1984); John P. Rumrich, *Milton Unbound: Controversy and Reinterpretation* (Cambridge: Cambridge University Press, 1996); and Laura Lunger Knoppers, *Historicizing Milton: Spectacle, Power, and Poetry in Restoration England* (Athens: University of Georgia Press, 1994).

defeatist and places Milton amidst a host of oppositional voices like George Sikes, George Wither, Andrew Marvell, and Richard Overton.[20] In her study of dissenting literature as "politically motivated," Sharon Achinstein "explores how the discourse of charismatic authority, and its opposite, the self-disciplined political subject, registered an important engagement with the complex political consequences of religious radicalism."[21] The poetics of withdrawal can have a revolutionary thrust.

Reading for radicalism, the last three chapters of this study focus on Restoration authors outside the hegemonic culture. Family metaphors circulated not just in wider national debates but also in counterdiscourses, which reinterpreted family metaphors to give them more egalitarian or radical meanings. Having to define themselves outside the mainstream, such authors turned to the still dominant language of family to define their separate identities. Thus family remained a productive language of political, social, and religious experiment. What appears to be withdrawal was instead a reimagination of alternative communities. Furthermore, while courtly culture was misogynistic, women played a larger role in marginalized communities. Even the strongly paternalistic republicanism of Lee's *Lucius Junius Brutus* acknowledges women's importance in defining citizenship while Dryden's *Absalom and Achitophel* includes no significant part for women. The civil wars gave women greater opportunity to participate in political and religious life. In the 1640s, women were involved in enclosure and fen riots, demonstrated in London, and petitioned Parliament; they numbered among the Levellers seeking social and economic justice.[22] Keith Thomas suggests that women were also numerically prominent in the separatist churches, playing a disproportionate role, as religious authority was a means by which women could challenge patriarchy.[23] Along with the democratization of gender relations, the English Revolution produced figurations of family with more significant roles for women and for wives.

[20] Norbrook, *Writing the English Republic*, 435–36.
[21] Sharon Achinstein, *Literature and Dissent in Milton's England* (Cambridge: Cambridge University Press, 2003), 11, 21.
[22] Patricia Higgins, "The Reactions of Women, with Special Reference to Women Petitioners," in Brian Manning, ed., *Politics, Religion and the English Civil War* (London: Edward Arnold, 1973), 179–222; and Ann Marie McEntee, "'The [Un]Civill-Sisterhood of Oranges and Lemons': Female Petitioners and Demonstrators, 1642–53," in James Holstun, ed., *Pamphlet Wars: Prose in the English Revolution* (London: F. Cass, 1992), 92–111.
[23] Keith V. Thomas, "Women and the Civil War Sects," *Past and Present* 13 (1958), 42–62. See also Patricia Crawford, "Historians, Women and the Civil War Sects, 1640–1660," in *Rulers, Religion and Rhetoric in Early Modern England: A Festschrift for Geoffrey Elton from his Australasian Friends* (Sydney: Parergon, 1988), 19–32; and Claire Cross, "'He-goats before the Flocks': A Note on the Part Played by Women in the Founding of Some Civil War Churches," *Studies in Church History* 8 (1972), 195–202.

Deployed in assaults on the monarchy that helped break down traditional society, the family metaphor also forged new communities. The contestation over family metaphors was national and local. In its local manifestations, family tropes constituted communities contiguous or even opposed to the nation. A complete account of the family metaphor must examine its uses in separate communities. The next chapters address how various marginalized authors developed communal identities separate from, though still in dialogue with, national culture. While Milton, part of a resistant republican culture, remains fully engaged with the larger debates over family and state, Margaret Cavendish, sidelined by her gender and her affiliations with feminized old Cavaliers, offers a more covert critique of monarchy. Finally, the Quakers, forming a separatist family of dissenters, rearticulated national concerns within the boundaries of their peculiar community. In reimagining community distinct from mainstream Restoration culture, these authors meditate on the gender implications of the family metaphor to expose the conflict of authority inherent in patriarchalism.

CHAPTER 5

Execrable sons and second Adams: family politics in Paradise Lost

GENESIS, *PARADISE LOST*, AND PATRIARCHAL THEORIES OF THE STATE

In the first invocation of *Paradise Lost*, the narrator asks his Heavenly muse what caused the fall, what "Mov'd our Grand Parents in that happy State, / Favour'd of Heav'n so highly, to fall off / From thir Creator" (1.29–31).[1] The language of "Grand Parents" and "happy State" is reminiscent of patriarchal political theory. Beyond the familial language, the epic poem also reexamines the original social compact. In its reworking of family metaphors in the context of Genesis, *Paradise Lost* can be compared to a number of major works of political philosophy in the period. Given that the story of the fall is an aetiology of human society, Genesis was remarkably resonant for family-based politics in the seventeenth century. Mary Ann Radzinowicz suggests that the Genesis story can be contrasted with the myth of Utopia, another garden state: "in Milton's day utopia seldom was, whereas the Genesis myth not only could be but repeatedly was, made to argue social and political reform."[2] But these two myths tend to inhabit different genres of writing. Even when not arguing directly for reform, utopias are often political theory in the form of fiction, while arguments for political reform using Genesis tend to be biblical exegesis. Milton combines utopia with Genesis to address fundamental questions of political obligation.

The language of family in *Paradise Lost* is not accidental. Having had to confront the family analogy in the regicide tracts, Milton continues in *Paradise Lost* to grapple with this important strand of political debate. While his biblical original supplies some of the rationale for presenting the

---

[1] Roy Flannagan, ed., *The Riverside Milton* (Boston and New York: Houghton Mifflin, 1998). All references to *Paradise Lost* are from this edition and cited parenthetically.

[2] Mary Ann Radzinowicz, "The Politics of *Paradise Lost*," in Kevin Sharpe and Steven N. Zwicker, eds., *Politics of Discourse: The Literature and History of Seventeenth-Century England* (Berkeley: University of California Press, 1987), 218.

143

relations in familial terms, he emphasizes family and expands on its scope in his elaboration of Genesis: much of the exploration of the relationship between God and the Son is not biblical. Since the language of family already has political meaning for his contemporaries, by using this language Milton can subtly present his arguments for reorganizing state and society, even arguments against the Stuart monarchy.

The most trenchant statement of patriarchal theory of the state, Sir Robert Filmer's *Patriarcha*, unabashedly uses Genesis to make its claims for the authority of the father: "creation made man prince of his posterity. And indeed not only Adam but the succeeding patriarchs had, by right of fatherhood, royal authority over their children."[3] A political philosophy based on biblical exegesis, Filmer's argument derives power not only from the authority of the Bible but also from his claim to go back to the very beginning of human society. Considered a historical method, biblical exegesis is favored also by Milton, whose writings are so peppered with quotations from the Bible that in many pamphlets they overwhelm his prose. Other political philosophers who engaged with the issue of family-based politics also turned to Genesis. John Locke, for instance, rebuts Filmer by reinterpreting Genesis in his *Two Treatises of Government*, as I will discuss in the epilogue. Although not primarily an exegesis of the Bible, Thomas Hobbes's postulation of a state of nature too owes something to Genesis and its myth of origins. It is probably no coincidence that Milton compares the defeated Satan in Book I to the mythical beast from the Book of Job, Leviathan (1.201), whose name served as the title of Hobbes's infamous work: Milton may be critiquing Hobbes's revision of the nature of creation.

As a political theorist, Milton is not theoretical and abstract, basing his arguments on history instead.[4] He shares with Filmer an interest in exploring the role of parents in relation to government, but he comes to radically different conclusions. As in the prose pamphlets, Milton reworks Stuart family metaphors to present a radical, republican political philosophy. While Filmer uses the story of Genesis to conflate fatherhood and monarchy, Milton denies Adam a greater status. Through the fall, Adam is "brought down / To dwell on eeven ground now with [his] Sons" (11.347–48). Moreover, there is no suggestion that the prelapsarian Adam would be made king. Monarchy is reserved only for God. Breaking the link between

---

[3] Robert Filmer, *Patriarcha*, in Johann P. Sommerville, ed., *Patriarcha and Other Writings* (Cambridge: Cambridge University Press, 1991), 6.

[4] For Milton's relation to history, see David Loewenstein, *Milton and the Drama of History: Historical Vision, Iconoclasm, and the Literary Imagination* (Cambridge: Cambridge University Press, 1990).

father and king, Milton reinterprets the account of the first human state. Reading *Paradise Lost* in the context of the tradition of patriarchal political thought makes it evident how Milton continued to engage Stuart family politics in the Restoration.

THE DIVINE FAMILY CIRCLE

In *Paradise Lost*, as in Milton's polemical tracts, society is understood in terms of family. In Heaven, the Messiah is referred to as the Son and defined by his familial relation to God the Father. In many ways, this is also true of the other figures in *Paradise Lost*. Although God's creation of angels is not depicted, it is significant that Satan raises doubts about God's paternity to justify the rebellion, making it a denial of family relations. God, in contrast, affirms family ties, calling the unfallen angels "my Sons / Invincible" (6.46–47). Before the rebellion, the angels are united in worshipping God "as sons of one great Sire / Hymning th' Eternal Father" (6.95–96). While the Messiah has a special position as God's "onely Son" (5.603) and his "begotten Son" (5.835, 7.163), all of creation is arguably God's family. The Son himself refers to Adam as God's "youngest Son" (3.151). After the fall, when God clothes the guilty Adam and Eve, he does so "As Father of his Family" (10.213).

The familial structure of society is extended into the human and the postlapsarian world. Even before the fall, Adam and Eve are known as parents to the human race: they are "our first Parents" (4.6); Adam is "our general Sire" (4.144) and "Patriarch of Mankind" (5.506) and Eve our "general Mother" (4.492). God himself, when leading the new-born Eve back to Adam, tells her that she "to him [Adam] shalt beare / Multitudes like thy self, and thence be call'd / Mother of the human Race" (4.473–75). These parental titles are repeated and emphasized though we see Adam and Eve in the role of spouses. After the fall, in Michael's vision, the whole world is depicted as a family. Lamenting the murderous impulses of men, Adam exclaims, "for of whom such massacher / Make they but of thir Brethren, men of men?" (11.679–80). The relation between men is fraternal while human history is a tragic family history of fratricide, bad marriages, and sons dishonoring fathers.

The "execrable son" of my title is Nimrod from Book 12. The episode recounting Nimrod's establishment of the first empire and the building of the tower of Babel and its subsequent dissolution has been identified as Milton's clearest expression of republicanism in *Paradise Lost*. Milton portrays the establishment of a king as the destruction of the peace and order of a people who have dwelled "Long time in peace by Families and Tribes / Under paternal rule" (12.23–24). Nimrod destroys a peaceful republic to erect a monarchy: "not content / With fair equalitie, fraternal state" (12.25–26), he replaces a state of equal brothers with a tyrannical kingship. That this tranquil world, which Nimrod overturns, is characterized by "paternal rule" may seem antithetical to a "fraternal state," but it is not inherently contradictory for a republican state to be also one where fathers rule households. While the relation of citizens, understood as male, to each other is fraternal, their relation to others (women, children and servants in the household) is paternal. Another instance of how Milton adapts the family metaphor to give it a radical meaning, this passage makes it very clear that paternal rule is not the same as rule by a king. It goes further than Milton's reversal of the analogy linking king and father in the *First Defence*, in which he makes the people parents to the king. Here Milton denies that the relation between king and people is familial, arguing that earthly kingship destroys the family. Rebutting the royalist conflation of father and king, he suggests that the first human king is a bad brother who ignores family obligations. In making himself king, Nimrod also tries to displace God. With the building of Babel, the institution of kingship depicted as usurpation of authority has as its ultimate goal God's very throne.

Milton's interpretation of scripture challenges patriarchalism. Adam is "fatherly displeas'd" (12.63) and pronounces Nimrod "O execrable Son so to aspire / Above his Brethren, to himself assuming / Authority usurpt" (12.64–66). Since patriarchalist theorists trace kingly authority back to Adam, his censorious fatherly proclamations are not just another voice critical of monarchy. Because Milton's father rebukes the over-ambitious son, it is clear that a king is no father. In addition, by making Adam, the first father, condemn the origin of kings, Milton calls patriarchalist myth into question. In their interpretations of human history, both Michael and Adam take positions that appear republican. As a result of the fall, fathers no longer have dominance, not even the "first Father" (8.298). Before the fall, Adam's descendents might have come "to celebrate / And reverence thir great Progenitor" (11.345–46). With the fall, however, Adam loses "this preeminence" and is "brought down / To dwell on eeven ground now with [his] Sons" (11.347–48). The first father no longer has authority over his sons. In structuring society as a family, Milton does not insist on the authority of fathers. He does not force obedience even to God, who is both king and father. We can choose to obey or freely choose to fall.

Nimrod's seizing of power parallels the aetiology of the rule of the Greek gods recounted in a simile in Book 1:

> *Titan* Heav'ns first born
> With his enormous brood, and birthright seis'd
> By younger *Saturn*, he from mightier *Jove*
> His own and *Rhea's* Son like measure found;
> So *Jove* usurping reign'd.   (1.510–14)

The Greco-Roman gods are reduced to petty tyrants, ruling through force. Their reigns are marked by failed family relations: Saturn, though younger, seizes control to dominate his elder brothers, and Jove overthrows his own father to become the supreme god. Instead of familial love, we have fraternal war. A cataclysmic change (Jove's usurpation) results in the rigid hierarchy of rule by a king.

Satan's rebellion has interesting parallels with the embedded cautionary tales of Nimrod and of Jove, and thus, it can be read as their lessons writ large. Satan, too, rebels against his father, God, and brother, the Son. Civil disobedience is family disloyalty. Indeed, in *Paradise Lost*, each becomes a figure for the other. The war in Heaven is described as a wonder of sorts by Raphael to Adam because it pits brother against brother, more accustomed to feasting together. This fraternal war is also referred to as an "Intestine War" (6.259), that is, a civil war. Milton also puns on the word "civil": "Warr seem'd a civil Game / To this uproar" (6.667–68). While the comparison asserts an incommensurability between heavenly war and human war, at the same time it also links the two and brings to mind the recent civil wars fresh in the memory of Milton's readers, who remember them as fraternal wars. If Satan's revolt is seen as a family quarrel, then the lesson offered by the example of the rebellious son Nimrod applies. That lesson is a conception of both family and body politic that emphasizes equality among its members. Seditious attempts to dominate constitute a breaking of union. The gravity of such betrayal can be expressed only by the most horrific of family crimes: patricide and fratricide, crimes that Milton himself was accused of, and responded to, in the *Second Defence*. Here he throws the accusations back at the royalists.

In his rebellion Satan denies God's paternity and rejects brotherly love. When Abdiel argues that the angels cannot be equal to the Son because they were made by God and the Son jointly, Satan proclaims the angels to be without parents: "We know no time when we were not as now; / Know none before us, self-begot, self-rais'd / By our own quick'ning power" (5.859–61). Although close to Milton's argument about the people's creation of the king in the *First Defence*, Satan's argument must be read alongside the passages on Nimrod and Jove. Heavenly kingship is a special case. As Blair Worden argues, Satan falsely applies republicanism in this and in other speeches, using the language of freedom and tyranny only to aspire to be a monarch himself.[5] As important is Satan's act of disowning the family of God.[6] Refusing to acknowledge God's exaltation of the Son, Satan contests the Son's part in creation, that the angels are "the work / Of secondarie hands, by task transferd / From Father to his Son" (5.853–55), and ends up denying his God, since to reject one is also to reject the other. Satan's rejection of community is emphasized by his dependence on his own memory in his account of the angels' origin rather than on collective memory.

Denying his familial ties to God, the Son, and the faithful angels, Satan embraces a new family – Sin and Death – whose relations are perverted and solipsistic. Sin was born of Satan's envy and his "bold conspiracy against Heav'ns King" (2.751). Satan's birth pangs, as it were, are characterized by great pain and physical distress, impairing his faculty of sight. He cannot see past Sin's outward beauty and becomes enamored of his own image in her. (This narcissistic moment is repeated by Eve, but with a different end.) Satan compounds his error by having incestuous sex with Sin, which creates his monstrous progeny.[7] Satan is self-divided in multiplying himself in Sin, Death, and the hell hounds, his grandchildren. He also brings about other kinds of divisions: he divides Heaven by his insurrection, and, most of all, he divides himself from God.[8] Satan's incest is symptomatic of his inability to go outside his self: his family members are but extensions of himself. There may also be a mocking reference to royalist family metaphors

[5] Blair Worden, "Milton's Republicanism and the Tyranny of Heaven," in Gisela Bock, Quentin Skinner, and Maurizio Viroli, eds., *Machiavelli and Republicanism* (Cambridge: Cambridge University Press, 1990), 236 ff.

[6] Merritt Y. Hughes, "Satan and the 'Myth' of the Tyrant," in Millar MacLure and F. W. Watt, eds., *Essays in English Literature from the Renaissance to the Victorian Age Presented to A. S. P. Woodhouse* (Toronto: University of Toronto Press, 1964); Stevie Davies, *Images of Kingship in* Paradise Lost: *Milton's Politics and Christian Liberty* (Columbia: University of Missouri Press, 1983), 3–88; Michael Wilding, *Dragons Teeth: Literature in the English Revolution* (Oxford: Oxford University Press, 1987), 226–31; and Joan S. Bennett, *Reviving Liberty: Radical Christian Humanism in Milton's Great Poems* (Cambridge, Mass.: Harvard University Press, 1989) have all argued for the association of Satan with human tyrants. Stevie Davies is the only one, however, who has broached the subject of family in relation to tyranny. Even so, she only addresses fathers, not family in general as I do.

[7] For early modern incest, see Bruce Thomas Boehrer, *Monarchy and Incest in Renaissance England: Literature, Culture, Kinship, and Kingship* (Philadelphia: University of Pennsylvania Press, 1992). His conclusion that "As a rethinking of family-based politics, [Milton's] work is a profoundly brave and sophisticated failure" (137) does not account for how Milton has shifted the terms of the argument.

[8] While critics have pointed out various possible sources for Milton's conception of Sin (including Homer's Scylla, Ovid's Echidna, and Spenser's Duessa), the close parallel of Milton's account with that of John Gower's allegorical geneology of Sin in *Mirour de l'Omme* has only been noted by John S. P. Tatlock, "Milton's Sin and Death," *Modern Language Notes* 21.8 (1906): 239–40.

here: incest is what we get when we conflate the two royalist metaphors of monarch as father and monarch as lover or spouse.

Satan, Sin, and Death perversely parody the holy trinity.[9] Death is Satan's "only son" (2.728), as the Son is God's. Satan's encounter with Death, where Death tries to kill Satan, reveals a deeply divided family. Death has trouble recognizing his own father. Repulsed, Satan recognizes neither daughter nor son. Furthermore, when Satan attempts to pass through the gates of hell, Death challenges Satan and proclaims his sovereignty in hell, asserting his greater power over his father (not to mention over his mother in the rape): "I reign King, and to enrage thee more, / Thy King and Lord" (2.698–99). Death's kingship is another reversal of family hierarchy. In this case, Satan is not a father who gracefully yields his position to a mature son, but a sinful father punished by having his son reign over him. Tellingly, the overturning of family hierarchy is associated also with kings. Finally, Satan's degradation of family is also evident in his relation to Beelzebub, his "neerest Mate" (1.192) and "Companion dear" (5.673), names normally reserved for a wife, and so indicates "a perversion of the normal marriage relationship."[10] Rejecting God's community, forming his own inwardly directed trinity – characteristically, Satan chooses to find his own way to the newly created earth alone – Satan turns family inside out and produces confusion. While he complains about God's arbitrariness, Satan himself is a rigid authoritarian. As he sits "High on a Throne of Royal State" in hell, addressing the fallen angels, Satan claims that "the fixt Laws of Heav'n / Did first create [Satan] your Leader" (2.18–19). Though changed in his external appearance, he takes pride in "that fixt mind, / And high disdain, from sence of injur'd merit" (1.97–98). Defiantly embracing his new fallen circumstance, Satan claims "A mind not to be chang'd by Place or Time" (1.253). Out of despair, he revels in his obduracy. Satan's insistence on a strict and static hierarchy makes him less a revolutionary than a tyrant.[11]

God's kingship differs from Satan's in fundamental ways, with flexibility its main defining characteristic. Because in many ways family and state are identical in the prelapsarian world of *Paradise Lost*, the flexible family hierarchy of the poem has direct implications for political hierarchy. Both familial and political hierarchies are intertwined and interpreted as

[9] John Halkett, *Milton and the Idea of Matrimony: A Study of the Divorce Tracts and* Paradise Lost (New Haven: Yale University Press, 1970), 100.

[10] Flannagan, ed., *Paradise Lost* 1.192 n.72.

[11] Joan Bennett dismisses the attempts by Romantic poets as well as more recent critics such as Christopher Kendrick to link "God with Charles I as monarchs and Satan with Cromwell and Milton as revolutionaries" (*Reviving Liberty*, 33); see Christopher Kendrick, *Milton: A Study in Ideology and Form* (London: Methuen, 1986), 93.

dynamic, flexible, and open to change based on reason and on merit. Mary Ann Radzinowicz cogently argues that Milton's hierarchy is "individualistic, voluntaristic, and meritocratic" and that while "Satan's actual example is of a frozen meritocracy or tyranny," Milton's God creates "not a static meritocracy in Heaven with fixed status for its members under unvarying law but an evolving, organic, unified totality."[12] My argument about God's dynamic and flexible hierarchy overlaps with much of hers, but I am more attentive to the familial structure of that hierarchy, grounding my discussion of hierarchy in the context of the political language of the family. Milton's dynamic and flexible family dismantles hierarchies and undermines traditional authorities, especially the authority of the father but also that of the elder brother, both of which are resonant metaphors for royalists in justifying the monarchy. In this regard, Abdiel is the characteristic Miltonic hero, who stands firm against Satan and his rebellious crew. While greater angels fall, the seraph Abdiel, a lesser angel, remains faithful, "Unshak'n, unseduc'd, unterrifi'd" (5.898), even though he is in a minority of one. Morally superior, Abdiel's stand makes him greater than Satan, thus overturning the initial hierarchy of angels. This flexible hierarchy where merit trumps original status has radical implications.

For Stevie Davies, what distinguishes God's kingship from Satan's and from earthly kingdoms is God's "fathering creativity: he is *pater patriae* politically in a literal way (as Creator)."[13] She contrasts the "barren lack of kinship" in Satan's relations with his hellish compatriots with God's kingship in which "the divine family extends itself infinitely outward."[14] While Satan's unholy trinity is an absolutist monarchy, for Davies, God's kingship is associated with the (maternal) imagery of fecundity, evidence of God's "paternal love for his creatures."[15] Although much of Davies's argument is persuasive, it is not God's fatherhood that justifies his kingship. Having denounced the royalist coupling of father and king in the prose tracts, Milton avoids having the roles of father and of king justify each other. Instead, different fatherhoods are associated with different sorts of kingship. Satan is a father, but he produces the evils of Sin and Death. Death too is a

---

[12] Mary Ann Radzinowicz, "The Politics of *Paradise Lost*," 211, 211, 224. See also William Shullenberger, "Wrestling with the Angel: *Paradise Lost* and Feminist Criticism," *Milton Quarterly* 20 (1986): 69–85; Charles W. Durham, "'To Stand Approv'd in Sight of God': Abdiel, Obedience, and Hierarchy in *Paradise Lost*," *Milton Quarterly* 26 (1992), 15–20; Teresa Michals, "'Sweet Gardening Labour': Merit and Hierarchy in *Paradise Lost*," *Exemplaria* 7 (1995), 499–514; and Michael Wilding, "'Thir Sex Not Equal Seem'd': Equality in *Paradise Lost*," in P. G. Stanwood, ed., *Of Poetry and Politics: New Essays on Milton and his World* (Binghamton: Center for Medieval and Early Renaissance Studies, State University of New York at Binghamton, 1995), 171–86.

[13] Davies, *Images of Kingship*, 8. See in particular ch. 5, "The Father-King," 164–94.

[14] *Ibid.*, 188, 189.   [15] *Ibid.*, 189.

father; his children are the result of rape and as king he devours his subjects. Indeed, by devouring people, Death makes them his subjects. While God happens to be both father and king, his rule is justified by reason: the fallen angels are described as those "who reason for thir Law refuse, / Right reason for thir Law, and for thir King / Messiah, who by right of merit Reigns" (6.41–43). This justification unlinks the conjunction of father and king in *Paradise Lost*. Moreover, these roles are defined very differently from the Stuart conception of father-kings. God is not the authoritarian father who governs over immature children. The analogy linking father and king, as the royalists understand it, falls far short of providing an adequate defense for his rule. When it comes to God, the analogy fails.

God's paternal relation to the Son is particularly prominent in Milton's dynamic reconceptualizing of family. The Son is central in more ways than one. If there is a chronological beginning to *Paradise Lost*, it is God's exaltation of the Son, which triggers the series of events related in the poem. Satan dislikes the exaltation as a disruption in the old hierarchy:

> he of the first,
> If not the first Arch-Angel, great in Power,
> In favour and in præeminence, yet fraught
> With envie against the Son of God, that day
> Honourd by his great Father, and proclaimd
> *Messiah* King anointed, could not beare
> Through pride that sight, & thought himself impaird.
>
> (5.659–65)

Whether or not Satan truly suffers a demotion or merely believes himself to have so suffered, the exaltation does institute a dramatic change: the Son now heads the angelic hierarchy as king. Suspicious of change, Satan uses God's exaltation of the Son as an excuse to justify his rebellion: "new Laws thou seest impos'd; / New Laws from him who reigns, new minds may raise / In us who serve" (5.679–81). His suspicion, however, lacks divine approval. Abdiel argues that the Son deserves his position because he was an agent of God's creation, "by whom / As by his Word the mighty Father made / All things" (5.835–37). Moreover, there are two exaltations of the Son, which can confuse. Chronologically, the first comes before Satan's rebellion while the second comes after the Son offers to save mankind. The Son's part in creation justifies the first by merit while the second is meritoriously earned by his future sacrifice: "His [Adam's] crime makes guiltie all his Sons, thy merit / Imputed shall absolve them" (3.290–91). By this deed, the Son "hast been found / By Merit more then Birthright Son of God, / Found worthiest to be so by being Good" (3.308–10). Furthermore, because Milton does not proceed chronologically, our interpretation of the poem has to take into account both the chronology of events and the sequence of the narrative. In terms of the narrative, the second exaltation of the Son in Book 3 comes before the first, which is in Book 6. Thus, what is presented first to the reader is the second exaltation, given under circumstances where the Son's merit is more evident.

Moreover, change is good in God's universe. The angels delight in something as mundane as the daily alternation of day and night. In an aside, Raphael says, "(For wee have also our Eevning and our Morn, / Wee ours for change delectable, not need)" (5.628–29). Day is not intrinsically good nor night bad. Not a dualistic universe, but a monist one, all matter here derives from God, from "one first matter" (5.472), its exact nature depending on closeness to God: "But more refin'd, more spiritous, and pure, / As neerer to him plac't or neerer tending" (5.475–76).[16] Matter can transmute into spirit, changing back into its divine essence as men's "bodies may at last turn all to Spirit, / Improv'd by tract of time, and wingd ascend / Ethereal" (5.497–99). A movement up God's hierarchy, such change is positive and an integral part of God's universe. What is potentially possible for man is realized by the Son, who moves up the hierarchy and gains greater glory when God declares him king. Milton's care in locating the event temporally emphasizes the fact of change. Even if the narrator must hedge about the heavenly concept of time, different from human time and yet having duration, the exaltation occurs in time, "on a day" (5.579). The exaltation of the Son is not simply a reconfirmation of what already is. Through chronology, Milton emphasizes the progression of events in order to highlight the progress signified by the event. Unlike Satan's fall, this is a divinely ordered change that is a change for the better.

Satan erroneously interprets the Son's exaltation as a reconfiguration of hierarchy that implies a downward change in his own status. Failing to understand that the exaltation is for the good of all the angels, Satan ignores God's command that instructs the angels to unify under the Son's rule:

> Under his great Vice-gerent Reign abide
> United as one individual Soule
> For ever happie: him who disobeyes
> Mee disobeyes, breaks union.
>
> (5.609–12)

---

[16] John Rumrich, *Milton Unbound: Controversy and Reinterpretation* (Cambridge: Cambridge University Press, 1996), argues that all matter, including chaos, originates in God. On Milton's monist universe, see John Roger, *The Matter of Revolution: Science, Poetry, and Politics in the Age of Milton* (Ithaca: Cornell University Press, 1996).

Stella Revard argues, "For in the decree God is stating that ruin will result when a creature, a part, separates himself from the creation, the whole. God has named the Son to kingship so as to make manifest visually and symbolically the union upon which the vitality of his creation depends."[17] The exaltation is designed to bring the heavenly community closer together. Abdiel contradicts Satan's claim that it diminishes the other angels: "how farr from thought / To make us less, bent rather to exalt / Our happie state under one Head more neer / United" (5.828–31). Rather, the angels are to form a tighter union. As Abdiel reminds Satan, through exaltation God becomes closer to the angels: "nor by his Reign obscur'd, / But more illustrious made, since he the Head / One of our number thus reduc't becomes" (5.8421–43). The ultimate goal is for God to become fully part of the union, for everything to be imbued with God: "God shall be All in All" (3.341). This means that mankind too will be incorporated into Heaven:

> till by degrees of merit rais'd
> They open to themselves at length the way
> Up hither, under long obedience tri'd,
> And Earth be chang'd to Heav'n, & Heav'n to Earth,
> One Kingdom, Joy and Union without end.
>
> (7.157–61)

Eventually, there will be no distinction of rank, no difference between Heaven and Earth. This potential for others to rise in hierarchy is ultimately that to which Satan objects. Occupying a position near the top as one of the brightest archangels, Satan wants the hierarchy to remain static.

God's universe, however, is far from static. Hierarchy in *Paradise Lost* is not a settled one but dynamic and responsive to changes or the addition of new members. The Son's elevation disturbs the balance in Heaven that Satan is accustomed to. But it also disturbs the balance of power between the Son and God the Father. The difference is that the Father facilitates this change and allows the Son to grow into his maturity. The Son's interaction with the Father shows a different model of father–son relations than that advocated by the Stuart kings. As the ultimate father, God declines to wield absolute authority over his son. The Son is treated not as a child who needs parental guidance but as a mature adult. Milton's argument from the prose tracts for Englishmen to be treated as men is repeated and extended in *Paradise Lost*. Here too he argues for a familial model of government that turns royalist conceptions on their heads, doing away with the royalists' unbridgeable gap between father and child.

---

[17] Stella Purce Revard, *The War in Heaven*: Paradise Lost *and the Tradition of Satan's Rebellion* (Ithaca: Cornell University Press, 1980), 57.

The exaltation of the Son is a ceremonial acknowledgment of his maturity. The war in Heaven is the arena in which the Son's maturity becomes manifest, even put to the test. God declares that the war was foreseen and permitted it "To honour his Anointed Son aveng'd / Upon his enemies, and to declare / All power on him transferr'd" (6.676–78). The transfer of power becomes evident in the Son's triumph over the enemies of the Father. In giving away power, the Father allows the Son to share in his authority. As William Empson wittily remarks, God "is envisaging his abdication."[18] The Son acts on his Father's behalf, but he is more than just his Father's agent. "Effulgence of [God's] Glorie," he becomes a "Second Omnipotence" (6.680, 684). The Son is the Father made visible. As "Divine Similitude" (3.384) who makes clear the Father's nature, the Son is perceived as the Father himself.

Milton's theological position on the relationship of the Son and Father is not always clear. John Rumrich, among others, argues that Milton was an Arian and therefore anti-trinitarian.[19] He points to *De Doctrina Christiana*, whose provenance is in dispute, but also notes that Milton's Arianism is evident in *Paradise Lost*. My argument supports such an interpretation. The Son is not identical to the Father from the start. Rather, he becomes the Father, taking on his attributes, as he grows into his maturity:

> Go then thou Mightiest in thy Fathers might,
> Ascend my Chariot, guide the rapid Wheeles
> That shake Heav'ns basis, bring forth all my Warr,
> My Bow and Thunder, my Almightie Arms
> Gird on, and Sword upon thy puissant Thigh.
>   (6.710–14)

Putting on his Father's armor, the Son assumes his Father's attribute of omnipotence. Despite Milton's much-vaunted opposition to epic values, the Son's debut in the paternal role is as a warrior. The Son drives the "Chariot of Paternal Deity" (6.750), possibly a reference to the Greek myth of Phaeton who tries to drive his father the sun-god Apollo's chariot but fails because of his youth.[20] Unlike Phaeton, who loses control of Apollo's

---

[18] William Empson, *Milton's God*, rev. edn (London: Chatto & Windus, 1965), 137.
[19] Rumrich, *Milton Unbound*, 40–46.
[20] In Ovid's account, when Phaeton asks to drive the chariot, Phoebus (Apollo) tries to dissuade him: "You seek a privilege that ill befits / Your growing years and strength so boyish still" (Ovid, *Metamorphoses*, trans. A. D. Melville [Oxford: Oxford University Press, 1986], 26). While the passage is usually treated as a reference to Ezekiel 1 and 10, Milton's allusions can be multilayered, simultaneously referring to the classical canon and to scripture, as his puns often are. For Milton's weaving of the Icarus myth into *Paradise Lost*, see David Quint, "Fear of Falling: Icarus, Phaeton, and the Lucretius in *Paradise Lost*," *Renaissance Quarterly* 57 (2004), 847–81.

chariot and falls to his death, the Son controls his Father's chariot beautifully and defeats the rebelling angels, proving himself no immature youth. There is also an equalizing between God and the Son: God calls him "My word, my wisdom, and effectual might, / All hast thou spok'n as my thoughts are, all / As my Eternal purpose hath decreed" (3.170–72). Speaking exactly as the Father would, he embodies the Father and puts his being into action. By the end of *Paradise Lost*, the Son has the power not only to destroy God's enemies, but also to enact God's judgment: "Vicegerent Son, to thee I have transferr'd / All Judgement, whether in Heav'n, or Earth, or Hell" (10.56–57). After the fall, the Son is sent as "both Judge and Saviour" (10.209) to Adam and Eve and "As Father of his Familie he clad / Thir nakedness with Skins of Beasts" (10.216–17). Acting as God here, the Son appears in the guise of a father. As Rumrich points out, "During the course of the epic action, the Son increases in stature, authority, and power, all at the Father's pleasure – an augmentation of being that would not be possible or needed if he were unlimited, infinite, immutable, and eternal."[21] In other words, the Son is taking over his Father's place. The ambiguity over Milton's position on the doctrine of the trinity in *Paradise Lost* may well stem from the Son's process of maturation.[22] Milton may at times seem to adhere to orthodox ideas about the holy trinity because the Son grows to become equal and identical to the Father. Redefining the family such that a son can take on a paternal role, Milton presents the Son as taking on the Father's political role. What is more, this role happens to be that of the king. The father-king of *Paradise Lost* is not James I's version of a father-king: for Milton, paradoxically, that role is played by a son.

FAMILY HIERARCHY IN THE STATE OF NATURE

Interpreting the exaltation of the Son as having the consequence of displacing him from his position of favor, Satan feels similarly beleaguered by God's new creation, man. Satan alleges that God is:

> Determin'd to advance into our room
> A Creature form'd of Earth, and him endow,
> Exalted from so base original,
> With Heav'nly spoils, our spoils. (9.148–51)

---

[21] John Rumrich, "Milton's Arianism: Why it Matters," in Stephen B. Dobranski and John P. Rumrich, eds., *Milton and Heresy* (Cambridge: Cambridge University Press, 1998), 81.

[22] There is further ambiguity about the Son's relation to the Father in the invocation to light: "Hail holy Light, ofspring of Heav'n first-born, / Or of th' Eternal coeternal beam" (3.1–2). The Son (Light) is either God's firstborn or has always existed with the Father.

Satan's envy is compounded by the gap he perceives between man and angel: made from clay, a lowly substance, man yet stands to inherit the riches of Heaven. Having lost the war in Heaven to the Son, Satan tries instead to attack man. From Satan's perspective, man becomes God's "new Favorite" (9.175), whom God advances in order to spite and to punish the rebellious angels. To Satan, God is a despotic monarch, who indiscriminately elevates undeserving commoners to titled positions and plays favorites.

Satan is right in that he and the fallen angels are being superseded by a lesser creature: as Beelzebub puts it in his speech concluding the parliament of hell, man is "less / In power and excellence, but favour'd more / Of him who rules above" (2.349–51). Adam is God's "creature late so lov'd, thy [God's] youngest Son" (3.151), as the Son notes when persuading God to show mercy to Adam. Although the "youngest Son," Adam replaces in God's favor Satan and the fallen angels, elder brothers who were created first. This pattern of lesser figures displacing greater ones and of younger sons displacing elder brothers is a leitmotif in *Paradise Lost*, demonstrating the flexibility of family roles. Milton overturns traditional family hierarchy to argue for the assignment of roles based on merit, making such displacements a reasonable and appropriate adaptation to changed circumstances. The idea of lesser figures eventually overtaking greater ones modifies Milton's presentation of gender hierarchy as well. Although Eve is created second, her secondariness is reconceived as something good, similar to the reconceptualization of the secondariness of younger sons.

When he falls, Satan is no longer fit to hold the high position as archangel. Man too is displaced when he falls. Adam's place is voluntarily taken by the Son, who is told by God, "Be thou in *Adams* room / The Head of all mankind, though *Adams* Son. / As in him perish all men, so in thee / As from a second root shall be restor'd" (3.285–88). This language is not unlike that of Book 9 when Satan complains that God is "Determin'd to advance [man] into our room" (9.148). The passages echo each other in the use of the word "room" for place. In God's pronouncement, the verb is "be," conveying the sense of stability that lacks the impression of violent and forceful ejection of the fallen angels implied by Satan's verb "advance." Satan interprets his displacement by man as an arbitrary act of God even though he chose to rebel. It is different with God. When God approves the Son's displacement of Adam, the displacement is designed ultimately to restore Adam to his former position. As the Messiah, the Son comes after Adam; he is in fact Adam's son. But as Adam's son, the Messiah replaces Adam in being the "Head of all mankind." The son becomes the father of his father. This displacement reverses the role of son and father. Matters are complicated by the fact that as co-creator the Son is Adam's father. In becoming man, the Son is deliberately changing places: he is the father reversing roles with his son. The double reversal highlights the flexibility of family hierarchy in the universe of Milton's God.

The displacements in *Paradise Lost* have positive connotations of reform and redemption. The Son also displaces Satan, who is very much the disinherited heir (or at least he acts as one), and this displacement signifies salvation for man. The Son and Satan parallel each other in their roles as savior. When God asks for someone to "be mortal to redeem / Mans mortal crime" (3.214–15), there is silence until the Son offers himself: "all the Heav'nly Quire stood mute, / And silence was in Heav'n: on mans behalf / Patron or Intercessor none appeerd / Much less that durst upon his own head draw / The deadly forfeiture, and ransom set" (3.217–21). Likewise, when Beelzebub asks for a volunteer to seek out the new world in order to restore them to their former condition, there is silence in Hell: "all sat mute, / Pondering the danger with deep thoughts; and each / In others count'nance read his own dismay / Astonisht" (2.420–23). Only Satan comes forward, seizing the moment to declare himself king, saying that he "should ill become this Throne, O Peers, / And this Imperial Sov'ranty" (2.445–46) if dangers deter him from the attempt. But Satan and the Son are very different sorts of saviors. The Son humbles himself, taking on mortal form and becoming the son of a man. Satan, however, seizes kingship in his role as savior to the fallen angels. Given that both Satan and the Son are kings, their different models of kingship present a stark contrast. Satan is an imperious and tyrannical monarch while the Son, crowned king, takes on the servant's role when he becomes man: he "disdain'd not to begin / Thenceforth the form of servant to assume, / As when he wash'd his servants feet" (10.213–15). The example of the Son presents us with an ideal of the king as public servant. Although chronologically the Son's offer to save man occurs before Satan's offer to search for the new world, in the narrative the Son's offer comes in Book 3 right after Satan's, recounted in Book 2. The Son replicates Satan's offer but he is the good Messiah, a second version that overturns the first. Structurally, the Son displaces Satan, but his offer also undoes the evil that Satan makes. Thus, being second is not automatically negative: at Judgment Day, the race of man will be revived by the Messiah, the "second root" (3.288), and after the flood "Man as from a second stock proceed" (12.7) from Noah, a type of Christ. Second starts are new beginnings with greater promise.

Milton's privileging of second starts and younger sons is biblical. He even obliquely refers to the prominent Old Testament story of Esau selling his birthright to his younger brother Jacob for a bowl of pottage, an account of a younger son displacing the firstborn to become his father's heir: escaping from Hell, Satan comes to the stairs to Heaven, which "Stairs were such as whereon *Jacob* saw /Angels ascending and descending, bands / Of Guardians bright, when he from *Esau* fled" (3.510–12). Roy Flannagan suggests, "Satan perceives something very like the ladder Jacob sees after he has cheated his brother Esau out of his birthright (Genesis 28.12–13). The comparison between Jacob in his sinful condition and Satan is apt, except that Jacob will repent and Satan cannot."[23] A simple comparison of Jacob and Satan, however, overlooks the context of Jacob's vision. Although Jacob, pretending to be his elder brother Esau, tricks his father Isaac into blessing him, Jacob gains his birthright because Esau fails to value it: "Thus Esau despised his birthright" (Genesis 25:34). Moreover, far from revealing his sinful condition, Jacob's dream of the stairs or ladder reveals rather the great plans that God has for him and his progeny. God promises:

the land whereon thou liest, to thee will I give it, and to thy seed; And thy seed shall be as the dust of the earth; and thou shalt spread abroad to the west, and to the east, and to the north, and to the south: and in thee and in thy seed shall all the families of the earth be blessed. (Genesis 28:13–14)

Jacob is not rebuked for taking Esau's birthright. In fact, the dream of the stairs to Heaven confirms his possession of that birthright in a more fundamental way. The Bible does not insist on rights of being firstborn. For instance, it is Jacob's younger son, Joseph, who prospers most and rises in status above his brothers: *his* dream of how he becomes greater than his brothers makes them jealous enough to sell him into slavery.

Likewise, Milton is careless of family hierarchy. He does not invest the eldest son with any particular distinction. The comparison between Jacob and Satan is less direct than may at first be supposed. The allusion to Jacob may simply be an allusion to the stairs, the subject of many commentaries. If the story of Jacob and Esau has a bearing on Satan, I suggest that it would be another example of how a younger brother becomes the hope of the future – as future patriarch, Jacob is the start of an empire through which God blesses the world – because the elder brother fails. Satan's relation to the Son has something of the dynamic between Jacob and Esau. God's exaltation of the Son is not unlike Isaac's blessing of Jacob. Satan thus can be compared not to Jacob but to Esau. Like Esau, Satan feels cheated of his birthright. Insofar as Satan is a version of Esau, the Son becomes the

---

[23] Flannagan, ed., *Paradise Lost* 3.503 n.136.

younger brother who inherits his father's wealth and position. Like Jacob, the Son is the instrument through which God will bless the world. The Son becomes the politically efficacious younger brother.

The prominence of younger sons in *Paradise Lost* suggests that Milton is asserting that new men will rise up to take the place of the old who failed. His use of younger brothers as metaphorical figures for a hoped-for revolution can be contextualized within the debate over younger sons in the period. Joan Thirsk shows that in the sixteenth and seventeenth centuries younger sons became a focal point for debates about and calls to reform the custom of primogeniture. She suggests that gentry families rose in prominence at the expense of their younger brothers, who were disadvantaged by primogeniture, and the younger son became a stock character like a stepmother or a mother-in-law: "During the sixteenth century to describe anyone as 'a younger son' was a short-hand way of summing up a host of grievances . . . *younger son* meant an angry young man, bearing more than his share of injustice and resentment, deprived of means by his father and elder brother, often hanging around his elder brother's house as a servant, completely dependent on his grace and favour."[24] The amount of literature on the subject suggests a crisis in the early modern family – at least for the gentry and noble classes. The situation worsened during the civil war and interregnum such that even the Levellers took up the cause of younger sons. For the Diggers, the younger brother became a symbol of economic and, given the property basis of citizenship, political disenfranchisement: "The Diggers turned the terms 'elder brother' and 'younger brother' into synonyms for the propertied, and unpropertied classes. Covetous landlords and lords of manors generally were referred to as elder brothers and the poor commoners, cheated of their commons, as younger brothers."[25] The younger brother thus was a particularly resonant metaphor for dispossion.[26] In *Paradise Lost*, Milton transforms the younger brother into a figure for change. This positive interpretation was already part of the discourse around younger brothers. Criticizing primogeniture, Thomas Wilson, a younger son of a gentleman, found one consolation: "This I must confess doth us good someways, for it makes us industrious to apply ourselves to letters or to armes whereby many times we become my master elder brothers' masters, or at least their betters in honour and reputation, while he lyves att home like a mome and knowes the sound of no bell but his

---

[24] Joan Thirsk, "Younger Sons in the Seventeenth Century," *History* 54 (1969), 360.   [25] *Ibid.*, 369.
[26] One widely advocated solution for the problem of younger sons was to send them to colonize the New World. Interestingly, Satan calls earth the new world and sets out to conquer it for hell.

own."[27] Milton takes up the stereotypes of the lazy elder brother and of the meritorious younger brother to present a family and a political state where hierarchy does not predetermine status. His younger sons eventually become masters through merit and industry. The younger brother becomes a metaphor for disinherited citizens who merit politically significant roles.

The literature on younger sons in the early modern period suggests that family hierarchy was felt to be oppressive by some.[28] This literature also suggests that such a hierarchy was unstable and subject to contestation. Milton's contribution to this discussion undermines the authority of elder brothers and of fathers. While the Stuart kings justify rule on the basis of a stable family hierarchy, Milton disrupts family order, advancing instead a political state where merit and youth rather than age and authority prevail. Unsurprisingly, when family order is disrupted, so are traditional gender relations. In her summary of over three decades of scholarship on gender and *Paradise Lost*, Diane McColley argues, "Milton does not need to be defended by means of allowances for the assumptions of his time; Milton himself struck off the chains of custom."[29] McColley strikes exactly the right note. Not making anachronistic and extravagant claims for a feminist Milton, she nonetheless recognizes the ways in which Milton's writings have promoted liberty for women as well as for men, emphasizing Adam's and Eve's individual attributes rather than their unequal relation to each other. I concur and add that Adam and Eve's inequality is not irrevocably fixed, as hierarchy in *Paradise Lost* is always subject to revision. In undermining the authority of elder brothers and of fathers, Milton also destabilizes gender hierarchies.

Given the positive connotations associated with being second, Adam and Eve present a complex and fascinating case. We need to revise our understanding of what it means for Eve to be made second. There has been a lively debate on the nature of Eve's subjectivity and her submission to Adam. From an earlier consensus that Milton embraced the traditional evil Eve, we have gone through a feminist reassessment of *Paradise Lost* to a postfeminist challenge of defenses of Milton. Among these recent

---

[27] F. J. Fisher, ed., *The State of England Anno Dom. 1600 by Thomas Wilson*, Camden Miscellany, xvi, Camden Society, Third Series, lii (1936), 24; quoted in Thirsk, "Younger Sons," 360.

[28] See Keith Thomas, "Age and Authority in Early Modern England," *Proceedings of the British Academy* 62 (1976), 205–48; Ilana Krausman Ben-Amos, *Adolescence and Youth in Early Modern England* (New Haven: Yale University Press, 1994); and Paul Griffiths, *Youth and Authority: Formative Experiences in England, 1560–1640* (Oxford: Clarendon Press, 1996).

[29] Diane K. McColley, "Milton and the Sexes," in Dennis Danielson, ed., *The Cambridge Companion to Milton*, 2nd edn (Cambridge: Cambridge University Press, 1999), 177. See also McColley, *Milton's Eve* (Urbana: University of Illinois Press, 1983).

challenges is Mary Nyquist's influential essay on gendered subjectivity in Milton, which argues against McColley's suggestion that Eve possesses an individual psychology. Nyquist contends that because Eve was created for Adam her subjectivity is necessarily secondary; Eve's subjectivity is part of Adam's personhood rather than wholly her own. But this account is in fact the opposite of Adam's experience of Eve. Against Nyquist's insistence that Milton's interpretation of Genesis, especially his contractual understanding of marriage, produces "an individualism paradigmatically masculine, autonomous, articulate, and preternaturally awake to the implications of entering into relations with others," Linda Gregerson contends that patriarchalism makes Eve the "normative" postlapsarian subject: every fallen Christian is in a relationship of "reciprocity within hierarchy" with God.[30]

These readings of Eve's secondariness are cogent and insightful. But the question of priority can also be approached by considering the possibility that second may be better than first. Nyquist herself points to seventeenth-century texts that rework this question of priority. In favoring the more egalitarian Priestly ("P") creation text over the masculinist Yahwist ("J") creation account, Rachel Speght's *A Mouzell for Melastomus, the Cynicall Bayter of, and Foule Mouthed Barker Against Evahs Sex* (1617), Ester Sowernam's *Ester Hath Hang'd Haman: A Defense of Women, Against The Author of the Arraignment of Women* (1617), and Alexander Niccholes's *A Discourse, of Marriage and Wiving, and Annotations Upon All the Books of the Old and New Testaments* (1615) all reverse the conventional interpretation of Eve's (and woman's) place in the hierarchy. Nyquist writes, "In the restricted intellectual economy of the 'Querelle,' orthodox views of male superiority are frequently countered by paradoxical assertions of female superiority. Lastness is therefore placed in the service of overturning firstness."[31] Milton makes this sort of paradoxical argument with Eve as well as with other figures in the poem. James Turner finds the opposition between Eve's equality and submission to be a central ambiguity in the poem: he calls it an "irresolvable doubleness at the heart of Milton's apprehension of wedded love – a contradiction that lies dormant in Genesis and the Pauline tradition."[32] This ambiguity, I suggest, derives from Milton's contradictory privileging of secondness.

---

[30] Mary Nyquist, "The Genesis of Gendered Subjectivity in the Divorce Tracts and in *Paradise Lost*," in Nyquist and Margaret W. Ferguson, eds., *Re-membering Milton: Essays on the Texts and Traditions* (New York: Methuen, 1987), 114; Linda Gregerson, *The Reformation of the Subject: Spenser, Milton, and the English Protestant Epic* (Cambridge: Cambridge University Press, 1995), 196.

[31] Nyquist, "Genesis," 107.

[32] James Grantham Turner, *One Flesh: Paradisal Marriage and Sexual Relations in the Age of Milton* (Oxford: Clarendon Press, 1987), 286.

Nyquist suggests that if Eve were to have related the story of her creation second – following the order of creation – rather than before Adam's story, there is the danger that Derrida's logic of the supplement might come into play, and Eve would appear superior.[33] She thus shies away from following this line of argument to its logical end. In fact, the logic of the supplement does come into play, even though Eve tells her story first, because of Eve's secondary nature. But I want to locate instead a historicized notion of secondariness. Milton's language of supplementarity is a biblical one, with examples like Jacob and Esau from the Old Testament. Eve's position as second ultimately confers on her greater honor than Adam. First, salvation comes through her as mother of mankind. Second, Eve's status as mother makes possible family and community.

As God's final and youngest creation, Eve stands in analogical relation to younger sons. Like younger sons, Eve has a prominent political role in *Paradise Lost*. When the prelapsarian Adam awakens Eve, he calls her "My fairest, my espous'd, my latest found, / Heav'ns last best gift, my ever new delight" (5.18–19). The lines can be compared to the Song of Songs: "My beloved spake, and said unto me, Rise up, my love, my fair one, and come away" (Song of Songs 2.10). What Milton adds to the verses is the emphasis on Eve's lastness and bestness. This emphasis also imbues Eve with an aura of newness. Adam's naming of Eve as "Best image of my self and dearer half" (5.95) may suggest her secondary and imitative nature. But it also aligns her with the Son, who is "Divine Similitude" (3.384). If man, dear to God, is not "the least / Though last created" (3.276–77), then woman, the very last creation, cannot be least simply by virtue of when she happens to have been created. Even the Virgin Mary has the status of being second to Eve. When Raphael first greets Eve, he connects her to the future Virgin Mary: "On whom the Angel *Haile* / Bestowd, the holy salutation us'd / Long after to blest *Marie*, second *Eve*" (5.385–87). Although Mary follows Eve, her secondariness does not diminish her: Mary, who gives birth to God, is in fact greater than the first Eve. Yet, the passage does not disparage Eve either; the link made between Eve and Mary reflects positively on both. Milton does not make the traditional distinction between a sinful Eve and a pure Mary: they both play important maternal roles. Even after the fall, Eve is instrumental in bringing about salvation: her "Seed shall bruise our Foe" (11.155).

The relation between greater and lesser is imprecise and equivocal, as can be seen from Adam's discussion with Raphael about the movement

[33] Nyquist, "Genesis," 119.

of the heavenly bodies. When Adam wonders why God created greater celestial bodies to give light to the lesser earth, Raphael reproves him for his unwarranted assumption about hierarchy: "That bodies bright and greater should not serve / The less not bright, nor Heav'n such journies run, / Earth sitting still" (8.87–89). Instead, Adam is told to "consider first, that Great / Or Bright inferrs not Excellence" (8.90–91). The question about the hierarchical relation between Adam and Eve is similarly complex. The courtier-like Eve has the power to coerce and to persuade, despite her inferiority.[34] Rejecting a hierarchy of precedence, Milton is also remarkably coy about establishing a hierarchy based on gender. The sun, gendered male in the poem, appears to Adam to revolve around a feminine earth: "the Sun that barren shines, / Whose vertue on it self workes no effect, / But in the fruitful Earth; there first receavd / His beams, unactive else, thir vigour find" (8.94–97). This way of perceiving the relations between greater and lesser calls into question assumptions about servitude and rule. Milton makes the apparent gender hierarchy between Adam and Eve much more open to debate than we suppose. One line has been most offensive in its assumption of gender inequality: "He for God only, she for God in him" (4.299). But as some scholars note, the line may be part of Satan's reflection. It is the first time Satan sees Adam and Eve, whose happiness arouses his jealousy. The accuracy of his perception is doubtful. The passage is riddled with the modifier "seemed": Adam and Eve "seemd Lords of all" (4.290), they "worthie seemd" (4.291), and "thir sex not equal seemd" (296). Furthermore, though Eve's curly hair "impli'd / Subjection" (4.307–08), her submission is "requir'd with gentle sway" (4.308) and "by her yielded, by him best receivd" (4.309). Eve's submission is predicated on her own freedom of will to submit and cannot be forced.

It is far from clear that Eve is inferior to Adam. Adam reacts to Eve as though she is the superior creature: transported by "passion" (8.530) or "commotion strange" (8.431), Adam finds "so absolute she seems / And in her self compleat, so well to know / Her own, that what she will to do or say, / Seems wisest, vertuousest, discreetest, best" (8.547–50). Even Adam feels that Eve's secondariness in creation does not accurately describe her: Eve is "As one intended first, not after made / Occasionally" (8.555–56). Adam is not necessarily wrong about Eve being wisest and best, for Milton invokes the analogy between Adam and Solomon to present prelapsarian

[34] For Eve as courtier, see Michael C. Schoenfeldt, "Gender and Conduct in *Paradise Lost*," in James Grantham Turner, ed., *Sexuality and Gender in Early Modern Europe: Institutions, Texts, Images* (Cambridge: Cambridge University Press, 1993), 310–38.

conjugal love as the love of wisdom made manifest.[35] Raphael appears to rebuke Adam for overvaluing Eve, but what he actually tells Adam is not to attribute "overmuch to things / Less excellent" (8.565–66). Adam's fault is to overvalue Eve for her beauty. Focusing on "the charm of Beauties powerful glance," Adam accuses God of bestowing on Eve "Too much of Ornament, in outward shew / Elaborate, of inward less exact" (8.538–39). Raphael chides Adam, "For what admir'st thou, what transports thee so, / An outside?" (8.567–68). Frowning on Adam's invention of a false hierarchy, he tells Adam that Eve is "worthy well / Thy cherishing, thy honouring, and thy love, / Not thy subjection: weigh her with thy self; / Then value" (8.568–71). While Raphael sees Eve as subordinate to Adam, the image of weighing suggests a balance that shifts as it finds its equilibrium. Where that equilibrium lies is uncertain. Moreover, Raphael needs to advise Adam on how to lead: "Oft times nothing profits more / Then self esteem, grounded on just and right / Well manag'd; of that skill the more thou know'st, / The more she will acknowledge thee her Head" (8.571–74). Prompted by Adam's doubts about his own value, Raphael's advice debunks any notion of inherent superiority. Adam has to be coached on how to be a leader; he is not a natural.

Despite being warned not to overvalue Eve, we are in fact asked to acknowledge her powerful attractions. The various descriptions of Eve, including Adam's, convey not just her beauty but also her poise and her magisterial presence. Adam uses a political term for a king in describing Eve, calling her "absolute." Satan calls her "Empress" (9.626), and in the guise of the serpent flatters her, "no Fair to thine / Equivalent or second, which compel'd / Mee thus, though importune perhaps, to come / And gaze, and worship thee of right declar'd / Sovran of Creatures, universal Dame" (9.608–12). Satan is of course trying to seduce Eve into eating the fruit, but he does not lack for admiration when he first sees Adam and Eve. Expressed in an internal soliloquy, in which he is not speaking to persuade an audience, Satan's praise is at least an honest reaction even if misguided. Scholars have noted passages that describe Eve in queenly terms and have found in them something positive. Albert Labriola sees the cult of Elizabeth underlying the language of monarchy and speculates that such praise may constitute a Miltonic challenge to patriarchy.[36] In her fascinating work on female authority, Katherine Eggert disagrees with Labriola; but her own conclusion

---

[35] Theresa M. DiPasquale, "'Heav'n's Last Best Gift': Eve and Wisdom in *Paradise Lost*," *Modern Philology* 95 (1997), 44–67.

[36] Albert C. Labriola, "Milton's Eve and the Cult of Elizabeth I," *Journal of English and Germanic Philology* 95 (1996), 38–51.

comes surprisingly close to his in its liberatory possibilities. Eggert suggests that because Eve's monarchical aspects are present at the moment when she exerts her will, Eve's "'Virgin Majesty' figures forth not only the divorce tracts' domineering shrew, but also their newly emancipated husband, who scorns external determination of his fate in the manner of the *Mask*'s virgin Lady and who hence becomes an essential constituent of the republican state." Eschewing a one-to-one correspondence according to sex between the husband and wife of the divorce tracts and Adam and Eve in *Paradise Lost*, Eggert links Eve with the self-governing husband of the divorce tracts. The feminine king Charles is berated for being ruled by his tyrannous wife, but this fallen world of female rule, Eggert says, is set against the very different Elizabethan queenship. She argues that Eve's "exertions of self-will – because they are associated as they are with a feminine sovereignty reminiscent of Elizabeth's – form a foundation in paradise for a republican government."[37] If Eggert is right that Eve's queenship and wilfulness serve as a basis for assertions of republican self-will, even though Eve is not unambiguously good, then she must not be condemned simply for her independence and self-sufficiency. The scene in which she is enamored of her own image in the lake is not evidence of her sinfulness or even a foreshadowing of the fall to come. This self-sufficiency may in fact make her the appropriate agent for the salvation of mankind. Although the first to fall, she is the first to seek peace with Adam and so the first truly to repent. Eve does not answer Adam's condemnation with harsh words of her own but instead "at his feet / Fell humble, and imbracing them, besaught / His peace" (10.911–13).

I also read the scene where Eve has to be led away from her own image, and from a barren love, to be joined to Adam, more sympathetically than Christine Froula, who argues that Eve is being schooled into submission by the voice of patriarchy.[38] While Eve pines "with vain desire" (4.466), God marries her to Adam, to whom she "shalt beare / Multitudes like [her] self, and thence be call'd / Mother of human Race" (4.473–75). Inserted into a family structure and hierarchy, Eve is given a role and a place in community. Although one could argue that Eve's role as wife oppresses her, as I have shown, family need not be a patriarchal construct. Milton's conception of family, in the tracts as well as in *Paradise Lost*, is remarkably free from assumptions of unquestioned patriarchal hierarchy. In fact, in *Paradise*

[37] Katherine Eggert, *Showing Like a Queen: Female Authority and Literary Experiment in Spenser, Shakespeare, and Milton* (Philadelphia: University of Pennsylvania Press, 2000), 192, 194.
[38] Christine Froula, "When Eve Reads Milton: Undoing the Canonical Economy," *Critical Inquiry* 10 (1983), 321–47.

Lost, he also overturns the gender bias of his regicide tracts that envision community as essentially male. In the epic poem, it is Eve, a woman, who makes possible the community of brothers. Marriage is given great importance in *Paradise Lost*. Many scholars have commented on Milton's regard for companionate marriage. It has not been sufficiently emphasized that for Milton companionate marriage is the foundation for society, even a society of men. In the *Doctrine and Discipline of Divorce*, Milton writes that the three major ends of matrimony are "Godly society, next civill, and thirdly, that of the mariage-bed."[39] Marriage is not only private but also has its public and societal components: it enables both civil society as well as religious community. In *Paradise Lost*, the epic narrator's paean to wedded love makes similarly large claims for marriage: "wedded Love" is the origin of "Relations dear, and all the Charities / Of Father, Son, and Brother" (4.750, 756–57). Remarkably, marriage enables not just family relations but relations among men. Eve is crucial. There would be no marriage without her. Without her, there would be no paternal or fraternal relationships, no community.

When Adam bitterly inveighs against Eve, asking why God, though populating heaven with "Spirits Masculine," would create this "noveltie" (10.890, 891) and wishing men could reproduce without women, he is fallen. Attempting to shift blame that is rightly his, Adam wrongly finds fault with what had been a source of possibility and hope – Eve's newness. Adam is also wrong about angels; we learn in the catalogue of fallen angels in Book 1 that angels are bigendered. Angels can adopt whatever form, male or female, they wish; conversely, gender makes no sense with the angels. Adam eventually recants and acknowledges Eve's importance, an importance that does not diminish even after the fall: "Whence Haile to thee, / *Eve* rightly call'd, Mother of all Mankind, / Mother of all things living, since by thee / Man is to live, and all things live for Man" (11.158–61). After the fall, Eve still makes family and community possible. She is all the more "Mother" because man will be saved by her son.

Eve herself does not fail to fulfill the promise of being second. The last speech in the poem, surprisingly, belongs to Eve. She gets the last word in the poem, a final speech that emphasizes her redemptive role. Meeting Adam, who has just returned from being shown visions of the future by Michael, Eve is comforted by the promise of salvation: "though all by mee is lost, . . . By mee the Promis'd Seed shall all restore" (12.621–23). Even

---

[39] Ernst Sirluck, ed., *Complete Prose Works of John Milton*, vol. II (New Haven: Yale University Press, 1959), 268.

as she acknowledges her part in the fall, Eve looks forward to the future, not to private consolations but to a public renewal: the coming of Christ who will "all restore." Given that *Paradise Lost*, though published in 1667, was completed only three years after the Restoration, the word "restore" recalls the late civil wars and the subsequent return of monarchy. Rather than denoting Milton's capitulation, however, the word has a more radical subtext.[40] For Michael's vision of human history, which Eve's speech sums up and to which it responds, is a shaming narrative of how human society recurrently degenerates into tyrannical monarchy. The restoration Eve anticipates will do away with such sinful human institutions. Milton reappropriates the word "restore" to mean a godly reordering of the civic space. The poem's ending has been read as portraying the fall as a *felix culpa*:[41] Eve's reference to the "Promis'd Seed" is essentially hopeful. Satan's triumph is not permanent. There will be another, greater restoration. Suggestively, at the very end of the epic, Milton leaves Adam and Eve still in the vicinity of paradise: "The World was all before them, where to choose / Thir place of rest, and Providence thir guide: / They hand in hand with wandring steps and slow, / Through *Eden* took thir solitarie way" (12.646–49).

By letting Eve articulate the desire for political renewal and change, Milton emphasizes the importance of the politically disenfranchised.[42] Although Eve does not have access to the vision, nonetheless she speaks the final words. Adam tacitly endorses Eve's claim, not correcting or modifying her words one jot: "*Adam* heard / Well pleas'd, but answer'd not" (12.624–25). Although Eve is not shown the visions, in her dream she receives the main message, and most importantly, it is through her that this political dream will come true. Eve, the ostensibly inferior woman, becomes greater than Adam in her role as mother of mankind and of the Savior. Like the Son and like Abdiel, Eve is another lesser figure who upsets the initial hierarchy, this time the gender hierarchy. The last shall be first, and the first last. Although Eve is the first to fall, it is through her that Christ brings salvation to men. Milton's hierarchies – both gender and family – are characterized by

---

[40] In her biblical epic Lucy Hutchinson uses the word "restoration" with a similar radical, dissenting edge: describing the great flood of Genesis, the narrator wonders, "What will full Restoration be, if this / But the first daybreak of God's favour is?" (*Order and Disorder*, ed. David Norbrook [Oxford: Blackwell, 2001], canto 8, lines 27–28). See David Loewenstein, *Representing Revolution in Milton and His Contemporaries: Religion, Politics, and Polemics in Radical Puritanism* (Cambridge: Cambridge University Press, 2001).

[41] Arthur O. Lovejoy, "Milton and the Paradox of the Fortunate Fall," *ELH* 4 (1937), 161–79. For a rebuttal, see Virginia R. Mollenkott, "Milton's Rejection of the Fortunate Fall," *Milton Quarterly* 6 (1972), 1–5.

[42] Whether or not Milton believes renewal possible, some of his contemporaries – including Fifth Monarchists preparing for the coming of King Jesus to dethrone Charles II – thought it imminent.

flexibility and dynamism, shifting with changing circumstance, depending on the merit of individuals. He is no feminist, but neither is he the patriarchal bogey first identified by Virginia Woolf and perpetuated by Sandra Gilbert and Susan Gubar. In his study of the receptions of sexual difference in *Paradise Lost* from the eighteenth century to the present day, Joseph Wittreich points out, "Not just most of the participants in the culture wars, but some feminists have forgotten that a patriarchal Milton, a bruisingly misogynistic Milton, is an early invention of Milton's male readership; that such conceptualizations figure, in the inaugural phase of Milton criticism, as part of a challenge to and devaluation of feminism itself."[43] Milton's world is mutable, with the possibility for men to rise as well as for them to fall. As Raphael tells Adam, "God made thee perfet, not immutable" (5.524). Eve's expression of hope for renewal at the end of *Paradise Lost* is a fitting end for a poem that favors lesser figures; a poem that looks forward to the new generation, figured as younger brothers; a poem that vigorously asserts that new men will rise up to take the place of the old.

[43] Joseph Wittreich, "Milton's Transgressive Maneuvers: Receptions (Then and Now) and the Sexual Politics of *Paradise Lost*," in Stephen B. Dobranski and John P. Rumrich, eds., *Milton and Heresy* (Cambridge: Cambridge University Press, 1998), 258.

CHAPTER 6

Marriage and monarchy: Margaret Cavendish's Blazing World *and the fictions of queenly rule*

NEW MONARCHY, OLD CAVALIERS

On the eve of the Restoration, William Cavendish, the Earl of Newcastle, later to become duke, wrote a book of advice for the future Charles II. In it, he advocates the use of ceremony to maintain royal authority, urging Charles "to shew your Selfe Gloryously, to your People; Like a God, for the Holly writt sayes, wee have Calld you Godds – & when the people sees you thus, they will Downe of their knees, which is worshipp, & pray for you with trembling Feare, & Love."[1] Besides comparing kings to gods, Newcastle also employs the Stuart marriage analogy to describe the king's relation to his people: "the king, & the Comonweath is no more to be Separated Then Christe & his Church" (72). With these overtones of divine-right kingship, it is not surprising that Newcastle's views take an absolutist cast. Thus church and law are to be "Bound upp under your Majesties prerogative" (34), that is the king should have transcendent authority over both. Newcastle warns against attempts by both churchmen and lawyers to appropriate sovereignty for themselves. While acknowledging that the king cannot go against God's law, he claims that churchmen "expound Gods will to bee what is best for their Advantage, & then they are kinges, & Rule" (34). Similarly, lawyers claim special knowledge of the law: "The Lawyeres sayes The kinge is to bee obayd, butt not againeste the Lawe, – & the – Lawyeres will Expound the Lawe to their beste advantage to Rule – & thus Robb your Majestie of your subiects, to bee their Subiects" (34). The authority to interpret scripture and law must be retained by the sovereign. In other words, the king is unlimited by scripture or positive law in any practical sense insofar as the king, as well as churchmen and lawyers, can interpret in ways that favor his case.

---

[1] Thomas P. Slaughter, ed., *Ideology and Politics on the Eve of Restoration: Newcastle's Advice to Charles II* (Philadelphia: American Philosophical Society, 1984), 44–45. Further references are given parenthetically.

In his "Advice," Newcastle adopts a Machiavellian pragmatic and amoral politics.[2] On the one hand, the king must have sufficient money and arms, that which gives power real force; on the other, ceremony and religion are ideological tools to secure the seeming consent of subjects. Machiavellian expedience thus allies Newcastle with Hobbes, a client of the Cavendishes, who also confers on the king supremacy in civil law and religion. Despite his urging Charles to follow the example of Elizabeth I's politics of love in her relations with subjects, Newcastle does more than simply hark back to Elizabethan times. Given the Machiavellian and Hobbesian subtexts of "Advice," its emphasis on ceremony is not simply a reactionary valorization of tradition. Traditional motifs, such as the marriage analogy, are given new meaning.

It is true that Newcastle had no significant political role to play in the Restoration. Although a valued member of Charles I and Henrietta Maria's court – he won the coveted position of tutor to the young Prince Charles, and during the wars he contributed a large part of his estate to the king's cause – Newcastle's position was no longer the same after the Restoration. From a different generation than the new king, he lived through the reigns of the previous two Stuart monarchs and was sadly out of step with the style of the new court. Newcastle did not have the ear of the adult Charles II, who was not inclined to follow the advice of his deceased father's or his mother's courtiers, but instead gathered a set of his own trusted advisors. In giving William the title of duke, Charles II was doing no more than acknowledging services to his unfortunate father. It was not only religious dissenters who had had to retreat with the Restoration; royalists who did not fit in the new court found themselves marginalized, no longer of the king's counsel.

Newcastle was among a group of Cavaliers hoping to be rewarded for their loyalty, compensated for their losses, and restored to their former wealth and standing. His resources considerably strained, Charles II could not fully fulfill their hopes. To make matters worse, he also needed to reward those parliamentarians, like General Monck, who made his restoration possible. Having expected to triumph over their enemies, the Cavaliers became discontented with Charles II and bitterly resented the king's apparent favor to parliamentarians. As early as 1661, in response to complaints

---

[2] For Newcastle's Machiavellism, see Arthur S. Turberville, *A History of Welbeck Abbey and its Owners*, vol. I, 1539–1755 (London: Faber & Faber, 1938), 61; Gloria Italiano Anzilotti, "Foreword," *An English Prince: Newcastle's Machiavellian Political Guide to Charles II* (Pisa: Giardini Editori e Stampatori, 1988), 59–75; and Conal Condren, "Casuistry to Newcastle: 'The Prince' in the World of the Book," in Nicholas Phillipson and Quentin Skinner, eds., *Political Discourse in Early Modern Britain* (Cambridge: Cambridge University Press, 1993), 164–86.

about offices not going to Cavaliers, Ormond, lord steward, surveyed the royal household to discover only two former Cromwellians among the servants, a porter and a sculleryman.[3] Yet popular perception continued to find the king insufficiently generous. In 1665, Samuel Pepys notes widespread Cavalier discontent: "the discontented Cavaliers that thinks [*sic*] their Loyalty is not considered."[4] He quotes Sir James Bunch saying, "this is the time for you . . . that were for Oliver heretofore; you are full of imployment, and we poor Cavaliers sit still and can get nothing."[5] The emphasis in Newcastle's "Advice" on rewarding friends and punishing enemies was a familiar note sounded by Cavaliers in the first period of the Restoration. At least up until 1670, Charles II was seen as too ready to appease his father's enemies and too tardy in rewarding friends. In 1670–1, when Charles supported the new Conventicle Act, the Cavaliers gained confidence in him, though that confidence quickly vanished when by the end of 1672 Charles's secret alliance with Catholic France was revealed. It became apparent that Charles favored tolerating Protestant dissenters so as to allow for the toleration of Catholics.[6]

The first decade of the Restoration was no unmitigated victory for the Cavaliers. In "Advice," Newcastle recycles earlier royalist ideas and concerns in this new context. Aiming to regain pre-civil war preeminence, royalists like Newcastle returned to themes of the Caroline period, including use of the family analogy, in an attempt to reconstitute their community. The new context, however, meant that the reiteration of family metaphors cannot exactly replicate Caroline past. The marriage analogy was undermined by Charles II's sexual promiscuity, and more damagingly, by Cavalier perception of him as politically promiscuous, favoring old parliamentarian enemies over Cavaliers. In the Restoration, the family-state analogy was not just an articulation of royal identity but rather, in the hands of royalists like Newcastle, an assertion of group identity. Hence, in "Advice," Newcastle stresses not just ceremonies that act as social glue, but also the king's dependence on a strong aristocracy. It was the aristocracy who "as the sinews of warr, mayntayneing them selves, & his [Charles I's] warr, almoste att their owne Charge, & held out beyond all Expectation, – itt was neyther the Church, nor the Lawe, that kepte upp the king so long, butt parte of

---

[3] Paul H. Hardacre, *The Royalists during the Puritan Revolution* (The Hague: Martinus Nijhoff, 1956), 147.

[4] Samuel Pepys, *The Diary of Samuel Pepys*, ed. Robert Latham and William Matthews, 11 vols. (Berkeley and Los Angeles: University of California Press, 2000), VI:303.

[5] *Ibid.*, VI:329–30.

[6] John Miller, *After the Civil Wars: English Politics and Government in the Reign of Charles II* (Harlow, UK: Pearson/Longman, 2000), 200–02.

the Nobilety, & Gentery" (46). After all, Newcastle says, "the worste in the Nobility is, but to pull downe one king, & sett upp an other, so that they are always for monarkey, butt the Comons, pull downe Roote, & branch, & utterly distroyes monarky" (47). When royalists subscribe to divine-right monarchy they do so out of class loyalty as well. Newcastle even seems to suggest that the aristocracy share in the king's divinity. In one copper-cut illustration from his lavishly produced manual on horsemanship, *La Méthode Nouvelle de dresser les Chevaux* (1658), a crowned Newcastle rides a centaur-driven chariot in a circle of horses bowing down before him, a remarkable assertion of semi-divine powers on his part.

This chapter considers one royalist rearticulation of Caroline values in the Restoration. I focus not on Newcastle, however, but on his wife, Margaret Cavendish, whose dissection of monarchy is remarkably attuned to the concerns of the Old Cavaliers and their sense of their own marginality. With a restored king, and moreover one with unpopular policies, Cavendish is less concerned with justifying monarchy than to imagine a place for royalists. She is no less obsessed than other Cavaliers with place-getting. In her biography of her husband, Cavendish describes in great detail the losses Newcastle sustained, lamenting that the law "shew'd no favour to him, besides that the Act of Oblivion proved a great hinderance and obstruction to those his Designs, as it did no less to all the Royal Party."[7] She even draws up a table itemizing the value of Newcastle's properties from a 1641 survey to show by how much his estate was reduced in the wars. By 1667, the publication date of her biography, Cavendish, grandly claiming objectivity, did not perhaps have reason to hope for preferment:

But being so much as I am above base Profit, or any Preferment whatsoever, I cannot fear to be suspected of Flattery, in declaring to the world the Merits, Wealth, Power, Loyalty, and Fortunes of my Noble Lord, who hath done great Actions, suffered great Losses, endured a long Banishment for his Loyalty to his King and Countrey; and leads now, like another *Scipio*, a quiet Countrey-life. (Sig. D2v–D3)

But, a defense of Newcastle's conduct during the civil war and an accounting of his material losses, Cavendish's *Life* is hagiography put to the service of the new Restoration party politics. For Newcastle did not in fact entirely retire from public life. In 1661 he was among the royalist gentry who wanted to recoup their impropriated tithes in a bill passed by the House of Lords (but stopped by Commons). Participating in local politics, he held a lieutenancy in the late 1670s, but was also politically allied with the powerful Sir Thomas

---

[7] Cavendish, *The Life of the Thrice Noble, High, and Puissant Prince William Cavendishe* (London, 1675), 117. Further references are given parenthetically.

Osborne, Earl of Danby, who came to power after Edward Hyde, Earl of Clarendon's fall. Even as late as the 1685 general elections, despite his ill-health, Newcastle attended the election at Nottingham to ensure support for the Tories.[8]

The Cavendishes' retirement to Welbeck Castle was no simple political withdrawal, especially considering Margaret Cavendish's strenuous efforts in publishing her writings. Hero Chalmers persuasively demonstrates how Cavendish's flamboyant self-display, both in print and in person, serves to defend her husband's social status. Cavendish's fortuitous meeting with Henry Lawes, which introduced her to a royalist literary circle, authorized her writing "as a gesture of political opposition on the part of dispossessed royalists"; "as the legal function of his identity," Cavendish serves as her husband's "surrogate."[9] In the context of aristocratic magnificence, Cavendish's self-display is consonant with an ideal of wifely obedience. Focusing on the interregnum period, Chalmers notes that the Restoration entailed modulations in her "rhetoric of fame" and that "ideals of heroic femininity so current during the royalist struggles of the 1640s and 1650s could still have a resonance after the Restoration."[10] Such resonance is not surprising if we consider the perceived marginalization of Old Cavaliers in the Restoration. Together with a rhetoric of isolation, Cavendish's modes of self-display champion Cavalier values embodied by her husband. Her political gestures were made not in defiance of her husband's authority but under its aegis. Cavendish claims, "If I had never married the person I have, I do beleeve I should never have writ so, as to have adventured to divulge my works."[11] She portrays herself as a happy, loving wife: the frontispiece to the 1656 edition of *Natures Pictures* shows her with Newcastle, his children, their spouses, and friends in a warm familial circle around the fireplace. This self-portrayal harks back to Caroline idealization of Charles I and Henrietta Maria's marriage, with the royal union symbolizing the loving rapprochement of monarchy and people. At the same time, the domestic image criticizes Cromwellian politics and celebrates royalist community.

The fact that Cavendish still operated under her husband's aegis can disguise at a casual glance the shift in gender roles. While women's legal designation as *femme couverte* still applied, gender relationships nonetheless

---

[8] Miller, *After the Civil Wars*, 178, 224, 288.
[9] Hero Chalmers, "Dismantling the Myth of 'Mad Madge': The Cultural Context of Margaret Cavendish's Authorial Self-Presentation," *Women's Writing* 4.3 (1997), 324–25.
[10] *Ibid.*, 333.
[11] Cavendish, *The Worlds Olio* (1655), sig. E3v. Further references are given parenthetically.

have changed. As petitioner, Cavendish represented her husband before Parliament; as the author of his biography, she represented him in print. Much has been written on female sectaries and their effect on public religious life. In addition, women of all political persuasions petitioned Parliament on a range of issues from private property disputes to matters of public concern such as trade regulations and the conduct of criminal trials. Women petitioners claimed the right to influence the way Parliament governed the country by insisting that they "have a very equal share and interest with men in the commonwealth."[12] Cavendish's example, as one such petitioner hoping to gain a pension, suggests a change also in the roles of aristocratic women.[13] The shift in gender roles, initiated in the civil wars and interregnum, was hard to reverse in the Restoration.

Something of the sort happened between the Cavaliers and the king. While there may not have been drastic political or constitutional changes, Cavaliers' relationship with the king also changed. Resentful of the Restoration settlement, they became less enthusiastic about the king they helped restore to the throne. Pepys captures the mood of the Cavaliers in a 1667 comment: "It is strange how . . . everybody doth nowadays reflect upon Oliver and commend him, so brave things he did and made all the neighbour princes fear him; while here a prince, come in with all the love and prayers and good liking of his people, and have given greater signs of loyallty and willingness to serve him with their estates then ever was done by any people, hath lost all so soon."[14] In her analysis of Restoration politics, Cavendish strikingly represents Old Cavaliers like her husband as feminized by their position in the new order. Figuring Cavalier marginality in gendered terms, Cavendish could at once envision a more important role for women to play in governance and still support Cavalier ideals. She does so by extending greater political roles only to aristocratic women. In her imaginative writings, Cavaliers like Newcastle, feminized because marginalized, come to share greater equality with their wives.

Women's greater participation in political life is rarely accounted for in political theory of the period. Hobbes posits an initial equality between men and women in the state of nature, but women quickly lose that equality with childbearing. Carole Pateman argues that Hobbes elides over the need

---

[12] *England's Moderate Messenger* (London, 1649), cited by Ann Marie McEntee, "'The [Un]Civill-Sisterhood of Oranges and Lemons': Female Petitioners and Demonstrators, 1642–53," in James Holstun, ed., *Pamphlet Wars: Prose in the English Revolution* (London: F. Cass, 1992), 98.

[13] Susan Wiseman, "Margaret Cavendish among the Prophets: Performance Ideologies and Gender in and after the English Civil War," *Women's Writing* 6.1 (1999), 95–111, relates the performance of female visionaries to female performance on stage.

[14] Pepys, *Diary*, VIII:332.

for a prior sexual contract before there can be a social contract among men.[15] In modern scholarship, there is frequently too an elision of women out of the history of political thought. Quite simply, histories of political thought that focus on high political theory and their canonical texts cannot account for women's political ideas. We need to turn to imaginative works of fiction and other genres of writing. Cavendish is a natural figure for such reassessment.

Modern scholars have started to take Cavendish seriously as a natural philosopher, putting her work in the context of seventeenth-century science, but they have been slower to treat Cavendish seriously as a political theorist.[16] This is in part due to Cavendish's own demurrals about women in politics. In *Philosophical Letters* (1664), after evaluating the first part of Hobbes's *Leviathan* as natural philosophy, Cavendish claims that because matters of government do not concern her as a woman, she refrains from commenting on the rest of the work, which is overtly political: "First, That a Woman is not imployed in State Affairs, unless an absolute Queen. Next, That to study the Politicks, is but loss of Time, unless a man were sure to be a Favourite to an absolute Prince. Thirdly, That it is but a deceiving Profession, and requires more Craft then Wisdom."[17] Such statements must be read in the context of Cavalier resentment, as part of a rhetoric of isolation. Not only did Cavendish know about her husband's "Advice," a work of politics by a man who failed to become the prince's favorite, but it has been suggested that her "Judgment's Commonwealth" bears comparison with Newcastle's longer work.[18] Furthermore, *The World's Olio* (1655), the massive, hodge-podge volume collecting "Judgment's Commonwealth," contains other material on political subjects, including short histories of English monarchs.

---

[15] Carole Pateman, *The Sexual Contract* (Stanford: Stanford University Press, 1988).

[16] This is changing: Victoria Kahn, *Wayward Contracts: The Crisis of Political Obligation in England, 1640–1674* (Princeton: Princeton University Press, 2004), which includes Cavendish, offers, among other things, a subtle analysis of the marriage contract as analogy for the political contract. See also Margaret Cavendish, *Political Writings*, ed. Susan James (Cambridge: Cambridge University Press, 2003).

[17] Cavendish, *Philosophical Letters: or, Modest Reflections Upon Some Opinions in Natural Philosophy* (London, 1664), Letter XIII, 47, sig. N2.

[18] Ellayne Fowler, "Margaret Cavendish and the Ideal Commonwealth," *Utopian Studies* 7.1 (1996), 38–48. For Cavendish's "Christianized Machiavellianism," see David Norbrook, "Women, the Republic of Letters, and the Public Sphere," *Criticism* 46.2 (2004), 299–30. For differences in the political views of Cavendish and her husband, see Hilda L. Smith, "'A General War amongst the Men . . . but None amongst the Women': Political Differences between Margaret and William Cavendish," in Howard Nenner, ed., *Politics and the Political Imagination in Later Stuart Britain: Essays Presented to Lois Green Schwoerer* (Rochester: University of Rochester Press, 1997), 143–60.

Cavendish's rethinking of monarchy, and the political uses to which literary forms can be put, is shown by the example of the poem concluding *The World's Olio*, in which she imagines an ideal judge-king who is "a Father to the Common-wealth" (217). Such a king must not be driven by paranoid fears, otherwise "with this Fear a Tyrant he becomes, / And then he Massacres, and Martyrdoms / All his best Subjects, free from factious strife, / That Loyal are, . . . / But scorn to flatter, or applaud his Crimes" (218). In imagining this ideal king, she seems to be chiding the exiled Prince Charles for lack of martial valor. Cavendish is not concerned in the slightest about the common man. Rather, she cares about the king's relation with his "best subjects," the aristocracy. Newcastle's maxim that "the king can doe no wrong, & it is moste true, for hee is Above the Law" (54) does not apply when it touches the well-being of nobles. The best subjects may criticize the king while commoners should not dispute his prerogative. Cavendish's notion of a fit king and how he must indeed fit himself to the position is such that she can imagine a monarchy that can devolve onto someone other than a hereditary successor. The ideal king must be a man of courage and action; he must not be overly religious, overly inclined to "lazy Praying," for "such faint-hearted Prince, is fitter for / A private life, than Kingdome that's in War; / And fitter to Obey, than to Command, / Or Rule and Reign, in Peace, War, Sea or Land; / And fitter far it were, whilst he doth live, / That he the Sovereign Power up did give / Unto a Kinsman, or himself did choose / A Wise and Valiant man, that Power to use" (219). The king can choose to yield sovereignty to a "Kinsman," which preserves the notion of divine right, but Cavendish offers another choice, that of a "Wise and Valiant man," one not of royal blood, to use monarchical power and become *de facto* king, even if the sovereign maintains his title.

The impersonal formulation, "fitter far it were," leaves ambiguous how the state is to be put right if the king happens to be unfit. He seems to be expected to abdicate. However, there is no suggestion of a forced ejection though Charles I's beheading must loom over these lines. In her later and best-known work, *The Description of a New World, Called The Blazing World* (1666), Cavendish would provide answers about the means. Her "Wise and Valiant" chancellor turns out not to be a man at all but aristocratic women – queens and their female courtiers. By giving female characters vast scope in the state, Cavendish rewrites monarchy as partnership. She portrays wives usurping their husbands' powers. In *Sociable Letters* (1664), Cavendish claims that women are not tied, nor bound to State or Crown; we are free, not Sworn to Allegiance, nor do we take the Oath of Supremacy; we are not made Citizens of the Common-wealth, . . . and if we be not Citizens in the Commonwealth, I know no reason we should be Subjects to the Commonwealth. And the truth is, we are no Subjects, unless it be to our Husbands, and not alwayes to them, for sometimes we usurp their Authority, or else by flattery we get their good wills to govern.[19]

Women stand both inside and outside politics, wielding political power indirectly and circuitously. This formulation makes peculiar sense of the analogy between household and polity. The domestic revolution necessarily has political ramifications. The restructuring of the wife's role in the house-hold transfers to the state when her husband happens to be an emperor of a world, as is the case in *Blazing World*. In rewriting patriarchalism, Milton treats the problem of gender by viewing femaleness in analogical position to the younger son. Although inferior, both younger son and the wife can in his mutable world rise to greater positions. Milton's analogy reenvisions political as well as domestic hierarchies in revolutionary ways, even if the gender hierarchy may itself be reinforced in the process. In *Blazing World*, Cavendish makes the wife not analogous to the younger son but instead to the absolute monarch.

HEROIC QUEENS: FIGURATIONS OF HENRIETTA MARIA

The Blazing World, as with so much of her work, has often been read in ways that emphasize how Cavendish discursively produces an isolated, private, interior self, one that "retreats to the empire of the mind."[20] But her many invocations of "fancy" do not simply betray a mind that prefers the private imagination to the public, external world. In joining *The Blazing World* to *Observations upon Experimental Philosophy* (1666), a work of "fancy" to a treatise on natural philosophy, Cavendish suggests a link between fancy and reason. In the prefatorial address preceding *The Blazing World*, "To the

---

[19] James Fitzmaurice, ed., *Sociable Letters* (New York and London: Garland Publishing, 1997), 25. Further references are cited parenthetically.
[20] Catherine Gallagher, "Embracing the Absolute: The Politics of the Female Subject in Seventeenth-Century England," *Genders* 1 (1988), 27. Despite points of disagreement, my work is indebted to Gallagher's seminal analysis of the link between the absolute monarch and the absolute self. Recent scholarship is moving away from seeing Cavendish as an oddity: Anna Battigelli, *Margaret Cavendish: Exiles of the Mind* (Lexington: University Press of Kentucky, 1998), the first monograph on Cavendish, is an intellectual biography that locates her within political, religious, and philosophical thought, particularly the Platonism of Henrietta Maria's court; and Emma L. Rees, *Margaret Cavendish: Gender, Genre, Exile* (Manchester: Manchester University Press, 2003), examines her innovations with genre by paying attention to her reading of Lucretius, Plato, Homer, and others.

Reader," she explicitly claims, "when I distinguish *fancy* from *reason*; I mean
not as if fancy were not made by the rational parts of matter."[21] Although
she views both as different processes, nonetheless both are to her "actions
of the rational parts of matter" (124). More interestingly, what Cavendish
calls works of fancy are more, not less, politically engaged than her natural
philosophy, which she calls her works of reason.[22] For instance, she describes
the *Blazing World* as having the following three parts: "the first part whereof
is *romancical*, the second philosophical, and the third is merely *fancy*, or
(as I may call it) *fantastical*" (124). *The Blazing World* is divided into two
formal parts. The three parts that Cavendish alludes to probably refer first
to the Lady's adventures, in which the Lady finds herself in a new world and
marries the Emperor of that world (the romance); second to the Empress's
enquiry into the nature of matter and spirit (natural philosophy); and third
to the war in the Empress's own world, in which the Empress uses her
forces from the Blazing World to help the sovereign of her native country
become an absolute monarch of his world (the fantasy). It is the third,
which Cavendish calls "fancy" or "fantastical," that is the most political of
the work, as it is concerned with empire-building.

The political dimension of Cavendish's "fancy," the imagination, is
best understood when put in the context of Caroline court culture. As
R. Malcolm Smuts points out, Charles's court was far more cosmopolitan
than James's or Elizabeth's; both Charles and his courtiers had spent time
in the European courts of Madrid, Paris, Florence, and Rome; his queen
was from a major Catholic dynasty of the continent.[23] Like his father,
Charles adopted a foreign policy that favored peace. Both he and Henrietta Maria fostered the court's taste for fine art and theater, cultivating
such artists as Rubens, Van Dyck, and Inigo Jones. Under such circumstances, art was not neutral. Certainly, the divisions of the civil war ensured
that art and art forms that the Caroline court favored acquired specific
political associations: Smuts suggests that "prewar culture of the court provided materials used to construct a partisan royalist tradition in the 1640s
and after."[24] Bearing affinities with Caroline courtly culture in its evoca-
tion of the themes of Caroline masques, Cavendish's art, the product of

---

[21] Kate Lilley, ed., *Blazing World and Other Writings* (London: Penguin, 1992), 123. Further references
are from this edition and cited parenthetically.

[22] This is not to deny that Cavendish's works of natural philosophy have a political ideology: see John
Rogers, *The Matter of Revolution: Science, Poetry, and Politics in the Age of Milton* (Ithaca: Cornell
University Press, 1996), chapter 6.

[23] R. Malcolm Smuts, *Court Culture and the Origins of a Royalist Tradition in Early Stuart England*
(Philadelphia: University of Pennsylvania Press, 1987).

[24] *Ibid.*, 6.

her "fancy," is deeply influenced by the values of the Caroline court. In the *Blazing World*, Cavendish's engagement with Caroline court culture is manifest in her adoption of images and themes surrounding Henrietta Maria. Here I focus on two related aspects: martial queens, part of Henrietta Maria's self-portrayal, and masque imagery.

The Blazing World's Empress is represented as a martial monarch, signaled by her imperial clothes, dazzlingly covered with multi-colored diamonds and pearls. She holds in her left hand "a buckler, to signify the defence of her dominions" and in her right "a spear made of a white diamond, cut like the tail of a blazing star, which signified that she was ready to assault those that proved her enemies" (133). Dressed in these robes – the description of her clothes is more or less repeated in the second part – the Empress leads the Blazing World navy into her native world as a warrior woman. This representation of the Empress has been read as an appropriation of Elizabethan iconography.[25] A closer model is Henrietta Maria with her self-fashioning as a *femme forte*, the singular heroic woman.

Carol Barash believes Cavendish adopted her flamboyant behavior from the *frondeuses*.[26] During the Fronde, a series of popular rebellions against the monarchy between 1648 and 1653, women *frondeuses* played a prominent role as military commanders and as political leaders, often in male dress, appearing as though real-life Amazons were walking the streets of Paris. Anne Marie d'Orléans, the "Grande Mademoiselle," niece of Anne of Austria and cousin to the king, turned the king's own canons against him. The rebellion finally collapsed, a failure Joan DeJean attributes partly to the lack of solidarity among *frondeuses* unwilling to submerge their vanity for a greater common cause.[27] Cavendish's masculine dress and her custom of styling herself "princess" on the title pages of her books were manners straight from the *frondeuses*. She would have witnessed the beginning of Fronde uprising, for the Newcastles left Paris in 1648, and personally observed women taking on male roles. Her response to such gender-crossing was mixed. The Fronde's more democratic politics were in opposition to her royalism, and having fled from the civil war in England, Cavendish would hardly have welcomed the idea of a civil war in France. Her allusion to the civil unrest that the Fronde rebellion brought to Paris in Letter 172 of

[25] Claire Jowitt, "Imperial Dreams? Margaret Cavendish and the Cult of Elizabeth," *Women's Writing* 4.3 (1997), 383–99.

[26] Carol Barash, *English Women's Poetry, 1649–1714: Politics, Community, and Linguistic Authority* (Oxford: Clarendon Press, 1996), 35.

[27] Joan DeJean, *Tender Geographies: Women and the Origins of the Novel in France* (New York: Columbia University Press, 1991), 42.

Sociable Letters shows serious misgivings: "I am so full of Fear, as I write this Letter with great Difficulty, for all this City hath been in an Uproar, and all through a Factious Division betwixt the Common Council, and those they call the Lords, which are the Higher Magistrates, the Common People gather together in Multitudes, Pretending for the Right of their Privileges, but it is thought the Design is to Plunder the Merchants Houses and the Churches" (183). For Cavendish, it would have seemed all too much like the overturning of her world in England.

Cavendish need not look to France for examples of the *femme forte*; she found them at home. Henrietta Maria took on martial characters in masques and even played an active role in the civil war, at one time leading her army triumphantly into Oxford. As a young girl, Cavendish had also seen the formidable Marie de Medici, Henrietta Maria's mother, entertained in Colchester. Sophie Tomlinson argues that the correspondence between Lady Sanspareille's behavior from Cavendish's *Youths Glory and Deaths Banquet* and Francis Osborne's comment on Elizabeth I's public speaking as "something too Theatrical for a virgine Prince" suggests that Cavendish's fantasy of performance is based on female monarchs.[28] In his diary Samuel Pepys compares Cavendish to Queen Christina of Sweden: when Cavendish came to court in 1667, "There [was] as much expectation of her coming to Court . . . as if it were the Queen of Sweden" that a great crowd gathered to try to catch a glimpse of her.[29] As Tomlinson points out, Pepys's comment can be understood as a reference to Queen Christina's posturing as a *femme forte*. Bulstrode Whitelocke records Christina's masculine clothing and behavior: she wore "a jackett such as men weare" and "a black velvet cappe . . . which she used to put off and on as men doe their hattes."[30] In her biography of Newcastle, Cavendish describes Henrietta Maria as a copy of her father: "Her Majesty shewed as much Courage as every any person could do; for Her undaunted and generous Spirit was like her Royal Birth deriving it self from that unparrallel'd King Her Father, whose Heroick Actions will be in perpetual Memory" (37–38).

Henrietta Maria's particular brand of *femme forte*, as discussed in Chapter 1, features heroic wives, and it is this version that Cavendish borrows. While this is most fully developed in the *Blazing World*, her other

---

[28] Sophie Tomlinson, "'My Brain the Stage': Margaret Cavendish and the Fantasy of Female Performance," in Clare Brant and Diane Purkiss, eds., *Women, Texts and Histories 1575–1760* (London and New York: Routledge, 1992), 146–47; Francis Osborne, *Historical Memoires on the Reigns of Queen Elizabeth and King James* (London, 1658), 60.

[29] Pepys, *Diary*, VIII:163–4.

[30] Bulstrode Whitelocke, *A Journal of the Swedish Embassy in the Years 1653 and 1654*, 2 vols. (London, 1772), 1:234.

fictions also are fascinated with wives playing public roles and even eclipsing their husbands. The heroine of *Bell in Campo*, a play touching directly on the civil war, forms a female army when the men refuse to take women into battle. Appointed "Generalless, [their] Instructeress, Ruler and Commanderess," Lady Victoria exhorts the women to study military arts so that the men "believe we are fit to be Copartners in their Governments, and to help to rule the World" and shows herself the equal of her husband, the Lord General.[31] Not accepting her exclusion, the heroic wife performs deeds of valor to equal her husband in love and to share in his government of the state. Intertwining love and women's militarism, *Bell in Campo* suggests love depends on the woman taking on a male role. Proving more successful than the men's army, the women are called the "*Amazonian* Army" (595). The stage directions suggest that they adopt male clothing: "*Enter two women like* Amazons" (596). Finally, the men capitulate, addressing the women as "You Goddesses on Earth, who have the power and dominion over men, 'tis you we worship and adore" (616). Not desiring to rule over men, the women are instead "willing upon their submissions to be friends" (617). As *femme fortes*, the women inspire admiration and wonder; as in so many of Cavendish's fictions, the figure inspiring wonder is addressed as divinity though the women simply want equality. In *The Blazing World*, female heroism also takes the form of a military victory. The Empress patriotically leads an army from the Blazing World to defend her native country of ESFI (the acronyms probably stand for England, Scotland, France and Ireland). As *femme forte*, the Empress reveals a ferocious determination to quell all opposition. Going beyond defense, she forces the rest of the world to submit to her native country. She sets resisting cities on fire with fire-stones that burn when wet, placing the fire-stones under houses and waiting for rain. When one kingdom with a dry climate proves particularly recalcitrant, she, "being desirous to make it stoop" (214), waits for the annual flood to burn their houses down.

Despite the Empress's savagery, war in *The Blazing World* is largely represented as illusionist art. The Empress's war strategy includes having the bird-men and fish-men surround her with torches made of fire-stone to create a surprising effect: the torches "being many thousands, made a terrible show; for it appeared as if all the air and sea had been of a flaming fire; and all that were upon the sea, or near it, did verily believe, the time of judgement, or the last day was come, which made them all fall down and

---

[31] Cavendish, *Playes Written by the Thrice Noble, Illustrious and Excellent Princess, the Lady Marchioness of Newcastle* (London, 1662), 588–89. Further references are given parenthetically.

pray" (208). The Empress wages war partly by putting on a "show" reminiscent of the theatricality of Caroline masque. She uses the same technique to appear before the general and commanders of her native country "in a splendorous light, surrounded with fire" (209). Like Henrietta Maria, for whom Inigo Jones created images of light and motion in such masques as *Luminalia, or The Festival of Light* (1638) to represent her as the Platonic ideal of Beauty, the Empress is often surrounded by light.[32] At the very beginning, she survives the cold, outliving her kidnappers, because of "the *light of her beauty*, the heat of her youth, and protection of the gods" (126, my emphasis). Images of light proliferate around her when she becomes the Empress, including extensive use of light in the chapels she builds, another instance of masque-like show. *The Blazing World* ends with a description of courtly entertainments: the narrative closes with the Emperor, the Empress, and their nobles dancing to music. As masque-like theater, the war in the second part of *The Blazing World* ends in a manner typical of masques, offering the peaceful closure of a communal dance.

By making war into a masque and by giving the Empress imperial clothes that are not only beautiful but also fashioned with sartorial art symbolizing her martial role, Cavendish aestheticizes political actions and roles, and in turn she gives aesthetic objects political meaning. This relation between art and politics is especially clear with the problem of religion in *The Blazing World*. In this matter, the Empress is most like Henrietta Maria, who proselytized her Catholic religion in England primarily through art. Erika Veevers argues that not only were there implicit connections between Henrietta Maria's cult of Platonic love and her Catholicism (the former a version of the explicit worship of the Virgin Mary of the latter), there were also links between her elaborate court entertainments and the ceremonialism and theatricality of the Catholic mass.[33] Like Henrietta Maria, the Empress tries to convert the people of the Blazing World to her religion, understood as Christian though not marked as Catholic in Cavendish's narrative: "wherefore she consulted with her own thoughts, whether it was possible to convert them all to her own religion, and to that end she resolved to build churches, and make also up a congregation of women, whereof she intended to be the head herself, and to instruct them in several points of her religion" (162). Interestingly, this community of women parallels the one that Henrietta Maria formed at court. Among the women in Henrietta

---

[32] For the light imagery created by Inigo Jones for Henrietta Maria in the masques, see Erica Veevers, *Images of Love and Religion: Queen Henrietta Maria and Court Entertainments* (Cambridge: Cambridge University Press, 1989), ch. 4, "The Queen's Masques," 110–49, *passim*.

[33] *Ibid.*, ch. 3, "The Queen's Religion," 75–109, *passim*.

Maria's *précieux* group were a number of prominent nobles with strong Catholic sympathies; they both performed in Henrietta Maria's masques and attended mass with her.[34] There were fears that this circle of women would corrupt the court and the king into Catholicism, just as the Empress attempts to convert the country by first converting a group of women.[35]

Like the Empress, Henrietta Maria built two chapels, one at Somerset House and another at St. James's Palace. Inigo Jones, who designed sets for masques, was the architect. The first mass performed at the chapel in Somerset House in 1636, according to Malcolm Smuts, was a spectacular example of Henrietta Maria's use of art to advance the Catholic cause. Using theatrical mechanisms, including a "machine" to display the host, Jones represented "a Paradise of glory, forty feet in height" and raised the whole scene above seven ranges of clouds "in which were figures of archangels, of cherubim, of seraphim, to the number of two hundred, some adoring the Holy Sacrament, others singing and playing on all sorts of musical instruments, the whole painted according to the rules of perspective."[36] The whole display was illuminated with 400 lights such that the mass resembled a masque, making such an impression on Charles that he spent an hour and a half studying it afterwards. Henrietta Maria's chapels drew considerable numbers of curious non-Catholic visitors. Cavendish may even have had the opportunity to view the Queen's chapel at St. James's Palace, located in the area of London that her family frequented during the years before the civil war when they spent winters in the city. Amusing themselves by going to plays, they would also go "in the Spring time to visit the Spring garden, Hide-park, and the like places,"[37] all of which are around St. James's Palace and the fashionable Pall Mall area.

The effects that the Empress uses for her chapels are similarly dramatic. She builds two chapels "one above another" (163), one lined with diamonds and on top of that with fire-stone and the other with star-stone in order to produce contrasting effects. In the chapel lined with fire-stone where she "preached sermons of terror to the wicked" (164), she contrives to make the chapel seem on fire by mechanical devices to produce an illusion of hell fires: "when she would have that chapel where the fire-stone was, appear all in a flame, she had by the means of artificial-pipes, water conveyed into

---

[34] For a list of prominent masquers, including known or suspected Catholics, see *ibid.*, 86–88.

[35] See George F. Sensabaugh, "Platonic Love and the Puritan Rebellion," *Studies in Philology* 37 (1940), 457–81; and Smuts, *Court Culture*, chapter 8, "Religion," 217–240, *passim*.

[36] Thomas Birch, ed., *The Court and Times of Charles I*, 2 vols. (London: H. Colburn, 1848), II:311. Quoted in Smuts, *Court Culture*, 228–29.

[37] Margaret Cavendish, "A True Relation of my Birth, Breeding, and Life," *Natures Pictures Drawn by Fancies Pencil to the Life* (London, 1656), 372–73, sig. Bbb2v-Bbb3.

it, which by turning the cock, did, as out of a fountain, spring over all the room, and as long as the fire-stone was wet, the chapel seemed to be all in a flaming fire" (163–64). But the chapel lined with star-stone "did only cast a splendorous and comfortable light" and so there she "preached sermons of comfort" to the repentant (164). The Empress's congregation, like Henrietta Maria's, is supposed to draw meaning from the picture presented to them[38]: "as that chapel was an emblem of Hell, so this was an emblem of Heaven" (164). The Empress herself, like Henrietta Maria in her masques, is the main actor, appearing "like an angel" (164). She converts the people of the Blazing World by persuading them through the use of art: "And thus the Empress, by art, and her own ingenuity, did not only convert the Blazing World to her own religion, but kept them in a constant belief, without enforcement or blood-shed; for she knew well, that belief was a thing not to be forced or pressed upon the people, but to be instilled into their minds by gentle persuasions" (164). Like Henrietta Maria, who encouraged a cult of Neoplatonic love, viewed suspiciously by Puritans as a scheme to lead the court into Catholicism, the Empress relies on love to maintain her people's religious loyalty: "for fear, though it makes people obey, yet does it not last so long, nor is it so sure a means to keep them to their duties, as love" (164).

Cavendish may well be poking mild fun at Henrietta Maria. The similarity of the mechanical and artificial means of the Empress's chapels to that of the chapels and masques of Henrietta Maria is clear when we consider Ben Jonson's vituperation directed against Inigo Jones and his machines after their falling out:

> O Showes! Showes! Mighty Showes!
> The Eloquence of Masques! What need of prose,
> Or Verse, or sense, t'express Immortall you?
> You are the Spectacles of State! 'Tis true
> Court Hiero-gly-phicks! & all Artes afford,
> In the mere perspective of an Inch board!
> You aske me noe more then certeyne politique Eyes!
> Eyes, that can pierce into the Misteryes
> Of many Coulors! read them! & reveale
> Mythology, there, painted on slit-deale!
> O, to make Boardes to speake! There is a taske!
> Painting, & Carpentry, are the Soule of Masque![39]

---

[38] Veevers discusses how "the Queen liked to find religious significance in 'picture'" (*Images*, 126).

[39] Jonson, "An Expostulation with Inigo Jones," lines 39–50, in *Ben Jonson*, ed. C. H. Herford, Percy and Evelyn Simpson, 11 vols. (Oxford: Clarendon Press, 1925–52), VIII:403–04.

In *A Tale of a Tub* (1633), Jonson satirizes Jones with the character of In-and-In Medlay, a joiner who creates a masque for Squire Tub; like Jones, Medlay claims authorship but Jonson dismisses him as "The Worke-man, Sir! the artificer! I grant you."[40] It is interesting to note that in 1634, Jonson prepared a masque for the king and queen, *Love's Welcome at Bolsover*, in which he again satirizes Jones, and it was performed at William Newcastle's Bolsover Castle. It would be a decade before Margaret would meet William in Paris, but her many allusions to Jonson suggest that she might have known the masque.

Nonetheless, Cavendish understands the ideological purposes of Caroline masques, dramatizing in her *Blazing World* its use in mythologizing love between ruler and subjects. The chapels and the war are examples of theatrical art that bring subjects to love the Empress as ruler. They do so by doling out a judicious portion of fear as well, illustrating Newcastle's revision of the Machiavellian dictum that it is better to be feared than loved: in "Advice," Newcastle argues that it is best to have "Both, Love, & feare, mixte together as occation Serves" (68). Cavendish places a greater emphasis on love: in *The Blazing World*, the Duchess, Cavendish's alter-ego, was discouraged from conquering another world because "conquerers seldom enjoy their conquest, for they being more feared than loved" (185). The chapels also illustrate Newcastle's Hobbesian insistence that religion be subsumed under the king's authority. Repeating Hobbes's lessons from *Behemoth* on the pernicious effects of universities on political stability, lessons found also in Newcastle's "Advice," Cavendish's Empress commands her scholars to "confine your disputations to your schools, lest besides the commonwealth of learning, they disturb also divinity and polity, religion and laws, and by that means draw an utter ruin and destruction both upon church and state" (162). Stability of the commonwealth is closely linked to that of the church, and both require the management of subjects' love through use of art. In recalling Caroline masques that mythologize love between ruler and subject, the *Blazing World* makes their central metaphors literal. Worshipping the Empress as divine, her subjects "could hardly be persuaded to believe her mortal, tendered her all the veneration and worship due to a deity" (132). In her native country, art again renders her divine to her people: she appears "like an angel, or some deity" and "all kneeled down before her, and worshipped her with all submission and reverence" (210). Their worship makes the metaphor literal. Using Caroline ideals, Cavendish portrays a divine-right monarchy, but her divine-right king is a woman.

[40] Jonson, *A Tale of a Tub* 5.3.23, in *ibid.*, III:85.

THE MONARCH'S TWO BODIES

Scholars who treat both the Duchess and the Empress as figures for Margaret Cavendish herself assume a near monomaniacal egotism on Cavendish's part.[41] Once the Empress is recognized as a figuration of Henrietta Maria, we find Cavendish writing a far more politically engaged work than we first expect. Like other writers who grapple with questions about government in the wake of the civil war, Cavendish too attempts to conceptualize a workable monarchy. For her, the queen has a major role. More than her other works, *The Blazing World* depicts monarchy as a partnership. Far from displaying a self that Gallagher calls "the writing subject, who is isolated and complete unto herself" (27), the self in *The Blazing World* is one that forms partnerships in ties of love and family, whether with spouses or with platonic lovers.

Although Cavendish justifies an absolute monarchy by arguing that it is natural to have one head, whether for a physical body or for the body politic, the monarchy that she actually portrays is quite different. In terms reminiscent of royalist justifications, the denizens of the Blazing World explain to the Empress that they prefer an absolute monarchy:

They answered, that as it was natural for one body to have but one head, so it was also natural for a politic body to have but one governor; and that a commonwealth, which had many governors was like a monster with many heads: besides, said they, a monarchy is a divine form of government, and agrees most with our religion; for as there is but one God, whom we all unanimously worship and adore with one faith, so we are resolved to have but one Emperor, to whom we all submit with one obedience. (134)

Like the Stuarts, the people of the Blazing World believe the king to be divinely appointed by God, but the one person mistaken for divinity is the Empress herself. With the appearance of the Empress, the monarchy of the Blazing World becomes a monarchy with two governors.

The two bodies of the monarch in *The Blazing World* are the married couple, the Emperor and Empress. Like the wife of Cavendish's *Sociable Letters*, the Empress gets her husband's "good will to govern": "the Emperor rejoicing, made her his wife, and gave her an absolute power to rule and govern all that world as she pleased" (132). But this wife governs not just a household but also an entire world, becoming an absolute monarch through marriage. Taking a far more active role than the Emperor, who only makes

---

[41] For instance, see Gallagher on Cavendish's defeated ambitions as a woman ("Embracing the Absolute," 27).

brief appearances in the narrative, the Empress is arguably *de facto* king. No passive monarch, the first thing she does is to become informed of their politics and religion: "But before all things, she having got a sovereign power from the Emperor over all the world, desired to be informed both of the manner of their religion and government, and to that end she called the priests and statesmen, to give her an account of either" (134). Through marriage, the absolute monarchy of the Emperor is converted into a monarchy of two, in which an actively intervening queen consort becomes effectively queen regnant.

By fictionalizing the marriage metaphor of the Caroline period in *The Blazing World*, Cavendish offers a transformed monarchy in which both king and queen play significant roles. But Cavendish further complicates her model of monarchy. She acknowledges the part that courtiers play by giving the Empress's favorite, the Duchess, a prominent role as an advisor. Government is also a partnership between monarchs and subjects. Another instance of how the text mythologizes the relation between monarchs and subjects as one of love, her platonic friendship with the Duchess becomes in turn a substitute marriage. Their meeting replicates the love at first sight that the Emperor experiences when he meets the Empress: "and truly their meeting did produce such an intimate friendship between them, that they became platonic lovers, although they were both females" (183). This "intimate" friendship is compared to the inseparability of a single body: "for between dear friends there's no concealment, they being like several parts of one united body" (183). This image easily recalls the biblical notion that in marriage the partners become one flesh.

The friendship is a substitute marriage, however, not simply because the women are platonic lovers but because they act as partners in government. When there is unrest in the Blazing World, the Duchess suggests that the cause is the Empress's innovations and she advises the Empress to return things to their original state. When the Empress hears about the invasion of her native country, the Emperor himself urges her to consult the Duchess: "but you having told me of your dear Platonic friend the Duchess of Newcastle, and of her good and profitable counsels, I would desire you to send for her soul, and confer with her about this business" (204). The consultation having turned into preparations for war, the Emperor drops out of sight while the women are closeted together "in a serious council" (205). The Empress follows the Duchess's advice because she "loved the Duchess as her own soul" (206). The Duchess and the Empress achieve a closeness not matched by the Empress's marriage to the Emperor, for the Empress invites the Duchess's soul, without a body in the Blazing World, to reside in her own body: "Your soul, said the Empress, shall live with my soul, in my body; for I shall only desire your counsel and advice" (206). This spatial intimacy implies a political closeness: the Empress's "desire" for the Duchess's counsel, and "only" hers, cannot be separated from the friendship. Just as in the Caroline court, both idealized marriage and platonic love exist side-by-side in Cavendish's *Blazing World*. As in *Bell in Campo*, where women who follow Lady Victoria's example are rewarded while women who yield to their cowardly natures are punished, the women of *The Blazing World* gain political clout not only through marriage but also through alliance with a queen. Such political closeness between queen and courtier again parallels Newcastle's suggestion in "Advice" that the king support the aristocracy. With this friendship, Cavendish presents the proper relation between Cavaliers and king. The gendering of the relationship as female suggests its marginality in the Restoration world.

Even the contentious world of the Duchess and her Duke is portrayed as one where alliances with powerful women matter. The Duke's misfortunes are allegorized as a contest between the lady Fortune, whom the Duke has slighted, and Honesty, whom he prefers and whose "foster-son" he is, who "bred him from his childhood, and made a perpetual friendship betwixt him and Gratitude, Charity and Generosity" (199). At the court where the Duchess tries to plead for the Duke's case and to smoothe over the difference between him and Fortune, all the major actors are gendered female. The friends of the Duke – Prudence and Honesty – and Fortune – Rashness and Folly – are all women. Moreover, even the Duke's soul, which cannot come to speak for him, is gendered female. Powerful women can do men harm or good. It is women who debate important questions in *The Blazing World*.

The women of the Blazing World, however, are excluded from church and state and strictly separated from governing members of society. Their priests and governors are eunuchs "to keep them from marriage: for women and children most commonly make disturbance both in church and state" (135). Women's influence is indirect yet they can affect public policy: "they so prevalent with their husbands and parents, that many times by their importunate persuasions, they cause as much, nay, more mischief secretly, than if they had the management of public affairs" (135). The most influential woman in the Blazing World, the Empress herself, becomes powerful precisely by the very route that the people fear, namely being "prevalent" with her husband. Unlike the other governors, the chief governor of the Blazing World, the Emperor, is no eunuch. He goes so far as to share his sovereignty openly with his wife. In reiterating the Caroline metaphor of the ideal marriage of king and queen during the Restoration, Cavendish reinterprets it. The absolutist monarchy becomes a monarchy headed by a woman. The Emperor of the Blazing World practically disappears, leaving the Empress in control of the government. Cavendish replaces the king with the figure of the aristocratic woman. Because the Empress depends on the Duchess's advice, the king is essentially displaced by a cabal of women.

It is difficult to make a sharp distinction, finally, between common women who usurp their husbands' authority and those who obtain it legitimately to become queens. The difficulty manifests itself in *The Blazing World* as a series of unstable substitutions. Not only does the Empress replace the Emperor as *de facto* king, she also has a spirit take the place of her soul when she travels with the Duchess's soul into the Duchess's world: "The Empress replied, she desired but one spirit to be viceroy of her body in the absence of her soul, . . . The spirits told her, . . . we will choose an honest and ingenious spirit, and such a one as shall so resemble your soul, that neither the Emperor, nor any of his subjects, although the most divine, shall know whether it be your own soul, or not" (189–90). The king's position is constantly being vacated, as if there is no need for a governor. Indeed, the Empress's active management of the state results in unrest. The deception, however, is not carried out completely without detection, as the spirits promise, for they neglect to take into account the replacement spirit's own emotions: "At last, a spirit came and told the Empress, that although neither the Emperor, nor any of his subjects knew that her soul was absent; yet the Empress's soul was so sad and melancholy, for want of his own beloved soul, that all the imperial court took notice of it" (195).

Moreover, the emotions of the Duchess herself come into play when she finds the Empress's soul become intimate with her husband's. The negotiations between the emotional demands of marriage and those of platonic love are tricky.[42] Although the Emperor does not become jealous, not so with the Duchess. When the Duchess's soul enters the Duke's body, the Empress's soul follows her, resulting in the Duke having "three souls in one body; and had there been but some such souls more, the Duke would have been like the Grand Signior in his seraglio, only it would have been a platonic seraglio" (194). The issue of sexual jealousy thus raised is quickly dismissed: "these two souls [the Duke's and the Empress's] became enamoured of each other; which the Duchess's soul perceiving, grew jealous at first, but then considering that no adultery could be committed amongst

---

[42] In her *Life*, Cavendish proudly asserts that William's love for his king was greater than that for his family, which may also be read as a complaint (235).

Platonic lovers, and that Platonism was divine, as being derived from divine
Plato, cast forth of her mind that Idea of jealousy" (194–95). Cavendish is
not so much mocking Plato as the Neoplatonism of Henrietta Maria's
court "derived" from Plato, especially with the capitalization of the word
"Idea." Alluding to Henrietta Maria's court, Cavendish attempts to solve
the conflict created by platonic love and by the doubling of the monarch.

Perhaps the biggest challenge to absolute monarchy is depicted in the
second part of *The Blazing World*. Using the art of the Blazing World, the
Empress forces other nations to submit to her native king with the "design
of making him the most powerful monarch of all that world" (212). The
Empress herself only wants his "grateful acknowledgment, and to declare
my power, love and loyalty to my native country; for although I am now a
great and absolute princess and empress of a whole world, yet I acknowledge
that once I was a subject of this kingdom, which is but a small part of this
world" (210). This acknowledgment is not simply a gesture. She requires
the king to recognize her superiority, even though she concedes that she
was his subject. She would have him honor her power in the present while
she admits her status as a subject only in the past. Her power denies his.
The second part of *The Blazing World* is a heroic account of how a woman
renews the state, contradicting the earlier depiction of a self-regenerating
government whose imperial race maintains its youthfulness by the means of
a gum that turns an old man young in the space of nine months. Although
Cavendish employs the birth metaphor in this episode, she also denies
the existence of a parent. In contrast, the Empress is the creator of the
absolute monarchy of the king of EFSI.[43] The Empress may have a natural
superiority, even sovereignty, that preserves her life in the beginning and
that leads to her being mistaken for a deity, but the absolutist power of the
king of her native land, a version of England, is in question. His absolutist
monarchy depends on the military might of a woman, his former subject.

For all the emphasis on unity in *The Blazing World*, including references
to the number one, the narrative suggests that the number for government
is two, perhaps even three, given the occasions when a third party interrupts the closed circle of a marriage. Although conventionally marriage is
understood as joining man and wife into one flesh, other numbers suggested for marriage are, oddly enough, six and two: "Then the Empress
asked, whether the number of six was a symbol of matrimony, as being
made up of male and female, for two into three is six. If any number can

---

[43] Interestingly, Cavendish writes that William Newcastle's estate "descended upon him most by
women" (*Life*, 121). Newcastle's grandmother was Bess of Hardwicke, made fabulously wealthy
by her four husbands.

be a symbol of matrimony, answered the spirits, it is not six, but two; if two may be allowed to be a number: for the act of matrimony is made up of two joined in one" (172). By suggesting that the number for matrimony is both one and two, the spirits posit a unity that is ultimately dividable. Again and again, images of unity are disrupted by subtle signs of division. When the Empress first approaches the seat of the kingdom, the high cliffs of the coast "seemed to be all one piece, without partitions; but at last drawing nearer, she perceived a cleft" (130). Like the seeming unity of the cliffs, the stateroom "was paved with green diamonds . . . so artificially, as it seemed but of one piece" (132). Rosemary Kegl usefully suggests that the "Mosaic-work" of Cavendish's Blazing World is associated with absolute rule "not only through its 'everlasting' display of artistry and conspicuous wealth but also through its very aesthetic," that is an aesthetic which differentiates rulers from the ruled.[44] I wish to add that such an aesthetic at once proclaims absolutism in the "seeming" unity and acknowledges that absolutism is not based on having a single king. Underlying Cavendish's absolute monarchies is a woman.

Even Turkish tyranny is represented as less than absolute. While the Empress thinks "the Grand Signior was the greatest; for his word was a law, and his power absolute," the Duchess disagrees out of patriotism, arguing that the Ottoman Emperor "cannot alter Mahomet's laws and religion; so that the law and church do govern the Emperor, and not the Emperor them" (191). Presumably it is otherwise with the English king. Indeed, religion proves a stumbling-block for the Empress herself. Her meddling with government and religion produces negative results. She finds much disturbance in the world, though the precise nature of that disturbance is not identified. The Duchess advises her "to introduce the same form of government again, which had been before; that is, to have but one sovereign, one religion, one law, and one language, so that all the world might be but as one united family, without divisions" (201). Although this advice does not specifically target the Empress's innovations in religion, religion is one of her key innovations, the only one described other than her founding of schools of philosophy. Significantly, the Empress has to be guided back to an absolutist model.

---

[44] Rosemary Kegl, "'The World I Have Made': Margaret Cavendish, Feminism, and the *Blazing-World*," in Valerie Traub, M. Lindsay Kaplan and Dympna Callaghan, eds., *Feminist Readings of Early Modern Culture: Emerging Subjects* (Cambridge: Cambridge University Press, 1996), 130. Kegl extracts the term "Mosaic-work" from John Evelyn's "An Account of Architects & Architecture" which is appended to his translation of Roland Freart's *A Parallel of the Antient Architecture with the Modern* (London, 1664), in which Evelyn describes "Mosaic-work" as an art favored by the ancient wealthy, which he also claims is "*best* approximated by the Queen Mother's parquet floors" (130).

By highlighting the power of queens and aristocratic wives, despite their potential for missteps, Cavendish appropriates the marriage metaphor of the Caroline court to imagine another world where a woman, though no virgin queen, may become absolute monarch. Viewing women as state-less, citizens of nowhere, Cavendish can only begin to see women as part of the state by imagining them as monarchs and not subjects. As importantly, in imagining women's place in the state, Cavendish views women as part of a corporate body, a group of women allied so closely that they sometimes merge into one being. Such a corporate body func-tions as an imaginary substitute for the ideal relationship between king and Cavaliers.

NOSTALGIA AND THE CONTEXT OF RESTORATION IMMORALITY

Sharing her husband's nostalgia for the world before the civil war, Cavendish evokes the myths and ruling metaphors of the Caroline court. This nostalgia explains some of the curiosities in *The Blazing World*, for instance, naming the Emperor's ruling seat and imperial city "Paradise" (130). During her interview with the spirits, the Empress suddenly asks them where paradise is located, "whether it was in the midst of the world as a center of pleasure? or whether it was the whole world, or a peculiar world by itself?" (170). The spirits' reply is rather insouciant: "Paradise was not in the world she came from, but in that world she lived in at present; and that it was the very same place where she kept her court, and where her palace stood, in the midst of the imperial city" (170). Cavendish appears to be playing a joke on her readers. The spirits' answer does not enlighten curious readers wanting to locate Eden. By reminding the Empress and readers of the name of the Emperor's city, and so seemingly locating paradise where the Empress is, the answer mocks human persistence in looking for paradise elsewhere. Yet, this answer also recalls the idealized pastoral settings of Caroline masques; many of the locations of romance in Cavendish are termed "paradise," perhaps also referring to the title of Walter Montague's masque for Henrietta Maria, *The Shepherd's Paradise* (performed 1633). The Blazing World is also a utopia because it is "Paradise." The spirits, seemingly serious, affirm that Adam fled "Out of this world, said they, you are now Empress of, into the world you came from" (170). Rachel Trubowitz suggests that "In reenchanting utopia, Cavendish reclaimed the genre for the royalist side as an instrument by which the magic of monarchy, custom, and tradition, which the Puritans had tried to eradicate through utopian visions of rationalized politics, culture, and religion, could be reinstated."[45] In the civil wars, romance became a peculiarly royalist genre. Rather than a simple reclaiming, the political disjunctions that Charles II presented to the Old Cavaliers means Cavendish's use of romance is both a reclaiming of royalist tradition and a critique of it.

Cavendish's nostalgia is intermixed with irony, stemming from the realization that the present world is no longer what it used to be. In particular, the new court set a very different moral tone from the previous one. Unlike Charles I and Henrietta Maria's sober court, Charles II's was known for its sexual immorality. Already the father of ten acknowledged bastards by five different women by 1670, Charles II's own extra-marital affairs were subjects of popular gossip. James Turner argues, *contra* Restoration historiography that would have political matters strictly separated from sexual ones, that the pressure of public business manifested itself in a sexual form in this period when the ruling monarch blatantly flaunted his illicit sexuality in defiance of all social rules: "the king's openly displayed priapism made it difficult to separate him into 'two bodies,' and mingled the public realm of political authority with the private emotions aroused by illicit sexuality: jealousy, excitement, furtive identification, and shame."[46] Such displays led to the identification of royal power with the royal libido. More damagingly, the enthralled king submits to his mistresses instead of ruling them. In 1663, Pepys recorded a conversation with Sir Thomas Carew about "the unhappy posture of things at this time; that the King doth mind nothing but pleasure and hates the very sight or thoughts of business. That my Lady Castlemayne rules him."[47] With the king ruled by lust and by his mistresses, Cavendish's fiction provides a countermodel of how he may appropriately yield authority to the queen, his lawful wife. Cavendish covertly chides Charles II for his mismanagement of the household as well as the state.

When we read the *Blazing World* in its Restoration context, the impossibility of transporting gold from the Blazing World to the Duchess's world takes on political significance. Gold is what would repair the Duke's losses during the civil war, and the Duchess wants only the amount that he lost, declining to take any of the diamonds of the Blazing World for herself. Gold signifies not only wealth but also position, and it is a reminder of the

[45] Rachel Trubowitz, "The Reenchantment of Utopia and the Female Monarchical Self: Margaret Cavendish's *Blazing World*," *Tulsa Studies in Women's Literature* 11 (1992), 236.

[46] James Grantham Turner, "Pepys and the Private Parts of Monarchy," in Gerald MacLean, ed., *Culture and Society in the Stuart Restoration: Literature, Drama, History* (Cambridge: Cambridge University Press, 1995), 106.

[47] Pepys, *Diary*, IV:136.

political clout that the Duke used to wield. The failure to transport the gold that would restore the Duke to his former wealth signals his political failure in the Restoration, just as the inability of his friends and wife to reconcile him with Fortune also represents such a failure. This failure is due to the impossibility of reconciling the Cavaliers' Caroline values and the values of the Restoration court. The physical barrier between the Blazing World and the Duchess's world symbolizes the problems of transferring *femme forte* values to Restoration England when the king is ruled not by his queen but by his quean.

CHAPTER 7

Marriage and discipline in early Quakerism

With beginnings in the 1650s, Quakers were one of several radical sects of the English Revolution. Initially enthusiastic and aggressive, the earliest Quakers engaged in flamboyant public proselytizing – including going into trances, prophesying, interrupting sermons, and "going naked as a sign."[1] Their itinerant preaching and their aggression broke statutes against offenses like vagrancy and blasphemy. By their religious practices – holding separatist meetings, refusing to pay tithes, refusing to give "hat-honour," and refusing to swear oaths – Quakers flouted the authority of the state. Set apart by their religious unorthodoxy – particularly their refusal to give deference to social superiors – their civil disobedience threatened the state. Parliament was particularly savage in the 1656 case of James Nayler, arrested for riding into Bristol with a group of women, singing and hailing him as Christ. This charismatic reenactment of the messianic entry made Quakers notorious.[2] Vehemently denouncing Nayler, Parliament debated the case for six weeks – with some members calling for his death. His punishment was severe: he stood in the pillory for two hours, was whipped 310 times, had his tongue bored through with a hot iron and his forehead branded with a B for blasphemer. The exaggerated reaction, Christopher Hill suggests, was due to fears by conservative elements of the government that religious toleration would get out of hand, fears that were fueled by the terrifying rapidity with which the Quaker movement was spreading.[3] Barry Reay even

---

[1] On this last practice, see Kenneth L. Carroll, "Early Quakers and 'Going Naked as a Sign,'" *Quaker History* 67 (1978), 69–87.

[2] For Nayler's biography, see Leo Damrosch, *The Sorrows of the Quaker Jesus: James Nayler and the Puritan Crackdown on the Free Spirit* (Cambridge, Mass.: Harvard University Press, 1996). For the early conflict between Fox and Nayler, see H. Larry Ingle, *First Among Friends: George Fox and the Creation of Quakerism* (New York and Oxford: Oxford University Press, 1994), 128–33, 141–50.

[3] Christopher Hill, *The World Turned Upside Down: Radical Ideas During the English Revolution* (London: Maurice Temple Smith, 1972; reprint Penguin, 1991), 249–51.

suggests that fear of Quakerism was crucial in destroying the Revolution: "hated as political radicals, as social and religious deviants, and in some cases as economic middlemen," Quakers "were a force for order" and "catalyst for popular traditionalism."[4]

The "enthusiastic" character of the movement became even more of a liability as the sect struggled for survival in the Restoration though they did not cease their aggressive activities: "A Cheshire parson could still be halted in mid-sermon by two Quakers equipped with a candle, with which they proposed to burn an offending text, while [Lord Mayor of London] Browne's hostility could hardly have been moderated when he was presented with a tract of exhortation addressed to the 'so-called Lord Mayor.'"[5] The movement had to change or expire. They suffered the brunt of punitive laws like the Conventicle Acts of 1664 and 1670 and the Quaker Act of 1662. Although attacked as "Roundheads,"[6] Quakers welcomed the return of the king. Charles II tried to protect them by absolving them from oaths, though his toleration of nonconformity was likely a strategy to offer toleration to Catholics. However, the Cavalier Parliament remained stubbornly intolerant and pushed through a series of repressive bills known as the Clarendon Code. Quaker quietism was a later development. Following several decades of persecution after the Stuart Restoration, the sect retreated into conservatism and attempted to integrate into the social and political mainstream, a process largely completed by the end of the seventeenth century.[7]

The history of the Quakers was not simply negative. Politically active, they had ties to the New Model Army, to the Levellers and to the interregnum government in the 1650s.[8] When the Revolution fell apart, they responded in creative ways to maintain their community, evolving to survive. They clearly thought of themselves as a distinct group: in a letter to King William toward the close of the seventeenth century, Margaret Fell wrote that "we have been a people for about forty-six years, and have lived under several reigns."[9] In rejecting social convention, they carried to the

---

[4] Barry Reay, *The Quakers and the English Revolution* (London: Temple Smith, 1985), 77–78.
[5] Ronald Hutton, *The Restoration: A Political and Religious History of England and Wales, 1658–1667* (Oxford: Clarendon Press, 1985), 168–69.
[6] Hill, *The World Turned Upside Down*, 188.
[7] See Reay, *The Quakers and the English Revolution*; Richard T. Vann, *The Social Development of English Quakerism, 1655–1755* (Cambridge, Mass.: Harvard University Press, 1969); and Phyllis Mack, *Visionary Women: Ecstatic Prophecy in Seventeenth-Century England* (Berkeley: University of California Press, 1992). All trace a similar trajectory though Mack focuses on Quaker women.
[8] M. E. Hirst, *The Quakers in Peace and War* (London: The Swarthmore Press, 1923); and Alan Cole, "Quakers and the English Revolution," *Past and Present* 10 (1956), 39–54.
[9] Quoted in Helen G. Crosfield, *Margaret Fox of Swarthmoor Hall* (London: Headley Brothers, 1913), 194.

extreme the puritan notion of the true church as a voluntary association of saints. Given the hostile reactions of outsiders, the Quakers' separate community was viewed as a rival to the state, especially threatening because it was a viable alternative. Tracing the rapid rise in the membership of Quakers from 500 in 1652 to 5,000 in 1654 to 20,000 in 1657 and 40,000 in 1660, Craig W. Horle provocatively suggests, "The Quakers became a state within a state, with a network of meetings for business as well as for worship."[10]

The Quaker state within a state was sustained by face-to-face encounters in the weekly and monthly prayer meetings and in direct business transactions. Traveling preachers bringing news connected Quaker communities and churches. The productive imagining of themselves as a people was conducted partly through oral exchange but also crucially for the Quakers through written material. Written communication was made necessary by distance. The Quaker practice of traveling to preach meant that family members were often separated. One of the ways in which Quakers maintained a sense of community was by letters. As their acknowledged leader, George Fox's letters to the various Quaker communities took on a pastoral cast; his correspondence functioned like the Pauline letters.[11] Letters conveyed news of distant church members; they advised and settled disputes; and they encouraged members to keep the faith in the face of persecution. Quakers not only generated texts, they were also great record-keepers, keeping accounts of their persecution, of their legal entanglements, and of the minutes of their meetings, all of which were stored in a central location. For instance, accounts of their persecution were sent to London to be recorded in a "Book of Sufferings." In addition, they actively published works both doctrinal and controversial.[12] Toward the latter end of the seventeenth

[10] Craig Horle, *The Quakers and the English Legal System 1660–1688* (Philadelphia: University of Pennsylvania Press, 1988), 15.

[11] For the similarity of Fox's letters to the Pauline letters, see John R. Knott, *Discourses of Martyrdom in English Literature, 1563–1694* (Cambridge: Cambridge University Press, 1993), 226–29. For the role of letters in building community among nonconformists, including the Quakers, see N. H. Keeble, *The Literary Culture of Nonconformity in Later Seventeenth-Century England* (Leicester: Leicester University Press, 1987), 88–89.

[12] Patricia Crawford's "Women's Published Writings 1600–1700," in Mary Prior, ed., *Women in English Society 1500–1800* (London and New York: Methuen, 1985), 211–31, a checklist of women's writings published in the seventeenth century, gives us some indication of the Quakers' reliance on print and writing. An overwhelming proportion of published women authors were Quakers, with Margaret Fell's works comprising 17 percent of the overall Quaker output. See also Arnold Lloyd, chapter 11, "The Quaker Press," *Quaker Social History, 1669–1738* (London: Longmans, 1950); Thomas O'Malley, "'Defying the Power and Tempering the Spirit.' A Review of Quaker Control over their Publications 1672–1689," *Journal of Ecclesiastical History* 33 (1982), 72–88; and Kate Peters, "Patterns of Quaker Authorship, 1652–1656," in "The Emergence of Quaker Writing: Dissenting

century and in the early eighteenth, they collected and reprinted sectarian writings in the process of canonizing certain figures in the movement (such as George Fox and Margaret Fell) and disavowing others (James Nayler and John Perrot).[13]

In bringing a far-flung community into being discursively through texts, the Quakers present on a smaller scale an example of the processes of Benedict Anderson's print nationalism.[14] Print enabled nationhood by making it possible for large numbers of people to know each other indirectly, to imagine themselves living in the same place and time, united by a common vernacular. Though they used both manuscript and print, Quakers conformed to this description in a number of ways. They too used print as a means of participating in the political process – petitioning Parliament, for instance, or arguing for their liberty of conscience. Criticizing Alan Cole and Barry Reay for underplaying the extent of Quaker involvement in politics, Kate Peters shows that Quakers used the printing press to enact an inclusive form of political participation, through which they expected to influence political and religious affairs and to establish a godly kingdom on earth.[15] The creation of the Quaker community was fostered by the division it created between outsiders and insiders. With the government provoked into imposing punitive laws that attempted to force conformity, both sides came to define the other as hostile, which in turn cemented Quaker group identity. Neil Keeble argues that Restoration persecution of religious nonconformity aided the consolidation of dissenting communities: their effect "was to forge the corporate identity of dissent."[16]

If the means of imagining the larger Quaker community was discursive, then the language and ideological framework with which Quakers imagined themselves as a distinct group demand attention. Some work has

Literature in Seventeenth-Century England," ed. Thomas N. Corns and David Loewenstein, special issue, *Prose Studies: History, Theory, Criticism* 17.3 (December 1994), 6–24.

[13] George Fox's epistles were published in 1698 and his doctrinal writings published as *Gospel-Truth Demonstrated, In a Collection of Doctrinal Books, Given Forth by That Faithful Minister of Jesus Christ, George Fox* (London, 1706); Margaret Fell's writings, including a short autobiography, were published as *A Brief Collection of Remarkable Passages and Occurrences Relating to the Birth, Education, Life, Conversion, Travels, Services, and Deep Sufferings of that Ancient Eminent, and Faithful Servant of the Lord, Margaret Fell* (London, 1710); and some of Robert Barclay's tracts were collected under the title *Truth Triumphant Through the Spiritual Warfare, Christian Labours and Writings of that Able and Faithful Servant of Jesus Christ, Robert Barclay* (London, 1692).

[14] Benedict Anderson, *Imagined Communities: Reflections on the Origin and Spread of Nationalism*, rev. edn (London: Verso, 1991). See also Elizabeth L. Eisenstein, *The Printing Press as an Agent of Change: Communications and Cultural Transformations in Early Modern Europe*, 2 vols. (Cambridge: Cambridge University Press, 1979).

[15] Kate Peters, *Print Culture and the Early Quakers* (Cambridge: Cambridge University Press, 2005).

[16] Keeble, *Literary Culture of Nonconformity*, 47.

been done on the repetitive, "incantatory" style of Quaker writing.[17] Analyzing the metaphors of Quaker writing provides a way of understanding their conceptual foundations. Richard Bauman and others note the unique Quaker category of living metaphors: Quaker sign performance "consisted in the physical acting out of originally verbal metaphors"[18]; these include the practice of going naked as a sign of their own or of their audience's sinful state. Scholars, however, have been more interested in the flamboyant examples, paying less attention to the Quaker metaphor of the family, which provided a fundamental structure for their imagined community. Conceiving their relations with fellow Quakers in familial terms, Quakers borrowed from and reinterpreted a common political language as part of a larger national contestation over the meaning of family and state. Just as the language of kinship and family enables the nation to ask sacrifices from its citizens, as Anderson argues, so too this language allows a structure in which Quakers can sacrifice for their faith. Moreover, while their choice of the particular form of the family metaphor had acquired monarchical associations – like James I, Quakers turned to Isaiah for the notion that leaders are "nursing fathers and mothers" – their emphasis on "nursing mothers" as well as "nursing fathers" disrupted royal use of Isaiah. Furthermore, as a gathered church, placing greater importance on obedience to God than to earthly authority, Quakers deemphasized the authority of both king and father.

In appropriating the common metaphor for the state, Quakers put political theory into practice. Although not as arresting a sign as going naked, the family living metaphor reveals more of the Quakers' internal organization. While for Benedict Anderson the demise of religion made modern nationalism possible, for the Quakers religion was a powerful force for communal identity. Quaker imagined community formed the middle level between the family or household and the larger nation. The history of the family metaphor was not simply a constitutionalist history. By moving away from an exclusive focus on high political theory, we can see the uses of the metaphor at more local levels of politics. The debates over family within the Quaker community reveal their struggle over authority, struggles that echoed national debates. Ultimately, family tropes both constructed

---

[17] Jackson I. Cope, "Seventeenth-Century Quaker Style," *PMLA* 71 (1956), 733, 734. See also Maurice A. Creasey, "'Inward' and 'Outward': A Study of Early Quaker Language," *Journal of the Friends' Historical Society*, Supplement 30 (1962), 3–24; and Luella Wright, *The Literary Life of the Early Friends, 1650–1725* (New York: Columbia University Press, 1932).

[18] Richard Bauman, *Let Your Words Be Few: Symbolism of Speaking and Silence among Seventeenth-Century Quakers* (Cambridge: Cambridge University Press, 1983), 86.

and destroyed Quaker community. There has been a renewed interest in the early millenarian and apocalyptic period of Quakerism,[19] but the early period of Quakerism was not simply the story of the hostility experienced in the encounter with unsympathetic outsiders. It was also marked by a series of internal dissensions threatening to fracture the sect.

From the start, gender was a faultline in the community. By taking on greater roles, women in the sects challenged patriarchy.[20] A case in point is the incident involving Nayler, condemned both within and without the sect for being misled by women. At issue was not theology since Nayler was simply performing the Quaker belief in the 'indwelling' spirit of God in man. Rather, sectarian unity was at risk because of gender conflicts. Patricia Crawford speculates that one of Nayler's female accomplices, Martha Simmonds, was an early Quaker leader whose role in the sect was elided by later historiography.[21] Christine Trevett argues, "It was *schism* rather than heresy . . . which Quakers were most fearful of at the time. Loyalty to George Fox seemed to be in jeopardy."[22] In the mid-1650s women were challenging male leaders and promoting alternative leaders to replace Fox, with whom they had become disaffected.[23] Gender of course always had the potential to create a rift in patriarchalism. Because of their extensive use of the family metaphor, Quakers' challenge to patriarchy was also a reformulation of patriarchalism. While they did not dismantle gender hierarchy, and indeed women's position in the sect would become a point of dissension, they respected female elders, giving women important roles. While James I emphasized the king as nursing father, Quakers looked to both men and women as nursing fathers *and* nursing mothers. And, while their gender troubles stemmed in part from outsiders' perception that Quakerism encouraged unruly women, Quakers did not necessarily

[19] Margaret J. M. Ezell, *Writing Women's Literary History* (Baltimore: Johns Hopkins University Press, 1993), ch. 5, "Breaking the Seventh Seal: Writings by Early Quaker Women," argues for a recovery of early Quaker women's writings occluded by both feminist and Quaker histories. See, generally, the special issue of *Prose Studies* 17.3 (December 1994).

[20] Hilary Hinds, *God's Englishwomen: Seventeenth-Century Radical Sectarian Writing and Feminist Criticism* (Manchester: Manchester University Press, 1996); and Katharine Gillespie, *Domesticity and Dissent in the Seventeenth Century: English Women Writers and the Public Sphere* (Cambridge: Cambridge University Press, 2004).

[21] Patricia Crawford, *Women and Religion in England, 1500–1720* (London and New York: Routledge, 1993), 176.

[22] Christine Trevett, *Women and Quakerism in the 17th Century* (York: The Ebor Press, 1991), 39. See also Ronald Knox, *Enthusiasm: A Chapter in the History of Religion* (Oxford: Clarendon Press, 1950); and Maryann S. Feola, "'Warringe with ye world': Fox's Relationship with Nayler," in Michael Mullett, ed., *New Light on George Fox, 1624–1691: A Collection of Essays* (York: The Ebor Press, 1993), 101–09.

[23] Maureen Bell, "Mary Westwood Quaker Publisher," *Publishing History* 23 (1988), 5–66, similarly finds disaffection among the female ranks.

agree among themselves about how far to take their principle of spiritual equality. Gender issues were expressed differently in the 1650s than after the Restoration. As the sect changed its character, the roles available for women within the sect also changed. Post-Restoration gender conflicts were over how much authority women had in the organization of the church. The interregnum female leaders attempted to carve for themselves public roles that offended the state. In the Restoration women gained positions in the administration of the sect, an innovation not imitated by the state. Thus, while the sect's internal dissensions repeated in miniature the larger nation's concerns about political authority and communal unity, Quakers offered an alternative solution to the problems and a novel interpretation of the family-state analogy.

FAMILY AND MARRIAGE

Seventeenth-century Quakers constructed their sect as a family to create a communal identity separate from a nation hostile to their beliefs and practices. Salutations such as "dear beloved Brethren and Sisters" are common, for example, in the letters of Margaret Fell published in her collected works of 1710. Quakers called each other brother and sister or simply friend. Familial language allowed them to imagine closer, affective bonds with fellow Quakers to strengthen sectarian unity. Marriage, in particular, became a crucial issue in the conflict between Quakers and state authorities. Refusing to acknowledge civil authority or to take oaths, the Quakers would not be married by either justices of the peace or by ministers of the Church of England, two legal ways of contracting marriages. Lacking legal sanction and having to refute accusations of fornication and adultery, Quakers ascribed great symbolic import to their marriages.

While they might borrow the language of brotherhood from the Pauline letters, Quaker use of familial language was more passionate, with the language sometimes turning ecstatic. After their convincement by George Fox, Margaret Fell and her household wrote letters that addressed him as "Our dear father in the Lord, for though we have ten thousand instructors in Christ, yet have we not many fathers, for in Christ Jesus thou hast begotten us through the Gospel, eternal praise be to our father."[24] Elevated above that of a mere teacher, Fox is given the active and primary part as

---

[24] Spence MS III, 24–26; quoted by Isabel Ross, *Margaret Fell, Mother of Quakerism* (London and New York: Longmans, Green, 1949), 36. The members of Fell's household who signed the letter were Thomas Salthouse, Ann Clayton, Mary Askew, her daughters Margaret and Bridget, and William Caton.

the generative father. The Gospel, a vessel for Fox to beget his followers, takes the secondary, female position. Fox's fatherly role is nurturing; he is the "bread of life," nursing his followers "with the breasts of consolation."[25] Endowed with female characteristics, Fox is a "nursing father" who provides spiritual food. In a seeming reversal of gender roles, the "nursing father" is a cultural ideal of early modern patriarchy because English Protestantism tended to emphasize the relation between God and son.[26] It also refers back to a medieval tradition of the maternal Christ, particularly in its mystical aspects.[27] At times the letter comes close to equating Fox with God the Father with potentially blasphemous invocations: "O thou fountain of eternal life, our souls thirsts [*sic*] after thee, for in thee alone is our life and peace, and without thee we have no peace, for our souls is much refreshed by seeing thee, and our lives is preserved by thee, O thou father of eternal felicity."[28] In addition, the metaphor of nursing mothers is equally common. Margaret Fell has long been called by that name. In 1654, Thomas Holme, a Quaker who was visited by Margaret Fell, Jr. in gaol in Chester, writes to Margaret Fell, Sr. praising her and her daughter and calling Fell, "A nursing Mother thou art who feeds the hungry with good things, but the fat with judgment, who kills and stays the living and raises the dead."[29] As Phyllis Mack points out, the archetypal female Quaker, who combines ecstatic prayer and public evangelizing with the mundane work of everyday life and Quaker committee work, is called "mother in Israel."[30] If Quakers are brothers and sisters, the elders of the community are viewed as fathers and mothers.

The metaphor of family allows the Quakers to maintain hierarchy but also to be more inclusive in their definition of community, and potentially more egalitarian. In *Gospel Family-Order, Being a Short Discourse Concerning the Ordering of Families, Both of Whites, Blacks and Indians* (1676), Fox writes that since God commanded Abraham to circumcise all his family, including servants purchased with money, Christians must have all of their families brought to the "Circumcision of the Spirit."[31] The tract, which purports to be a printing of Fox's speech at a meeting in the house of Thomas Rous

---

[25] *Ibid.*, 36.

[26] Debora Kuller Shuger, *Habits of Thought in the English Renaissance: Religion, Politics, and the Dominant Culture* (Berkeley: University of California Press, 1990), ch. 6, "Nursing Fathers: Patriarchy as a Cultural Ideal." For Quaker women's gender reversal, see Mack, *Visionary Women.*

[27] Caroline Walker Bynum, *Jesus as Mother: Studies in the Spirituality of the High Middle Ages* (Berkeley: University of California Press, 1982).

[28] Ross, *Margaret Fell*, 37.   [29] Swarthmore MSS. 1, 197; quoted in *ibid.*, 25.

[30] Mack, *Visionary Women*, 216.

[31] George Fox, *Gospel Family-Order* (1701), sig. A2v, 4. I draw quotations from the 1701 reprint edition. Further references are from this reprint edition and given parenthetically.

in Barbados in 1671 (though published five years later and likely edited and revised), proceeds from the premise that the family is a household to an argument that can be read as a precursor of the argument for the abolition of slavery.[32] Fox urges his audience to proselytize the other races, for "*Christ* dyed for all, both *Turks Barbarians, Tartarians* and *Ethyopians*; he dyed for the *Tawnes* and for the *Blacks*, as well as for you that are called *Whites*" (sig. A3v, 14). Names do not tell the whole truth about character even though racial distinctions do not break down completely. At the same time, Fox addresses his sermon mainly to the heads of families, implicitly equating fathers, heads of communities, and kings: "mark this, ye Elders, and Rulers, and Fathers of Families, who have Strangers and Sojourners in your Families, so as to see that you do perform your Duty, and bring them to do their Duty in the Covenant of Life, *Christ Jesus*" (sig. A4v, 8). In a letter to Charles II recorded in his journal, Fox addresses the king as an equal by calling him by the Quaker greeting of friend.[33] The interchangeability of the terms father, elder, and ruler suggests that church, community and nation are comparable to the family. With hierarchy emphasizing the unity of the group, the basic unit becomes the family rather than the individual. Furthermore, Fox's use of the word "family" has a suppleness that allows him to refer to the Jewish race as one family and at the same time to "whole Families of *Christians*" (sig. B2, 11]) in the plural. The inexact terminology allows him to slide easily from the nuclear family to the village community and to the nation.

The slipperiness is characteristic of minds accustomed to finding correspondences and analogues. Quakers easily turned marriage into a symbol. Fox viewed his late marriage to Margaret Fell as an example to all Christendom. Recounting his encounter with Walter Newton, who asked the reason for his marriage, Fox replies, "And I told him, as a testimony, that all might come up into the marriage as was in the beginning, and as a testimony that all might come up out of the wilderness to the marriage of the Lamb" (*Journal*, 557). Human marriage becomes a symbol for the marriage of Christ to the church. When Newton expressed surprise, believing marriage to be for procreation, Fox asserted that this mundane reason was beneath him. Some historians concluded that Fox and Fell did not have sexual intercourse, given their advanced ages and the fact that they were apart for most of their marriage. Whatever the truth was, Fox's

---

[32] For abolitionist strands in Quakerism, see Jerry W. Frost, "George Fox's Ambiguous Anti-Slavery Legacy," in Mullet, ed., *New Light on George Fox*, 69–88.

[33] John L. Nickalls, ed., *The Journal of George Fox*, rev. edn (Cambridge: Cambridge University Press, 1952), 423. Further references are given parenthetically.

answer exemplifies the Quaker drive to spiritualize the mundane, turning everyday actions into symbols and living testimonies. Turning marriages into metaphor, the Quakers engaged in a productive confusion of reality and trope. Because they took a concrete, recurring event – marriage – as a symbol of their faith, the "living metaphor" inhabited the space between reality and metaphor. Its hybrid nature is evident in the notion that the symbol could be tainted by improper acts. In an undated and unsigned manuscript in the Bristol MSS. V collection, "Right Marriage," Quakers are exhorted to keep themselves sexually pure before marriage for fear of defiling the symbol: "And marriage being a type of Christ and his spouse it ought to bee holy and ye man & ye woman ought to keep themselfes holy to their marriage day that the figure may bee kept clean."[34] As living metaphor, Quaker marriage is also a return to the prelapsarian origin. In *Concerning Marriage*, Fox contrasts the marriages of unbelievers with Quaker marriages modeled after Adam and Eve's: "But who comes together as it was in the beginning, comes over the *Jews*, *Gentiles*, and *Apostate Christians*."[35]

Given its symbolic importance, the Quakers developed their own distinctive marriage procedure. Through their "marriage discipline," they formed a communal identity, all the more because they suffered legal persecution for it.[36] In an unpublished paper, Margaret Fell instructs those wishing to marry to declare their intentions at meetings "so friends in the eternal truth may try & weigh the objection in the light, & if it bee found contrary to the truth, let it be condemned with the light."[37] Quakers are scrutinized by their fellow Quakers before they marry. Given the structure of meetings and the difficulty of traveling long distances, those who have the most say about any proposed marriage are other Quakers in the immediate community. Married Quakers are given great power in deciding whether to approve a match; this later becomes a dividing issue for the Quaker community. With the blessings of the community, the marriage is conducted largely as a verbal ritual prompted by the inner light, or divine spirit: "Then as they are moved of the Lord, by his power & in his fear, they may take each other in the meeting & speak what the unlimitted power & spirit gives

---

[34] Bristol MSS. v.112/113, 4, Friends' House, Bristol. I draw this source from a microfilm copy kept in the Library of the Society of Friends, London.

[35] George Fox, *Concerning Marriage: How God Made Them Male And Female in the Beginning* (London, 1661), sig. A3v–A4, 6–7.

[36] For the uses of suffering among Quakers, see Knott, *Discourses of Martyrdom*, chapter 7.

[37] Swarthmoor MSS. 8/1. Isabel Ross argues that this paper titled "Margaret Fell on Quaker Marriages 1656" proves that it was Fell who instituted marriage discipline rather than George Fox. See Ross, "Note on Margaret Fell's Epistle on Marriages," annotation to "Margaret Fell on Quaker Marriages 1656," Swarthmoor MSS. 8/1, Library of the Society of Friends, London.

utterance."[38] Marriage is turned into a spiritual act, even an act involving ecstatic prophecy. It is a curious combination of the spiritual and the mundane. While the married couple may be empowered by the divine to speak out, their friends must record the event to publicize it: they "draw a little note concerning that action of that day, which they were eye-witnesses of" and "set their hands to it. So that nothing bee acted among freinds in ye dark & so come under reproach."[39] The importance of form and procedure is evidenced by Fell's decision to conclude her paper by giving the form of the marriage certificate.

In "Right Marriage," the order of the marriage proceedings is modeled after the biblical example of Ruth's marriage to Boaz.

See how Boaz: would clear himselfe before hee did marry Ruth how & what hee said to his kinsman that if that hee would marry Ruth hee should or might and ye kinsman [said]: y^t Boaz may take her and redeem her Land & marry her for hee could not. And then Boaz said to some Elders which hee hath taken wth him in the gate of the City and to all the people yee [are] witnesses this day that I take Ruth to wife and all the people and the Elders y^t wee are with [God] . . . And this was a Marriage according to the Law of God.[40]

With property involved, Boaz is careful to recognize the priority of another. Only after the elders have witnessed that the kinsman with a prior claim has given up his right to Ruth's hand in marriage would Boaz offer for her. Public testimony is important because the metaphor is performative and requires an audience. Rejecting the authority of the priest as representative of the state, Quakers insist on another kind of public recognition. They substitute witnesses from their own community for the priest whose persona ordinarily is public and communal in the eyes of the law. The emphasis on keeping one's word in "Right Marriage" is consistent with the nature of Quaker marriages as verbal rituals, literally speech-acts. The prominent theme of public witnessing of marriages by the community in Quaker tracts highlights Quaker creation of tradition. Similarly, in *Concerning Marriage*, Fox lays claim to tradition by referring to Old Testament examples of marriages; in each of his examples – the marriages of Isaac to Rebecca, Jacob to Laban's daughter, Boaz to Ruth – witnesses are crucially present because "things were not done in a corner nor in a hole" (sig. A2, 3).

The importance of public witnessing is particularly evident in Margaret Fell and George Fox's certificate of marriage. Only a third of the certificate records the actual ceremony, while a major portion records the four times their intentions to marry were published, carefully noting the place

[38] *Ibid.*   [39] *Ibid.*   [40] Bristol MSS. v.112/113, 3.

and date of the declarations.[41] Even as living metaphor, marriage seems insufficient. Although the central focus, Fox and Fell's marriage commitment is amplified by the multiple testimonials of witnesses, an important component in the construction of community. This community is represented in a strikingly visual manner by the impressive total of ninety-four names at the bottom of the certificate, occupying most of the single sheet of manuscript. By this stage, the marriage as metaphor is no longer only made concrete as an event. It becomes a historical record, with public testimonies of friends at the marriage taken down for posterity.[42] The manuscript even tries to make sure that the order in which the proceedings are taken down accurately reflects the order in which words were spoken at the marriage. Margaret Fell's prayer is copied down on the second page of the manuscript, but in the top left corner is a marginal note – "Read not / this / now" – and after the title there is another note in darker ink, probably a later addition, which reads, "comes in after their marriage was accomplished: – & not here."[43] The manuscript recreates the event, possibly for Friends unable to attend. The annotations reflect its inadequacy as a text, its inability to capture the event in its entirety as it records each time when "many of ye testimonies were not taken in writing."[44]

The inadequacy of the written text becomes testimony to the plentitude of divine presence, which sanctions the marriage but defies verbal expression: "ffriends being so filled, & overcomed with ye power of ye Lord; & Testimonies that arose in themselves, to ye honorable marriage; then made mention off; that they could not writte G F words" (Portfolio 10. 53, p. 411). Physically overcome, Fox himself almost fell and "could not tell: whether he had A Body: or not a body" (Portfolio 10. 53, pp. 403–404). In a mystical experience, the mundane and the bodily are forgotten. This transcendence reflects the spiritualizing of Quaker marriages as close analogues to the marriage to God: in *The True Marriage Declared*, Fox says true marriage in the new covenant is "both inward and outward."[45] William Penn's testimony links the notion that Fox and Fell's marriage symbolizes marriage with God to the claim that Fox is a latter-day prophet. As another John

---

[41] Copy in Sarah Fell's handwriting, Thirnbeck MSS Vol. 367 no. 7, Library of the Society of Friends, London.
[42] There exists only a fragment of the manuscript, Portfolio 10.53, Library of the Society of Friends, London. It starts abruptly and ends tantalizingly with just the very beginning of George Fox's speech.
[43] Portfolio 10.53, 404. Pagination of the MS fragment starts with 403 and ends with 416.
[44] *Ibid.*, 403; further references are given parenthetically in the text.
[45] George Fox, *The True Marriage Declared: Or, Seven Testimonyes from the record of Scripture Concerning the True Marriages and Such As Are Not According to the Truth for Friends and All Others Concerned to Read in the Feare of the Lord* (London, 1679), sig. C2, 11. Further references are given parenthetically.

the Baptist heralding the second coming of Christ in the final days, Fox's marriage is "the true Character: Resemblance, & Expresse Image of that Inocent Marriage of ye lamb" (Portfolio 10. 53, p. 415). Penn's language collapses the two terms of the comparison. Referring to other Quaker writings, Nigel Smith notes, "Metaphorical abstractions break down the barrier between conceptions and things, or objective events."[46] Showing a similar habit of mind, Penn views the metaphor of the marriage with the Lamb as an actual event. Fox and Fell's marriage is equivalent to the heavenly one. They "Instrumentally" brought from out of the wilderness the "pure marriage" of Christ and church. Already living in the new covenant, they become icons.

If Fox and Fell are living examples, other Quakers play a complementary role as living witnesses. John Moon says, "ye Lord hath made us Liveing witnesses of that pretious life, that is made manifest in & Amongst us, – & that wee are made partakers of it" (Portfolio 10. 53, p. 409). The drama of marriage requires the active participation of all the actors. Some claim to have been expecting the marriage as part of God's plan. Miriam Moss claims to have a vision as far back as a decade earlier in 1657 when visiting Fell in Swarthmoor: "I was moved of ye Lord to goe into her garden wher I sitting in ye silence of my spirit, Then did ye Lord let me see, that GF: & mf were Joyned together in that one eternall spirit, & they should be Joyned together in that bond of love which could not be broken."[47] Most expressed their approval in typical phrases such as "having perfect unity with it" or "being satisfied in it." The repetition suggests a conventional language or the conventionality of oral testimony. It may also be a result of the scribe taking down what seemed most important in the testimonies. Despite their conventionality, phrases denoting agreement are significant because the marriage procedure is designed to elicit communal accord.

Looking to the inner light is the Quaker extension of the puritan appeal to individual conscience. By insisting on communal agreement in cases of marriage, the Quakers reinstitute and reemphasize a corporate identity. Although the reading of the banns in the established church may on the surface suggest a similar emphasis on communal agreement, for the Quakers, the practices of the Church of England have degenerated into mere ceremony. Quakers demand that the inner light of the community give spiritual and not merely formal assent. In *The True Marriage Declared,*

---

[46] Nigel Smith, *Perfection Proclaimed: Language and Literature in English Radical Religion, 1640–1660* (Oxford: Clarendon Press, 1989), 70. Smith gives an example from Fox's *Warning from the Lord* (1654), in which Fox says, "I saw a purity strike through Magistrates" (26).

[47] Portfolio 10.53, 410.

Fox argues that Anglican practice of having a priest preside over the ceremony is a renovation: "you cannot prove neither in the Old nor New Testament, that either Priest or Bishop, or *Jews* Priests or Christ or His Apostles married any, But Gods people took one another before wittnesses, and Recorded it in a Booke" (sig. B2, 7). Dismissing Anglican accusations of Quaker innovation in marriage rites, Fox shows that the Anglican practice is itself a departure from its Roman Catholic predecessor. Describing Quaker marriage in language that resonates with contemporary political events, Fox calls Quaker marriage part of the new dispensation and "in the restoration by Christ Jesus who came to restore man and woeman into the Image of God againe as they were in before" (sig. A1v, 2). The language of restoration hints at a parallel between spiritual renewal and the political reinstatement of the Stuarts. Spiritual renewal has political consequences: the restored marriage is part of a new order in one's relation with God and with one's community.

Given the symbolic freight of Quaker marriage, it was also a metaphor for particularly close relations between Quakers, as in the examples of Katharine Evans and Sarah Cheevers. Traveling together to preach in Catholic Malta, they viewed their relationship as a marriage. Evans and Cheevers were not unusual. Although investing marriage with great symbolic weight, Quakers did not necessarily endorse domesticity. With the example of their leaders, Fox and Fell, who were usually either in prison or traveling as part of their ministry, they reconciled separation and itinerant preaching with normalized family roles.[48] Traveling in same-sex pairs in order to avoid rumors of sexual scandal, Quakers, many of them women, also preached abroad. Elizabeth Hooton journeyed to Jamaica with Fox and was whipped out of Boston, while Mary Fisher was the only Quaker who managed to meet and proselytize the Grand Turk.[49] Intended to canonize the women as sufferers for the truth, Daniel Baker's compilation of Evans and Cheevers' narrative and letters, *This is a short Relation of some of the Cruel Sufferings (For the Truths sake) of Katharine Evans & Sarah Chevers* (1662), offers a fascinating and detailed example of Quaker deployment of family metaphors to create a corporate identity. Eschewing a linear narrative, Baker attempts to provide as complete a documentation of their travails as possible. The *Relation* reproduces narratives of the women's experiences juxtaposed with letters to family and friends. Its beginning is oddly recursive. After two pages detailing their arrival in Malta, Baker begins again

---

[48] Crosfield's biography of Fell depicts them as deaf to all but their divine calling (*Margaret Fox*, 165–66).
[49] Mabel Richmond Brailsford, *Quaker Women, 1650–1690* (London: Duckworth & Co., 1915).

with writing they had produced before leaving for Malta: "Here followeth a Copy of some more words which they had written before the former was given forth" (sig. B2, 3). The narrative is also interrupted by the women's writing in a wide range of genres – visions, verses, papers written to authorities, and epistles to family and friends – comprising about forty pages of text. More letters follow, ending with Baker's story of his own experiences in Malta. While the actual narrative depicts the women as independent actors resisting their Catholic inquisitors in a foreign country, the reprinted letters offer space for them to perform normalized family roles. While in the narrative the women are depicted as lone figures – especially when separated by their captors – in the letters they appear as part of a network of family and friends.

Insisting on their continuing connection with family, the *Relation* makes it clear that the women's long absence from home is not a repudiation of family life. Katharine Evans writes, "Most dear and faithful Husband, Friend and Brother, begotten of my Eternal Father, of the immortal Seed of the Covenant of Light, Life and Blessednesse, I have unity and fellowship with thee day and night, to my great refreshment and continual comfort, praises, praises be given to our God for evermore, who hath joined us together in that which neither Sea nor Land can separate or divide" (sig. H3, 53). Because it is constant and inseparable, presence in spirit is greater than mere physical presence. Evans thinks of her spouse as husband, friend, and brother all at once: the compounding of familial roles indicates how Quakers blur the line between household and the greater Quaker community. Writing to her husband and children, Cheevers claims to "have community with you in the Spirit: he that is joined to the Lord, is one spirit, one heart, one mind, one soul, to serve the Lord with one consent" (sig. I1, 57). Their faith binds family together more permanently and completely. Community in the spirit, imagined through metaphors of family, is privileged over a physical, earth-bound community. Thus, they maintain their membership in the spiritual family even when they seem most alone.

When separated by their persecutors, Evans and Cheevers use similar means to emphasize their solidarity with one another, keeping in contact through letters. The friars tempt the two women by misrepresenting one to the other, but they fail to weaken the women's faith because they "were guided by one Spirit, and spake one and the same thing in effect" (sig. D1, 17). In their perfect unity, Evans and Cheevers think of themselves as almost one person. Cheevers writes, "When we were separated, we spake one and the same thing, being guided by one Spirit, They would go from me to *Catharina*, they would bid her *speak as Sarah did*, and so she did to their condemnation" (sig. F4, 39). Acting and speaking with one accord, they create a corporate identity. This also happens on the level of the narrative voice itself. Rosemary Kegl argues cogently that the prose merges "into this first person pronoun the inseparable voices of Evans and of Chevers," and that the women "draw upon the language of mutuality to describe the bond produced by this 'yoke' of suffering," which together with the blurring of voices grants them authority by "emphasizing that they are one in God."[50]

The collapsing of individual identity is understood in terms of family. The blurring of voices and the language of mutuality are associated with the idea that the relationship is like a marriage. In her "Vision," Cheevers calls Evans a "dear and faithful yoke-fellow," a familiar term for spouses. In part, by imagining their relationship with a fellow traveler as a marriage, Quaker women subtly reform marriage into a more equal relationship, as it would be free from gender hierarchy. Evans and Cheevers try to maintain equality and to act with one undivided will. In addition, Quakers' pervasive use of the familial metaphor levels differences in relationships. All other Quakers are family members; a same-sex fellow preacher is a spouse; and one's husband is also a brother. Family metaphors enable Quakers to practice – not just imagine – a unified community without hierarchy.

However, perfect unity is a self-image Quakers did not always succeed in maintaining. Although their shared gender allowed Evans and Cheevers to be roughly equal, the relationship was not without its strains. They insisted on doing everything together as though any difference would make them unequal. Their tormentors' proposal to send Evans alone to Rome troubled Cheevers, who wonders "whether he [God] did not count me worthy" (sig. F3v, 38). The insistence on perfect unity created rifts in their relationship, for difference suggested hierarchy. Quaker unity was in part defined by a fear of hierarchy, later to be a dividing issue. Even with only a community of two, Evans and Cheevers found it difficult to maintain equal unity; so much more was the case for the more rigidified Society of Friends in the later Restoration.

[50] Rosemary Kegl, "Women's Preaching, Absolute Property, and the *Cruel Sufferings (For the Truths sake) of Katharine Evans & Sarah Chevers*," *Women's Studies* 24 (1994), 69, 70. Kegl argues that the women's marriage "is an ongoing process. In other words, its burden is to acknowledge the partners' mutual affection and mutual authority not only during the initial marriage contract but also during the subsequent, daily practices of married life." This model of the truly mutual marriage, where subordination has no place, "unsettles the logic of companionate marriages" (70).

Using the family metaphor both to establish hierarchy, and, as in the example of Evans and Cheevers, to level distinctions, Quakerism embodied a paradox. Quaker emphasis on "inner light," or divine promptings, gave equal authority to men and women. Elevating older women as "nursing mothers," Quakers expanded the scope of women's authority and made possible the leveling of the gender hierarchy. William C. Braithwaite notes among Quakers the "equality of men and women in spiritual privilege and responsibility."[51] More recently, Phyllis Mack shows how early Quakers transcended gender through the doctrine of perfection, with "its liquifying aspect, its potential for decomposing the individual, gendered personality and encouraging women and men to speak and act with the traditional attributes of both sexes."[52] Gender became disconnected from biological sex such that Quaker women could claim spiritual manhood: one Quaker woman said "that she was the Eternall Son of God; And when the men that heard her, told her that she was a woman, and therefore could not be the Son of God; She said, no, you are women, but I am a man."[53] Reversing their genders to claim a spiritual state that makes her not just a man but Christ himself, she chastizes her male detractors for their spiritual lack in the very terms they use to rebuke her. The Quaker use of gender to describe spiritual condition allowed women the liberating possibility of crossing gender lines, to think of themselves as men, at least spiritually. Quakers offered more scope for women's spiritual equality and participation in public preaching than other churches. But the symbolic use of gender also reemphasized the traditional negative associations with the female sex, and the androgynous ideal was hard to maintain in practice.

With the increasing need for conformity because of Restoration repression, hierarchy was reimposed within the sect. Given these contradictory impulses, women's authority became a contentious issue, contributing to schism.[54] The largest schism was led by John Wilkinson and John Story in the 1670s, as the "two Johns" rebelled against what they saw as Fox's

[51] William C. Braithwaite, *The Second Period of Quakerism*, 2nd edn (Cambridge: Cambridge University Press, 1961), 270.
[52] Mack, *Visionary Women*, 155.
[53] Francis Higginson, *A Brief Relation of the Irreligion of the Northern Quakers* (London, 1653), 3–4. Cited in Mack, *ibid.*, 157.
[54] Patricia Crawford argues that male sectarian leaders generally were caught between the criticism of outsiders for the disorderly women in their congregations and opposition from women within, and that women themselves were caught between conscience and duty to men, especially their husbands ("Historians, Women and the Civil War Sects, 1640–1660," in *Rulers, Religion and Rhetoric in Early Modern England: A Festschrift for Geoffrey Elton from his Australasian Friends* [Sydney: Parergon,

imposition of form and order, a kind of church government, in contradiction to the earliest Quaker belief that the individual must listen to
the inner promptings of the spirit. A major bone of contention was the
women's meetings, and closely allied to it, the practice of requiring young
couples wishing to marry to declare themselves at both the men's and the
women's meetings.[55] Fox's group was perceived to be instituting practices
that undermined men's authority. Fox had set up church hierarchy by for-
malizing the weekly and yearly meetings, both men's and women's, which
Richard Bauman, borrowing from Max Weber, aptly calls the "routinization
of charisma."[56] Although Wilkinson and Story framed their opposition to
Fox as a debate on imposed form in worship and church governance, the
issue became inflected by gender.

Fox's female supporters perceived the opposition to be against their wielding of authority in the church. While in the 1650s women attempted to
seize leadership through public preaching, given the charismatic character
of the Quaker sect at the time, after the Restoration they gained authority
through control of church government. Patricia Crawford argues that there
was a process of containment of women within the sect as a hierarchy of
male leaders was established.[57] Although largely true, her argument overlooks the opportunities open to women from the reorganization of the sect.
The regularization of women's meetings entailed a loss of the independence
available to enthusiastic female prophets and preachers. But through the
meetings women gained juridical power over young male Quakers wishing
to marry. The meetings gave women a powerful corporate identity. The
Wilkinson–Story schism was very importantly a controversy over women's
roles and gender relations, relations that had to be reconceptualized when

---

1988], 19–32). See also Keith V. Thomas, "Women and the Civil War Sects," *Past and Present* 13
(1958), 42–62; Claire Cross, "'He-goats before the flocks': A Note on the Part Played by Women in
the Founding of Some Civil War Churches," *Studies in Church History* 8 (1972), 195–202; and Rachel
Trubowitz, "Female Preachers and Male Wives: Gender and Authority in Civil War England," in
James Holstun, ed., *Pamphlet Wars: Prose in the English Revolution* (London: Frank Cass, 1992),
112–33.
[55] See Braithwaite, *The Second Period of Quakerism*, especially chapter 9.
[56] Bauman, *Let Your Words Be Few*, ch. 9, "Where Is The Power That Was At First? The Prophetic
Ministry and the Routinization of Charisma," 137–53. Max Weber argues that charisma "is undimin-
ished, consistent and effective only in statu nascendi . . . When the tide that lifted a charismatically
led group out of everyday life flows back into the channels of workaday routines, at least the 'pure'
form of charismatic domination will wane and turn into an 'institution'" (*Economy and Society:
An Outline of Interpretive Sociology*, ed. Guenther Roth and Claus Wittich, 2 vols. [Berkeley: University of California Press, 1978], II:1121). See also Arnold Lloyd, *Quaker Social History, 1669–1738*
(London: Longmans, 1950), ch. 2; Mack, *Visionary Women*, chs. 8–10; and Trevett, *Women and
Quakerism*, ch. 3.
[57] Crawford, *Women and Religion*, 162.

old notions about hierarchy sit uncomfortably beside new ones about God manifested in Friends, no matter gender or social class.

Opposition to women's meetings in the Wilkinson–Story controversy did not require a conservative interpretation of Pauline injunctions against women's speech. In contradistinction to Paul, William Rogers argues in *The Christian-Quaker* (1680) that both men and women must act when moved by God. At the same time, he opposes the submission of proposed marriages to women's meetings as an innovation, pointing out that Fox himself did not submit his proposal of marriage to the women's meetings even though at the time there was such a meeting in existence in Bristol where they married.[58] A huge, repetitive work in five parts, *The Christian-Quaker* provides an account from the perspective of the Wilkinson–Story faction. Answering the charge that he is destroying group unity, Rogers argues that he is not revealing names, except for a few of the major players. Moreover, he says, the division is already known to the outside world, and he claims that the other side started the publicizing of the schism with the publication of *An Epistle for True Love, Unity and Order in the Church of Christ* (1680), one of the defenses by women. The need for privacy in a public medium puts him in the difficult position of having to tell a history without names (Preface, sig. C3v). Rogers's arguments, and his settling for partial disclosure as a compromise, tell us much about Quaker reliance on the print medium, as do the numerous references to written documents in this and other tracts. Arnold Lloyd argues, "Quaker books exercised a deep consolidating influence on the Society during our period [1669–1738]."[59] While Quakers developed an emerging group identity through print, the permanence of writing also hastened the course of divisions.[60]

Believing that the women's meetings wield excessive authority in their exercise of the marriage discipline, Rogers contends that traditional hierarchies are overturned in a reenactment of Isaiah 3:12: "*As for my People, Children are their Oppressors, and Women rule over them. Oh, my Poeple [sic]! they which lead thee, cause thee to Err*" (part 1, sig. H4v, 64). Detecting a conspiracy, he believes the true aim of the women's meetings is the

---

[58] Rogers, *The Christian-Quaker, Distinguished from the Apostate & Innovator* (London, 1680), part 1, sig. H4v, 64. Further references are given parenthetically.

[59] Lloyd, *Quaker Social History*, 154. See, generally, Lloyd, ch. 11, "The Quaker Press," 147–56, and Ezell, *Writing Women's Literary History*, 141–45.

[60] Thomas O'Malley argues that the separatists were right to criticize Fox for seeking to gain control of Quaker printing in order to disseminate his views: "Fox was using the system of church government that he had established to impose his notions of uniformity on the movement through publications passed by the Second Day Meeting and the Meeting for Sufferings" ("'Defying the Powers and Tempering the Spirit,'" 85–86).

institution of the marriage discipline rather than charitable relief of the poor (part I, sig. IIv, 66). Resorting to antifeminist rhetoric, Rogers depicts Fox to be unduly influenced by women: "'tis a Shame for a Man to become an Instrument that *Womens Meetings* should be held" (part I, sig. IIv, 66). Accusing Fox of uxoriousness, he insinuates that Fell resembles Eve: "As the *Serpent* beguiled *Eve*, so *Eve* beguiled *Adam*, in prevailing upon him to eat of the *Forbidden Fruit which* she had eaten; and the Argument used by the *Serpent* to tempt *Eve* was this, *Ye shall be as Gods.* Even so are we persuaded, that there hath not been wanting unto him [Fox] (to speak comparitively [*sic*]) a tempting *Eve*, which hath been too aspiring after such a State" (part I, sig. M2v-M3, 92–93). While Fox depicts his marriage to Fell as that of Christ, the second Adam, to the church, his opponents turn that analogy against him to suggest a more appropriate analogy to the first fallen Adam and the sinful Eve. The bad influence of women recalls the example of the disgraced James Nayler, whose pride was fueled by the blasphemous adulation of women, as Rogers reminds Fox: "Hast thou forgotten, how Thou hast Testified against *James Naylor's* Spirit, whose great fall was *his owning*, or at least *not Reproving the Women*, when they Cryed with a Carnal Tongue *Hosanna* to him?" (part 4, sig. *m*4v, 96). Women's inherent sinful natures can corrupt men when they are allowed complete freedom of speech.

In *A Novelty: Or, a Government of Women* (1694), ex-Quaker William Mather similarly detects a conspiracy of women, criticizing the stubbornness of "such Women as has a secret Command of their Husbands Purses; together with those Preachers that reap Profit by such a Female Government."[61] Inveighing against submission to the devilish "*Female Authority* in Marriage," he compares the women's meetings to the "Government of the *Amazons*" (sig. A2v, 4).[62] Perceiving women's exercise of authority as monstrous, he emphasizes the opposition between young men and older women: "I do greatly desire to hear how they do to bear it, that a Young Man should refuse to submit to their Authority" (sig. A2v, 4). While Mather criticizes both male and female leaders for holding private meetings without giving a public account, he focuses on misgovernment by women and emphasizes the newness of their meetings, which are "unscriptural Female Government" (sig. B1v, 10). Although he finds marriage discipline burdensome, he believes submission to the women's meetings more irksome in

---

[61] William Mather, *A Novelty: Or, a Government of Women, Distinct from Men, Erected amongst some of the People, call'd Quakers* (London, 1694), sig. A1. Further references are given parenthetically.
[62] For sexual satires of women taking on male roles, see Sharon Achinstein, "Women on Top in the Pamphlet Literature of the English Revolution," *Women's Studies* 24 (1994), 131–63; and Susan Wiseman, "'Adam, the Father of all Flesh,' Porno-Political Rhetoric and Political Theory in and after the English Civil War," in Holstun, ed., *Pamphlet Wars*, 112–33.

requiring couples to travel long distances at their own cost. These couples have been so troubled with delays, even when relatives are satisfied, that some in desperation "have gone to a Priest upon the account of Marriage" (sig. B2, 11). Mather argues for exercising marriage discipline in public meetings rather than in "a Meeting of a few Women, (who may be Strangers to you [the couple])" (sig. B2v, 12). Repeatedly invoking the phrase "female Government," he displays a great fear of submitting to the authority of women uncontrolled by men.

While the conflict became inflected by gender, it was also one about authority, such that criticisms of male leaders were common. In *The Christian-Quaker*, William Rogers is troubled by the related issue of the authority of age: "In the Church of Christ, there are *Babes*, *Young Men*, and *Fathers*; there are the *Weak*, and the *Strong*: Suppose a Weak Brothers Faith Differs from his Brethren, must he be accounted *a Fool*, or an *Hipocrite*? Nay" (part 1, sig. D1v, 26). The repeated themes concern the curtailment of liberty of conscience as a consequence of the imposition of form and ritual, to which Rogers compares persecution by the state church. Arguing from spiritual equality, he calls for leveling social disparity. He uses familial metaphors to reconstitute the family of Friends into one free from the usual generational roles:

I now appeal to the impartial understanding Reader, whether according to this form of Government, one that is in the place of *Paul* a Father (who according to the aforesaid Author [Robert Blaykling, who supported Fox], hath right to rule over and command) may not have the testimony which he hath through the motion of Gods Spirit to publish unto the World for God, be *over-ruled* by *Timothy* a Son (when, according to the aforesaid Author, he ought to be *ruled* by *Paul* the Father) nay, perhaps by one that is of much lesser rank in the Body; if so be he hath a word of Exhortation on the behalf of Gods Truth, & is usually exercised therein in publick. (part 3, sig. D3v, 30)

Although Rogers objects to Fox's faction's use of familial metaphors to impose authority, he does not reject the metaphors but invests them with new meaning, imagining different, more equitable, roles for sons and fathers.

This concern about hierarchy and the authority of age is central to William Mucklow's *The Spirit of the Hat* (1673), ostensibly published by a hostile outsider who managed to acquire a work written by an anonymous Quaker.[63] Focusing on the problem of concentrating authority in a few hands in the meetings, this tract gives examples of the high-handedness

---

[63] Richard Mucklow, *The Spirit of the Hat: Or, the Government of the Quakers Among Themselves* (London, 1673), sig. A1. Subsequent references are given parenthetically.

of Quaker leaders, who "in their Selected Assemblies, . . . keep the Inferiors at so great a distance, and their Spirits are so over-awed, that they
dare not (but seldom) contradict the sayings of the most eminent Elders"
(sig. B7, 29). Imposition of hierarchical authority contradicts a central
tenet of Quakerism, which is that one acts according to the dictates of the
"indwelling spirit" of God. Ultimately, the conflict is between young and
old. The younger James Claypoole ended his quarrel with John Bolton by
apologizing, not because he genuinely changed his mind, but because of
their unequal positions. Arguing that the individual expression of young
members is suppressed by the group's older, powerful leaders, Mucklow
portrays the leadership in a contest of pride: "a few will sway a Meeting
which way they please, unless the *Peers* are in Competition, then they meet
as two great waters, ready to overwhelm one another, with their asserting
both *in the name of the Lord*" (sig. B7–B7v, 29–30).

Because the internal conflict is generational, marriage discipline becomes
an effective means of social control and punishment for insubordination
since it is the young who marry. Wishing to marry Rebecca Travers,
the younger, John Osgood had gone so far as to obtain permission at
the women's meeting (sig. B7v, 30). Despite the overwhelmingly positive
response from the women, however, Osgood encountered opposition at
the men's meeting because of an earlier disagreement with some of the
men, including John Bolton, on a theological point about whether to keep
one's hat on during prayer (sig. B7v, 30). Bolton insisted that Osgood
testify against the keeping on of one's hat before they would agree to
the marriage. Thus, marriage discipline could be used to ensure doctrinal conformity: "what greater temptation can a man meet withal to reduce
him to a conformity against his Conscience, than to deprive him of a
Person whom he most dearly loves?" (sig. B8v, 32). In conflict with individual conscience, marriage discipline is enforced by pitting the Quaker's
loyalty to church and community against love of (would-be) spouse and
family.

As such problems show, the demands of one's immediate family can come
into conflict with those of the imagined community. Accused of valuing
property above principles, the Wilkinson–Story faction in turn accuses
Fox of helping Mary Pennington secure her property while condemning
Rogers for doing so: Rogers asks, "If G. F. had so great a Care for *others,
not outwardly related to him,* I know no Reason why I may not take the
same Care for my *Wife* and *Children,* which are many" (*Christian-Quaker,*
part 5, sig. 7v, 46). Rogers assumes the priority of the immediate family
over the Quaker community, revealing that the familial metaphor for the

community can break down when money is involved and when one group seems to be favored over others. Given that the Quakers were dissenting outsiders to the nation, support from within the group, including trading with other Quakers, assumed a greater importance. Rogers complains that the accusations that Fox leveled against him caused other Quakers to cease trading with him, which trade he depended on "not only to provide for my Family, but to administer to the Relief of others also" (*Christian-Quaker*, Preface, sig. B3).

Partly, the conflict among the Quakers arises out of a drive toward corporatization that insists on wholly encompassing the lives of the members of the group. Perhaps the most extreme example of how the individual becomes subsumed in the group is the use to which Fox put his marriage to Margaret Fell. The author of *The Spirit of the Hat* rebukes Fox's overweening pride in equating his private, earthly marriage to the spiritual one between Christ and his church:

Such is the swelling pride of this *Luciferian*, that he gave forth a Paper, That *his Marriage with* Margaret Fell, *was a figure of the Marriage between Christ and the Church.* I may more justly believe it to be a figure of the great Apostasy from the Truth, and barrenness in the Truth.

He likewise declared, That *his Marriage was above the state of* Adam *in his Innocency, in the state of the second* Adam, *who never fell.* This Paper was so ill resented, and so much dislik'd, that it was call'd in again; and a rare thing it was to get a sight thereof, albeit through an accident, I had a a [*sic*] view of it. (sig. C5v, 42)

Although Fox's living metaphor was intended to shore up the Quakers' communal identity, the overemphasis of the group over the individual became divisive. In part, the problem arose from the way Fox elevated himself above the community. This example clearly reveals the problems in conflating individual and group identities, for the relatively powerless may find group identity dictated by the more powerful in terms distasteful to them.

In these schisms, gender was a lightning rod for conflicts over authority.[64] In order to uphold church hierarchy, Fox's faction was forced to defend women's authority. Modeled after Fell's *Womens Speaking Justified* (1666), Fox's *This Is An Encuragement To All the Women's Meetings In the World* (1676) compiles biblical examples of virtuous women to make the case

---

[64] The conflict over women's roles was not divided by gender. A number of men wrote tracts in defense of women's meetings, including John Pearson's *Anti-Christian Treachery Discovered and Its Way Blocked Up* (London, 1686?) and William Loddington's *The Good Order of Truth Justified* (London, 1685).

that it is godly for women to assemble in meetings.[65] More so than men, women have the domestic knowledge necessary to "admonish and exhort, reprove and rebuke" (sig. B2v, 20) the young. These verbs describe a strong and demanding authority figure. The metaphor of the "Nursing Mother" (sig. C6v, 44) makes women not just nurturers but also judges and teachers. Moreover, through his conceptualization of the Quaker community as a family, Fox sees women exercising this authority beyond their immediate families, so that "*the Elder Women should be as Mothers*; and a Mother is a Nurse, and Teacher, and Instructor of her Children, and *the Younger Women as Sisters, with all Purity*" (sig. E6v, 76). Women should be given authority, even authority over men, in maintaining order: "so in the Church here were women Instructers women prophets and Daughters Prophets" (sig. F5v, 90). Fox translates the spiritual equality of men and women into an even more threatening practical equality in managing church affairs.

In pamphlets defending their meetings, women on Fox's side in turn accused their opponents of disorder and discord while emphasizing the need to maintain order, peace, and unity, as for example in *An Epistle for True Love, Unity and Order* (1685).[66] Although defending order may be reactionary, the women gained from this conservatism, a conservatism evident in their envisioning of church as family, which they invoked to justify their authority. *A Living Testimony* (1685), signed by five women, argues that women ought to be respected as mothers and sisters: "such Elderly Women in the Truth, are to be intreated as Mothers, and so not to be Railed upon; and the Younger, as Sisters, with all Purity, and Widows, that are Widows indeed, are to be honoured."[67] It also argues for women's special domestic knowledge to justify their part in marriage discipline: "for many times we having seen, and do see more in the Young People and Widdows State and Condition, than some of the Men, because we are more amongst them" (sig. A2v, 4). As it turns out, the exercise of discipline is not only over young women but also over widows who wish to remarry. Since widows can be quite rich, marriage discipline gives the women's meetings much more power than it first appears.

---

[65] George Fox, *This Is An Encuragement To All the Women's Meetings in the World* (London, 1676), came under special attack in *The Christian-Quaker*, which repeatedly pointed out that Fox erred in holding up Micah's mother as a virtuous woman when the context in Judges 17 of the Old Testament plainly showed that she was idolatrous. References to Fox's tract are given parenthetically.

[66] Anne Whitehead and Mary Elson, *An Epistle for True Love, Unity and Order in the Church of Christ, Against the Spirit of Discord, Disorder and Confusion, &c.* (London, 1680), sig. B3v, 14.

[67] Mary Foster, Mary Elson, Anne Travice, Ruth Crowch, Susannah Dew, Mary Plumfield, *A Living Testimony From the Power and Spirit of our Lord Jesus Christ in our Faithful Womens Meeting and Christian Society [sic]* (London, 1685), sig. A2, 3. Further references are given parenthetically.

The Wilkinson–Story schism of the 1670s shows how the problem of maintaining group cohesion could quite easily be inflected by gender. Opposition to George Fox's leadership was framed in terms of opposition to the rule of women. Sometimes women were viewed as Fox's pawns in his attempt to consolidate his power and influence. At other times they were perceived as a corrupting influence. Often they were criticized in conventionally misogynistic terms. In *A Novelty*, William Mather derisively depicts the women as vain and pretentious, whose frivolous love of fine clothes shows them incapable of serious judgment: "And whether such *Women-Judges* ever did any Good, who come into the Seat of *Counsel*, rufling in gaudy flower'd Stuffs, or Silks, from Top to Toe, mincing with their Feet, *&c.* except their Gifts to the Poor" (sig. A3, 5). While Mather's denunciations are not confined to women but also encompass men, his use of the word "woman" tends to be pejorative. He laments that those who rule in the meetings are "most of them Ignorant ones, not knowing who gave them their usurped Power, yet will be as angry as a Woman, if you obey not their Wills, when you come before them" (sig. A4, 7).

Despite their notions of spiritual equality that distinguishes between the unlearned man and the spiritually learned woman, Quaker men were not unlike their peers in the established church or in the nation at large. They found powerful women threatening and tried to contain them. While Quaker ideas of spiritual equality allowed women active, speaking roles in the community, when women took on such roles they did not do so unchallenged. Women's public preaching was less threatening to the sect when it was directed at outsiders, even when they were highly confrontational and disrespectful of the authority of male priests. It was more controversial for women to assert equality within the sect, and Quaker women's leadership became a significant divisive issue. The struggle over women's authority was fiercer in the arena of social organization because the meaning of women's voices there was more troubling. A spiritually learned woman imbued with the "indwelling" spirit of God could, in that moment, become spiritually a man. This spiritual change in gender authorized her speaking. It was more difficult to maintain the notion of a gender shift with women who handled the daily business of church government.

In response to old prejudices about women's inferiority, Quaker women argued first from spiritual equality. They also argued that their participation in church government was an extension of women's traditional roles in the family. Quaker women argued for an expansion of their authority into church administration based on the authority they already possessed in the household. In their tracts, they portrayed themselves as good administrators of households: "For you know, that we are much in our families among our children maids, and servants, and may see more into their inclinations; and so see that none indulge any to looseness and evill, but restraine it."[68] Women's daily management of the household and their intimate knowledge of those they governed – children and servants – meant that they were best placed to act as moral guides. Quaker women maintained that their economic productivity gave them a voice in church affairs: "Since the priests claimes, and challenges a tithe, which belongs to women to pay, as well as the men, not only for widdows, but them that have husbands, as piggs, and geese, henns and eggs, hemp and flax, wooll and lamb: all which women may have a hand in: Soe it concerns the womens meetings, to looke strictly to every particular meeting, that every woman bring in their testimony against tithes, and that those testimonies be recorded."[69] Even married women, though only engaged in small-scale cottage business, had a tenth of the income they produced claimed by the state church, a claim that they had a part in resisting. Women's meetings took the responsibility of recording testimonies of women opposing tithes in accordance with Quaker principles. Because the practice of recording testimonies of Quaker suffering served to unify the sect, the women were insisting on their central place in the sect and refusing to be relegated to a peripheral role. In part, women's claim that their greater expertise in the household justified their authority in the church derived from the analogy that Quakerism made between church and family. Quakers' familial language of love and affection also implied a hierarchy of age and status based on the traditional family. Although perhaps ultimately patriarchal, this hierarchy could be appropriated by women to extend their authority from the household outward to the community of Quakers. Unlike the binary nature of the gender hierarchy, family hierarchy allowed women a place of respect and authority, whether from status or from age.

In response to challenges to their authority, Quaker women (and their supporters) resorted to several lines of defense. They insisted on their spiritual equality, a fundamental tenet in Quaker theology. They eloquently argued for women's right to speak, creatively interpreting the Pauline injunction for women's silence in church so as to limit its applicability. And they claimed roles of leadership within the sect based on their own experience as governors of households. Quaker women had no compunction about insisting on the prerogatives of seniority in order to argue for gender

---

[68] Milton D. Speizman and Jane C. Kronick, eds., "A Seventeenth-Century Quaker Women's Declaration," *Signs: Journal of Women in Culture and Society* 1 (1975), 242.

[69] *Ibid.*, 243.

equality. They could straightforwardly claim authority over servants and children. But their language of nursing mothers also allowed them maternal authority over other Quakers, authority with overtones of age and status. Paradoxically, then, Quaker women employed the rhetoric of hierarchy to claim authority. In their case, the authority of age was effectively used to counter gender authority claimed by men. Quaker women, and those who defended their leadership in the Quaker community, supported one hierarchy in order to contest another. While support for the authority of age and for a status hierarchy was fundamentally conservative, women's participation in public life and their rejection of patriarchal norms need not only take the form of aggressive preaching in the streets. Women also gained authority from their participation in the organization of a quietist sect. Conservatism offered a different set of opportunities to women, and it could, as in the case of the Quakers, be liberating for women.

With the Quakers, we come nearly full circle. Conflicts over authority that earlier divided the nation also tore the Quaker community apart toward the end of the seventeenth century. The Wilkinson–Story schism over marriage discipline mimicked in many ways the debate over episcopacy in the 1640s when Milton composed his antiprelatical tracts. In both contexts the familial metaphor appeared in various guises as well. But it was not simply an iterative history of mirrorings, echoes, and repetitions. While the issue of women's place initially hardly figured at all in the debates over form and government in the Church of England despite the frequent allusions to the church as mother, women became central to the controversy over the separatist churches. As a significant force in the Quaker community and full participants in its government, women also became a divisive issue among the Quakers. From James I's idea of the king as "nursing father" we arrive at the Quakers' appropriation of the idea of the "nursing mother" to define the role of women leaders at the local rather than national level. With metaphors of the family the Quakers not only conceptualized political and social organization of community but they also put these political ideas into actual practice.

Epilogue: the family-state analogy's eighteenth-century afterlife

The year 1698 saw the publication of John Locke's *Two Treatises of Government*, an enormously influential work in the development of liberalism in England and elsewhere; in France and America classical liberal movements even led to revolutions. Written in the context of the Exclusion Crisis, with a probable date of composition of 1679–80, the *Two Treatises* demanded the Glorious Revolution that came to pass in 1688.[1] Peter Laslett has shown that rather than a critique of Hobbes, as scholars have long assumed, Locke's *Two Treatises* has as its primary target the patriarchalism of Robert Filmer.[2] As a client of Lord Shaftesbury and a polemicist for the Whig party, Locke was involved in the attempt to exclude the Catholic James II from succeeding to the throne.[3] In support of James and hereditary succession Tories circulated Filmer's *Patriarcha* in manuscript. Whigs had to respond to patriarchalist theory as Filmer's 1630s treatise and his ideas of patriarchalism gained a new afterlife in the Revolutionary politics of the 1680s.

In refuting Filmer, Locke attacked the family-state analogy itself, breaking the analogy in order to make his argument for social contract and the natural freedom of men. Because the fifth commandment is so central to Filmer's thought, Locke first assaults the scriptural basis of Filmer's patriarchal argument by reinserting the female gender into Filmer's use of the commandment in the account of the origins of society. Accusing Filmer of treating the words "*and Mother*" as though they were "Apocriphal Words" (184), Locke mocks him for taking the fifth commandment as confirmation that royal power rests on paternal power and yet leaving out the second part of the fifth commandment enjoining honor and obedience to one's

---

[1] For the date of composition, see Peter Laslett, "Introduction," in John Locke, *Two Treatises of Government*, ed. Laslett (Cambridge: Cambridge University Press, 1988), 35, 65–66. All references to *Two Treatises* are from this edition and cited parenthetically.

[2] *Ibid.*, 50–52.

[3] For Locke's involvement with radical Whig politics, see Richard Ashcraft, *Revolutionary Politics and Locke's* Two Treatises of Government (Princeton: Princeton University Press, 1986).

mother. The commandment no more gave monarchical power to father than to mother: "For had our *A*[uthor]. set down this Command without Garbling, as God gave it, and joyned *Mother* to Father, every Reader would have seen that it had made directly against him, and that it was so far from Establishing the *Monarchical Power of the Father*, that it set up the *Mother* equal with him, and injoyn'd nothing but what was due in common, to both Father and Mother" (184–85). Interpreting the commandment to mean the equality of mother and father, Locke argues that it cannot support claims for absolute monarchy on the basis of parental power. Otherwise, mothers would surely share in that monarchy.

Women prove to be very useful for Locke in dismantling Filmer's argument. In disputing Filmer's claim that God granted dominion to Adam, Locke again reinserts a woman, this time Eve, into Filmer's scriptural evidence. Denying that God made Adam monarch simply by creating him, Locke avers that God granted the world to both Adam and Eve: "It is false that God made that Grant to Adam, as soon as he was Created, since though it stands in the Text immediately after his Creation, yet it is plain it could not be spoken to *Adam* till after *Eve* was made and brought to him" (152). According to Locke, Filmer is inconsistent in identifying as the original grant of Adam's government God's postlapsarian judgment that Adam would rule Eve. Logically, that ostensible grant is far removed from the act of creation, given only "after the Fall, when Adam was somewhat, at least in time, and very much, distant in condition from his Creation" (152). God was unlikely to be granting Adam the privileges of absolute monarchy while meting out punishments for eating the forbidden fruit: "if we will consider the occasion of what God says here to our first Parents, that he was Denouncing Judgment, and declaring his Wrath against them both, for their Disobedience, we cannot suppose that this was the time, wherein God was granting *Adam* Prerogatives and Priviledges, investing him with Dignity and Authority, Elevating him to Dominion and Monarchy" (172). Adam only "had accidentally a Superiority over" (172) Eve: with barely contained sarcasm, Locke says, "'twould be hard to imagine, that God, in the same Breath, should make him Universal *Monarch* over all Mankind, and a day labourer for his Life; turn him out of *Paradice, to till the Ground, ver.* 23. and at the same time, advance him to a Throne, and all the Priviledges and Ease of Absolute Power" (172). Eve's presence is crucial for Locke's refutation of Filmer. By alerting readers to the presence of the female sex in the critical passages, a presence that Filmer conveniently ignores, Locke interprets Genesis to show that there is no paternal basis for absolute monarchy.

Instead, Locke distinguishes between public and private, political and domestic dominion. The fifth commandment to honor one's father and mother can have only one application, referring either to the political domain or to the domestic. If the command is to obey the sovereign, then it excludes biological fathers, who "being equally Subjects and Slaves with their Children, can have no right by that Title, to any such *Honour or Obedience*, as contains in it Political Subjection" (189). If the command is to obey parents, "then it cannot concern Political Obedience, but a duty that is owing to Persons, who have no title to Sovereignty, nor any Political Authority as Magistrates over Subjects" (189). For Locke, father and ruler are "things inconsistent" (189). Likewise, he denies that Adam's sovereignty over Eve can be anything other than "Conjugal Power, not Political, the Power that every Husband hath to order the things of private Concernment in his Family, as Proprietor of the Goods and Land there, and to have his Will take place before that of his wife in all things of their common Concernment; but not a Political Power of Life and Death over her, much less over any body else" (174). His differentiation of father from ruler, domestic from political power, depends on a distinction between public and private spheres of influence. A father and husband may have supreme power in the household, but outside the domestic space, he lacks the absolute political power of Filmer's monarch.

For Filmer's natural subjection to the father-king, Locke substitutes men's consent. The social contract allows citizens to withdraw their loyalty and set up new governments: "For there are no Examples so frequent in History, both Sacred and Prophane, as those of Men withdrawing themselves, and their Obedience, from the Jurisdiction they were born under, and the Family or Community they were bred up in, and *setting up new Governments* in other places" (345). Like Milton, Locke bases society (including marriage) on contract, but unlike Milton, he has no use for the family analogy. Reconceiving the state as social contract and denying hereditary right (thus allowing Whigs to exclude James), Locke does away with the family metaphor. Even political subjection must be freely chosen, and Locke argues that the obedience of children is "no natural Tye or Engagement, but a voluntary Submission" (315) based on economic considerations, namely the children's desire to inherit their father's wealth. In essence, Locke separates family out as a private space outside the political realm.

Given the stature of Locke's *Two Treatises* in the modern history of political thought, his depoliticization and privatization of the family can be too easily taken as indicative of a contemporary trend. The standard historical account suggesting that the family becomes increasingly privatized in the period has been debunked by Ralph Houlbrooke's revisionary work, which shows little change in familial forms and functions between the fifteenth and the eighteenth centuries.[4] Houlbrooke's work demands a reevaluation of the privatization thesis. This study of the uses of the family metaphor traverses a period of nearly a hundred years, and yet, the experimenting with the family-state analogy does not seem to have ended with the close of the seventeenth century, no matter how neat such a closure would be. Traditional historical periodizations cannot dictate the demise of the family-state analogy. Rachel Weil has shown how Whig authors themselves varied in the way they adapted the analogy in their responses to Filmer; Locke's family-state distinction was not uniformly adopted by Whigs, and indeed the distinction for Locke was itself an *ad hoc* rejoinder to Filmer, not a fully coherent system.[5] The family continued to be a vital metaphor for the late seventeenth and early eighteenth centuries when there was indeed a married couple who ruled jointly (William and Mary), and later another queen (Anne) on the throne. Weil's analysis of the married queen, Mary, leads her to question the argument that increasingly women were consigned to the private familial space: "Mary's efficacy as a symbol lay in the fact that she straddled and even muddied the boundary between public and private, not that she was confined to one side of it." While she acknowledges the significance of the dichotomy, she also stresses the "elusiveness and malleability" of that divide.[6] In the Restoration, the family-state analogy has only shifted its contours in response to contemporary political concerns, especially in response to the emergence of party politics.

A brief glance at Mary Astell's *Reflections upon Marriage* (1700) provides another perspective on the evolution of the family-state analogy at the end of the seventeenth century. A Tory defender of sacral monarchy and opposed to the Williamite settlement, Astell challenges the Whig program in her works. She contests principally the ideas forwarded by Locke's *Two Treatises*, especially on liberty and property, though never explicitly naming him.[7] In opposition to Locke's attempt to sever the family from the political realm, Astell reinstates the family-state analogy. Although she shares some

---

[4] Ralph Houlbrooke, *The English Family 1450–1700* (London and New York: Longman, 1984).
[5] Rachel Weil, *Political Passions: Gender, the Family and Political Argument in England 1680–1714* (Manchester: Manchester University Press, 1999), 50–84. Weil also treats Algernon Sidney's *Discourses of Government* (London, 1698), William Lawrence's *Marriage by the Moral Law of God Vindicated* (London, 1680), and James Tyrrell's *Patriarcha Non Monarcha. The Patriarch Unmonarch'd* (London, 1681).
[6] *Ibid.*, 116, 17.
[7] For Astell's response to Locke, see Patricia Springborg, "Introduction," in Mary Astell, *Political Writings*, ed. Springborg (Cambridge: Cambridge University Press, 1996), xix–xxv. Further references to Astell's *Reflections upon Marriage* are from this edition and cited parenthetically.

of Filmer's assumptions, particularly about the analogous hierarchies of family and monarchical state, unlike Filmer, she questions the purported inferiority of women. As one example of a work contesting Locke's attempt to depoliticize the family, *Reflections* resurrects the family-state analogy in order to reimagine the family as vital to the state, but this time with a proto-feminist twist.[8] This study has discussed primarily how seventeenth-century authors recnvision family to propose new political structures. In disagreeing with Locke, Astell defends the traditional political structure, and in so doing, she revises the family as a space in which women can have active roles, and sometimes even become their husbands' superiors.

Disputing the Whig argument that England should not be an absolute monarchy, Astell wonders why there is absolute sovereignty in the family but not in the state: "if Absolute Sovereignty be not necessary in a State, how comes it to be so in a Family? or if in a Family why not in a State; since no Reason can be alledg'd for the one that will not hold more strongly for the other? If the Authority of the Husband so far as it extends, is sacred and inalienable, why not of the Prince?" (17). Assuming that family and state are comparable, Astell's strategy is similar to Locke's in refuting Filmer. She inserts gender into her opponent's argument to unravel it, expressing the problem of gender here as the husband's absolute sovereignty over his wife. To make domestic absolutism even less acceptable, Astell points out how husbands are elected in the way, according to Whigs, citizens freely choose their governors: "The Domestic Sovereign is without Dispute Elected, and the Stipulations and Contract are mutual, is it not then partial in Men to the last degree, to contend for, and practise that Arbitrary Dominion in their Families, which they abhor and exclaim against in the State?" (17). Because family and state are analogous, if absolute sovereignty in the state is unacceptable because citizens choose their kings, then absolute sovereignty is unacceptable in the family since wives choose their husbands. Knowing that men are unlikely to give up their husbandly prerogatives, Astell makes the argument for monarchical absolutism by showing how family hierarchy would change if Whig arguments were pursued to their logical end.

While acknowledging that a husband cannot legally take away his wife's life, unlike a despotic king, Astell describes the mental anguish and spiritual trauma that a tyrannical husband can cause his long-suffering wife: "What tho' a Husband can't deprive a Wife of Life without being responsible to the Law, he may however do what is much more grievous to a generous Mind,

---

[8] For a modern feminist biography, see Ruth Perry, *The Celebrated Mary Astell: An Early English Feminist* (Chicago: The University of Chicago Press, 1986).

render Life miserable, for which she has no Redress, scarce Pity which is afforded to every other Complainant" (18). While her vivid description of the wife's plight shares much with Milton's description of the condition of a husband suffering an incompatible wife in its emphasis on the oppression of the spirit, Astell's politics are poles apart from Milton's. The passage ends with a ringing cry against gender inequalities: "If all Men are born free, how is it that all Women are born slaves?" (18). These words may well be Astell's most famous. She scoffs at men who demand freedom for themselves but gladly oppress women, using Milton as the symbolic Whig figure: "how much soever Arbitrary Power may be dislik'd on a Throne, not *Milton* himself wou'd cry up Liberty to poor *Female Slaves*, or plead for the Lawfulness of Resisting a Private Tyranny" (46–47).

In recognizing gender inequalities, Astell does not demand equal rights for women. Rather, she advocates a reactionary politics, insisting on an absolute monarchy to mirror the absolute sovereignty of the husband. Her Tory politics also upholds strict class distinctions. Advising women not to marry below their rank, she argues that it is against the will of God for women to lower themselves socially:

For since GOD has plac'd different Ranks in the World, put some in a higher and some in a lower Station, for Order and Beauty's sake, and for many good Reasons; tho' it is both our Wisdom and Duty not only to submit with patience, but to be Thankful and well-satisfied when by his Providence we are brought low, yet there is no manner of Reason for us to Degrade our selves; on the contrary, much why we ought not. (52)

Her argument even has a religious dimension. Maintaining that a higher-class rank allows a woman more time to prepare for the afterlife and to do good to her social inferiors, Astell says that it is "ill Manners to Heaven, and an irreligious contempt of its Favours" (52–53) for a woman to lower herself to maintain a poor husband, which is "in the very literal Sense a caring for the things of the World" (53).

Astell's support of hereditary monarchy means that she can use class hierarchy to argue that some women are superior to some men, and so combat gender inequality in that fashion. Opposing the Whig cry for equality for all in the political domain, which Astell (correctly) interprets to mean equality only for men, she also dismisses the notion of class equality within the family: "A Husband indeed is thought by both Sexes so very valuable, that scarce a Man who can keep himself clean and make a Bow, but thinks he is good enough to pretend to any Woman, no matter for the Difference of Birth or Fortune, a Husband is such a Wonder-working Name as to make an Equality, or something more, whenever it is pronounc'd" (65–66). Astell's defense of class hierarchy in the state is a defense of women in the domestic sphere. Unlike Filmer, Astell makes class distinctions to argue that a man cannot be superior to his wife if he is socially inferior to her. A husband is not automatically head of the household.

Indeed, despite her Tory allegiance and her belief that the family and the state are analogous things, Astell's family does not have fixed gender roles. Using the Old Testament example of the woman from Shunem who entertains the prophet Elijah (from II Kings 4), Astell paints a portrait of a family where the wife is the head: "For whether it was not the Custom in *Shunem* for the Husband to Dictate, or whether her's was conscious of her superior Vertue, or whatever was the Reason, we find it is she who Governs, *dwelling* with great Honour and Satisfaction *among her own people*" (25). Astell emphasizes the woman's autonomy and authority: "The Text calls her a *Great Woman*, whilst her Husband is hardly taken notice of, and this no otherwise than as performing the Office of a Bailiff. It is *her* Piety and Hospitality that are Recorded, *She* invites the Prophet to *her House*; who converses with and is entertain'd by *her*. She gives her husband no account of *her* Affairs any further than to tell him her Designs that he may see them Executed" (25). Emphasizing also the woman's ownership of property, Astell points out that Elijah treats the woman as though she were the head of the household: "it is no more than what the Prophet encourages, for all his Addresses are to *her*, he takes no Notice of her Husband. His Benefits are confer'd on *her*, 'tis *she* and *her Household* whom he warns of a Famine, and 'tis *she* who appeals to the King for the Restitution of *her House and Land*" (26). In fact, she not only emphasizes the Shunemian woman's ownership of house and land, Astell also highlights the woman's leadership by designating the household as hers. The example of the Shunemian woman is important because she is an ordinary woman who governs the household and not a queen who by her political supremacy is also ruler in the house. While not arguing for the wholesale reformation of the conventional household, Astell allows for some flexibility in assigning family roles: "I wou'd not infer from hence that Women generally speaking, ought to govern in their Families when they have a Husband, but I think this Instance and Example is a sufficient Proof, that if by Custom or Contract, or the Laws of the Country, or Birth-right (as in the case of Sovereign Princesses) they have the supreme Authority, it is no Usurpation, nor do they Act contrary to Holy Scripture, nor consequently to the Law of Nature" (26). A staunch defender of hereditary monarchy, Astell refuses to reimagine the state as a domain where hierarchy can be flexible or abolished, but she does reimagine the family as a space where hierarchy is not fixed – there are circumstances that permit the wife to be head of household – even if only in a limited way. In her assertion that God "*is no Respecter of Persons, with whom there is neither Bond nor Free, Male nor Female, but they are all one in Christ Jesus*" (26), Astell echoes the Quaker claim for erasing gender difference in the spiritual realm.

At the end of *Reflections upon Marriage*, Astell calls not for women's freedom but reasserts men's right to govern in the household, offering the abused wife only the comfort that adversity makes her virtuous: "if any Woman think her self Injur'd, she has a Remedy in reserve which few Men will Envy or endeavour to Rob her of, the Exercise and Improvement of her Vertue here, and the Reward of it hereafter" (80). These words, the closing statement of *Reflections*, are tinged with bitter irony, but Astell is serious. While we may wish her less conservative and less resigned to the woman's lot, her use of the family analogy departs in significant ways from Filmer's. For her, a hierarchical view of the state can still produce a more malleable version of family.

Despite Locke and his assumptions we have inherited, Astell's example shows that the family-state analogy was far from dead at the end of the seventeenth century. Its persistence in the late seventeenth century and into the eighteenth can be detected in the politics of opposing Whigs and Tories that still reasoned in terms that assumed the correspondence between state and family. While Filmer's brand of patriarchalist politics did not last, the family was still a powerful way to think about the organization of the state. Rather than heralding the demise of the family-state analogy, the eighteenth century saw its survival and its reemergence in another form, like a political phoenix born out of the fires of the Glorious Revolution.

Index

Mather, William (*A Novelty: Or, a Government of
     Women, Distinct from Men, Erected
     amongst some of the People, call'd
     Quakers*), 214–15, 219
Mendle, Michael, 51
metaphor, 15–16
Milton, John, 7, 16, 140–41, 227
  and Arianism, 154
  and aristocratic republic, 70–71
  and gender, 54–58, 59, 60–61, 62, 160
  and parliament, 60, 61–62, 64–66, 69–70
  and *pater patriae*, 61, 69–70, 72–73
  and republicanism, 51–53, 59, 67–73
  and social contract, 65–67
  works:
     Animadversions, 55
     An Apology Against a Pamphlet, 54–55, 70
     Areopagitica, 71
     Commonplace Book, 53
     *Considerations Touching the Likeliest Means
        to Remove Hirelings Out of the Church*,
        74
     Doctrine and Discipline of Divorce, 53,
        57–58
     Eikonoklastes, 58n24, 58–59, 62, 69, 71
     First Defence of the English People (*Pro
        Populo Anglicano Defensio*), 49, 62–69,
        71, 72
     Of Education, 51
     Of Reformation, 51, 53, 55–56
     *Readie and Easie Way to Establish a Free
        Commonwealth*, 70, 74–75
     Reason of Church-government, 49, 53–54, 55,
        56, 69
     Second Defence (*Pro Populo Anglicano
        Defensio Secunda*), 72
     Tenure of Kings and Magistrates, 51, 61,
        71–72
     see also *Paradise Lost*
mixed constitution, 51
Mocket, Richard (*God and the King*), 1, 13
Moon, John, 207
Moses, 6, 66, 90, 107, 116, 122
Moss, Miriam, 207
du Moulin, Pierre (*Regii Sanguinis Clamor ad
     Coelum Adversus Paricidas Anglicanos*), 7
Mucklow, Richard (*The Spirit of the Hat: Or, the
     Government of the Quakers Among
     Themselves*), 215–16, 217
Mueller, Janel, 51

natural law, 63–66, 86, 108
Nayler, James, 195, 200
Nedham, Marchamont

works:
     *A New Conference Between the Ghosts of
        King Charles and Oliver Cromwell*, 125,
        126
     A New Meeting of Ghosts at Tyburn, 127
Neoplatonism, 41, 42, 182, 189–90
new historicism, 10
Norbrook, David, 9, 13, 17, 134, 140
Nyquist, Mary, 161–62

obedience, 32
Orgel, Stephen, 39, 42
Orlin, Lena Cowen, 31
Osgood, John, 216

Paradise Lost
  and Abdiel, 147, 150, 153
  and Adam, 156
  and Beelzebub, 149, 156
  and brothers, younger, 157–60
  and Death, 149
  and *felix culpa*, 167
  and hierarchy, flexible, 152–53
  and hierarchy of heavenly bodies, 162–63
  and marriage, 166
  and Michael, 166
  and Nimrod, 145–46
  and paternal state, 146
  and patriarchalism, 143–45, 146
  and patriarchy, 165–66, 168
  and Raphael, 162, 164, 168
  and republicanism, 145–46, 147
  and Sin, 148–49
  and social contract, 143
  and society as family, 145
  and tyranny, 145–47
  and Virgin Mary, 162
  see also Eve; God; Satan; the Son of God
Parker, Henry, 11–12, 64–65
Parliament, purged ('the Rump'), 74
Pateman, Carole, 77, 78n7, 174
pater patriae, 61, 69–70, 72–73, 105–06,
     108–09, 111–12, 113–14, 122, 134,
     138
patriarchalism, 1–2, 3–4, 5–6, 16–18, 36, 76–79,
     81–84, 85–86, 111, 135, 137, 143–45, 146,
     200, 222–23
patriarchy, 16–18, 141, 165–66, 168, 200
Paul, 84, 201, 213
Peltonen, Markku, 52
Penn, William, 206–07
Pennington, Mary, 216
Pepys, Samuel, 171, 174, 180, 193
Perrot, John, 198